For Jeanne,
with my best wishes.
Some angels have
halos, and some have
tails)!

Marilyn Jeffers Walton

2010

BADGE ON MY COLLAR II

TO SERVE WITH HONOR

Marilyn Jeffers Walton

author**HOUSE**®

AuthorHouse™
1663 Liberty Drive
Bloomington, IN 47403
www.authorhouse.com
Phone: 1-800-839-8640

First published by AuthorHouse 8/28/2009

ISBN: 978-1-4389-9511-3 (sc)

Printed in the United States of America
Bloomington, Indiana

This book is printed on acid-free paper.

Cover photograph, K-9 Rudi, courtesy of Dave Brown. Additional cover photography by R. Harold and Carolyn G. Kramer

Back cover photograph, members of the Saint Paul Police Canine Unit, courtesy of Mark Ficcadenti

Pete Renterria	*K-9 Lance*
Mike Ernster	*K-9 Buzz*
Author	
Dave Pavlak	*K-9 Chico*
Nicole Rasmussen	*K-9 Chase*
Dave Longbehn	*K-9 Kody*

Dedication

For the brave of heart who served with honor and valor

Officer Tim Jones and K-9 Laser
Saint Paul, Minnesota
Lost August 26, 1994

Deputy Matt Williams and K-9 Diogi
Polk City, Florida
Lost September 28, 2006

"There are no words......."

Acknowledgements

A debt of gratitude is owed to the following, who greatly contributed to the creation of this book.

John R. Walton
Russ Hess, Executive Director, USPCA
R.O. Rogers
John and Becki Johnston – Ace K-9
Tony Cerimele – A. Cerimele Photography
Debrah H. Muska – Animal Images
Binghamton Police Identification Unit
Gordon Leitz
Joanne Chanyi
Linda Sparks
Michael A. Spochart
Kimberly A. Schneider
Freda Babinski
Andy Revering
Ronald Macleod
Marion Lopizzo
Roger Mayer
Emily Schmidt
Jay Paquette

Jim Frost
Jan Ballard
Rob Vetsch & K-9 Charlie
Jay Thompson & K-9 Harley
Saint Paul, Minnesota, Police Department
U.S. Capitol Police

Contents

Preface

From the heathered Scottish Highlands to the rugged Australian land down under, K-9s are on patrol. Tracking through the Arctic blasts of Canadian winters or across the scorching desert heat of Arizona, they go where called. Thrashing through the dangerous jungles of Vietnam or patrolling through the magical green of England's Sherwood Forest, memorable and dedicated dogs of beauty and valor serve with courage and honor. Come along to the U.S. Capitol Building or hover in a helicopter over Indonesia with four-footed officers. Follow the hilarious tales of New Jersey's Tracker and witness the astonishing heroics of dogs, both young and old, from the East Coast to the Deep South. Whether accompanying a crack SWAT team or tenderly standing by the hospital bed of a sick child, these multi-faceted dogs will warm your heart.

In this sequel to *Badge on My Collar—A Chronicle of Courageous Canines,* Marilyn Jeffers Walton takes you around the globe to ride along with dogs whose stellar careers and unselfish sacrifices exemplify the brave character and profile of today's police canine. The common thread among the geographically-distant dogs is their love of handler, their bravery in the face of confrontation with the "bad guys" and their total willingness to surrender their very lives in order to protect their handlers and the public. Highly-trained, intelligent and steeped in the deepest measure of devotion, this international collection of K-9s casts a bright light on all dogs that protect and serve. They are truly the guardians of the night.

Foreword

As a dog handler, trainer and member of the Saint Paul Police Canine Unit for seventeen years, I have watched the evolution and deployment of police service dogs change. Early police service dogs were, at times, viewed as "attack dogs," used for crowd control and intimidation. They have since evolved into a valuable and effective tool used by the military and civilian law enforcement agencies around the world. This evolution is directly attributed to the dedication of professional trainers and handlers.

The modern police service dogs are more skilled, more highly-trained and more smartly deployed. As a result, these dogs are fulfilling a critical need in policing. Today's police service dog protects the public in ways never before thought possible. Whether searching for and finding dangerous criminals, locating illegal drugs, detecting explosives or deploying with modern-day SWAT teams, these dogs enhance officer safety and save lives. Their mere presence in a tense situation is enough to prevent the escalation of violence.

Marilyn Walton is an author who has spent a good deal of time learning about police service dogs and their capabilities, and she understands the intense bond between a dog and its handler. She has watched dogs train and ridden with them on patrol. In doing so, she has come to know their nature and understands the pain when the last full measure is given; as an officer or dog has made the ultimate sacrifice in the line of duty.

Walton's book is an introduction into the private world of K-9 that the public seldom sees. It is a collection of international stories that highlight the universal bond that all handlers share with their dogs and shows the sacrifices that officers and their dogs make every day protecting the citizens they serve. Using both humorous and poignant stories, she clears up any misconceptions anyone might have about the duties and devotion of today's police service dogs. As the stories suggest, it is no wonder one of the most common comments one hears in the K-9 world is, "He was the best partner I've ever had."

Few books have examined the valor and sacrifice of these dogs. In this sequel to *Badge on My Collar--A Chronicle of Courageous Canines*, Walton once again presents fifteen admirable dogs that have served with honor and will warm the reader's heart, while paying tribute to all who serve. Her examination of the service of dog handlers reveals to the reader why we, both handlers and dogs, are proud to wear the badge.

An everyday reminder of the handler-dog partnership for the handlers of Saint Paul Police Canine Unit is a tribute inscribed on a monument located in the Saint Paul Police Canine Cemetery on the grounds of the Timothy J. Jones Training Facility:

> ***"The valiant acts of those buried here are
> known only to God and to us..."***

Jon J. Sherwood
Police Officer
Dog Handler/Assistant Trainer
Saint Paul, Minnesota Police Canine Unit
K-9 Roscoe - 1991 - 2005
K-9 Benji - 2000 - present

K-9 Buffy

"Ambassadress Extraordinaire"

"My baby girl." It is such a simple and affectionate appellation for a police canine who is the sweetheart of the District of Columbia. K-9 Buffy, of the United States Capitol Police in Washington D.C., is not only an expert in bomb detection but has over the years become the public greeter in the nation's capital. Her friendly nature and winning ways combine to make her the ideal ambassadress of goodwill in the heart of the United States Government.

At seven-years-old, Buffy has been around long enough to know the ins and outs of working Washington. Members of Congress know the Grande Dame as the beautiful sable-coated dog that carefully patrols the confines of the U.S. Senate and House of Representatives making sure that the building is safe for all those who enter to conduct the nation's business. Year after year, the dog's toenails have clicked across the vast cold marble floor of the Capitol Rotunda as she walked proudly by the side of her handler, Jason Conlon. Together, they make sweeps of the heavily-populated areas where dignitaries, visitors and employees walk, ensuring that no explosives have been planted, thus keeping everyone safely out of harm's way.

Buffy's brush with aristocracy began with her Canadian breeding. She was born in Ontario, Canada, the offspring of two German shepherd dogs carrying prestigious pedigrees and impressive bloodlines, and like her parents, she was a registered canine with the Canadian Kennel Club. There was no doubt that

1

a well-bred animal of such notable lineage would enjoy much success entering the Canadian Kennel Club's competitions, but it was decided that instead she would be sold to a Florida kennel where her life would take a fully different twist. Accordingly, she was exported to the United States for possible police work.

At the sunny Florida kennel, far from her Canadian roots, Buffy and the other dogs were rigorously tested prior to selection by a police department for their potential operational ability. Impressed with the Canadian princess's credentials, the Capitol Police purchased her there and brought her to Washington where she was evaluated by trainers.

Immediately, Buffy showed great potential. From the start, the trainers noticed a strong retrieval drive in the dog. When a ball that a trainer had thrown for her landed in some bushes, Buffy encountered a sharp piercing thorn. The thorn cut her eye, but relying on her sensitive nose instead, she still managed to find the ball. When she found it, Buffy regally trotted out of the weeds carrying the ball in her mouth as she vigorously wagged her tail. Despite her injury from the thorn, she completed her training that day and went on to meet the officers who might eventually be matched with her. Along with other canines waiting to be assigned partners, day after day Buffy sat in her stark lonely kennel at the police facility, a far cry from the Canadian show ring.

In 2003, the K-9 sergeant for Jason's shift took all of the new handlers out to the site to introduce them to the canine recruits and to familiarize themselves with each dog's personality. Jason slowly walked past the row of cages inspecting each dog. At Buffy's kennel door, Jason briefly glanced at the smallish dog and noted that her dark sable coat needed a good brushing. With sad eyes, she sat next to a "present" she had left on the kennel floor. She had never been farther from her rich aristocratic Canadian heritage, and her demeanor seemed to reflect that sense of humiliation. Jason continued on past her and picked out another dog to walk.

Two weeks passed, and Jason visited the kennel again. Once again, he stopped and considered Buffy. Through her unkempt appearance, he saw the inner beauty of a "diamond in the rough." This time, he realized that with a little care and attention, she could fill the bill for a good police dog. Yet again, she had left another "present" on the cement floor. This time Jason cleaned it up, and in moving closer to her, he noticed she had a growth on her eye. After a veterinarian prescribed the appropriate medication, Jason took it upon himself to treat her eye each day. He felt the start of a bond with the bedraggled princess, and soon he was brushing the tangled coat restoring it to its former luxurious sheen.

Looking and feeling better, the dog once more exhibited her show-like qualities that had been hidden in the commonness and mundane surroundings of the police kennel. Her eyes were bright, and her exquisite rich coat gleamed. Each day, she looked forward to Jason's visits. She was not royalty, but she was certainly beginning to feel like it.

Shortly thereafter, Buffy and the other dogs were all chosen to start bomb detection training. Initially, every handler ran an exercise with a different dog, in effect, "trying them out." Over the first two weeks, the participants worked with the dogs in the class with no specific dog assigned to them. Gradually, they saw how each dog's methods and abilities differed. Some of the dogs worked very quickly racing forward like rockets to find the planted explosives. Lady that she was, Buffy was very slow and methodical in her search techniques having a distinct mind of her own. She took the time to meticulously check everything possible. Jason watched her as she attentively checked the alarm stickers on the bay windows of a seating hall recognizing that they were not part of the actual window. To her, even those were suspect.

Handlers who were more in tune with the faster dogs kept pulling Buffy along to encourage her to work faster. But she did not respond well to them and continued at her own leisurely, but careful pace. When Jason worked with her, he let her take her time, and given free rein, she excelled. When the training staff saw how well the two worked together, they decided that Jason and Buffy would be a perfect match.

Arduous training followed consisting of explosives detection, obedience, agility, healthcare of the dog and even grooming. Buffy always appreciated the grooming, ensuring that she would remain more beauty than beast. Within Washington D.C. and the surrounding areas, the dogs-in-training were exposed to potential situations and environments they might encounter on the job. Quickly, they were familiarized with escalators, seats, hotels and a wide variety of places where they might eventually search. The more they saw and were exposed to, the less likely they would be distracted when they needed to focus on the serious job of bomb detection.

Before too long, Buffy learned just about every odor that would indicate an explosive device. Monthly retraining and training with other agencies introduced her to the newest substances in a terrorist's arsenal so nothing would go undetected. Becoming highly-accomplished provided the one-time potential Canadian show girl an exciting police career using the skills she had so quickly honed. But best of all, she was permanently partnered with the kind officer that had lovingly tended to her sore eye and brushed her now-silky coat.

Bomb Detection K-9 School Graduation Day – 2003
Courtesy of Stephen Payne

Jason brought Buffy home with him to start her career in law enforcement, and she easily settled into his household. For the first few days at home she stayed in the outdoor kennel when he was not around. But after a week or two, he could tell she was well-behaved and would not be a problem in the house. Off duty, Buffy was the lady of the bachelor's household and demonstrated that to Jason's cat by holding him down with her firm paw to pinch bite him in an effort to groom him to her own high standards.

The new police partners still had things to learn together to perfect their working relationship. Jason had been a patrol officer before he became a K-9 officer, and over the years he had developed his own style of driving. The first time he went on a code run (lights and sirens) with Buffy, he took a turn too fast for her, and the elegant canine flew across the car with all legs flailing, most undignified for a girl of her refinement. From then on, she learned that when she heard the sirens, all she needed to do was lie down to prevent another out-of-control and embarrassing display.

Buffy was never required to attack in her training or assignments, but that did not preclude her from protecting Jason if the situation arose. As the soft winds of autumn splashed colorful leaves around the gleaming white Capitol building, Buffy and Jason walked a foot beat one night in its broad shadow. As the lingering evening darkened, they passed a large bush in the surrounding area, and suddenly Buffy hesitated and cocked one ear in its direction. Jason could not see or hear a thing. Nonetheless, he shone his flashlight in the direction of the bush illuminating a homeless and disheveled man who appeared to be sleeping in the protection of the bush's brittle branches. Jason ordered him out, since it was strictly forbidden for the man to be in that vicinity.

"You can't make me come out!" yelled the defiant vagrant.

Obviously knowing something was amiss, Buffy barked a warning to him.

"Is that a dog you've got there?" the sleepy man yelled through the branches.

When Jason assured him that it was, the man agreed to come out.

"Don't let that dog near me!" the man cried as he scrambled out of the bush and quickly disappeared into the cool night.

After the man's departure, Jason and Buffy examined the area for any suspicious items. Luckily, there were none, and the pair continued along the pathway to complete their assigned route that brisk fall night.

Even without specialized training, Buffy had sensed something was wrong, and Jason's close bond with her allowed him to correlate her unusual change of behavior and cautious steps indicating possible danger from a hidden man with unknown intentions. From that time on, he felt the same security from his bomb detection dog as other officers felt walking beside their specially-trained protective patrol dogs, and Jason knew that Buffy would never let him down. Her protective skills had never been professionally tested before, but the vagrant in the bush provided all the testing Jason felt she would ever need.

Far from her solitary days in her former police kennel, Buffy traveled with Jason wherever they were needed. She trotted through glamorous hotel lobbies and paraded proudly through airports, politely flying in the cabins of airliners. She loved every minute of her job as she increasingly moved in the powerful social circles of government. Buffy stayed in hotel rooms with Jason, and she was called to work the Republican National Convention in 2004, where she was required to conduct sweeps of the buildings where delegates and candidates would later gather.

While on that assignment, Buffy was called to New York Harbor to search aboard the USS Intrepid, the retired aircraft carrier turned into a museum. The decks of the ship had been walked upon by many influential and historical figures over decades, and now Buffy moved confidently across that deck on the most serious of missions. A member of Congress was to visit aboard ship so it was mandatory that Jason and Buffy sweep the ship for possible explosives.

Upon arrival, Jason found that the superstructure (the tall tower on the flight deck) needed to be searched. Shading his eyes from the sun and looking skyward, he saw that the ladders were narrow, steep and open. Buffy had never climbed such naval ladders before aboard a ship and doing so would present a challenge to even the most agile dog. At just fifty-seven pounds, no doubt carefully maintaining her petite girlish figure, Buffy showed no hesitation at attempting the climb. She skillfully climbed up the ladders as if it was routine, positioning each carefully-placed paw upon the rungs. Later, she had no difficulty navigating the restrictive and difficult passageways of the large sea-going vessel. The bomb tech watching her was very impressed with her agility and work ethic as she continued her methodical sweep of the area until all areas were deemed safe.

Returning to the capital, Buffy was an integral part of the traditions of Washington. Before the annual State of the Union addresses, the Capitol Police K-9s routinely swept the House of Representatives, and in 2004 the duty fell to Buffy and Jason. In the quiet chamber, Buffy walked along the colorful carpet where the most powerful figures in Washington would later gather and where legendary presidents and power brokers had spoken.

"It was an honor, privilege and a great responsibility," said Jason, "knowing that the President of the United States would speak there safely due to our protective sweep of the area."

Between security sweeps in Washington, Buffy began to shine as the canine hostess of Washington. Her friendly personality allowed her to graciously welcome visitors and guests to the Capitol. Those serving in Congress began to look for the furry Perle Mesta and accepted her friendly wag of the tail greeting as she made her rounds. As she worked among the inner circle of Washington's elite, no experienced socialite could have conducted herself with more grace among such luminaries.

Beyond that, Buffy showed her ability to interact with all varieties and ages of people. When Jason's grandfather and wheelchair-bound grandmother visited Washington, he watched as Buffy greeted the woman for the first time at Union Station. Soft steps and sensitivity prevailed, and soon Buffy placed both her dainty paws gently in the woman's lap and softly reached up to lick the smiling face. Buffy was the great dispenser of canine kisses, and over the years she found many happy recipients.

Children that Buffy encountered loved her as much as she loved them. Her most rewarding encounters with them came through the Make-A-Wish Foundation, which provided unforgettable experiences for terminally-ill children. Buffy seemed to know instinctively that any child in a wheelchair needed that little extra-gentle touch or lick on the face. She innately understood that the children were special cases requiring her undivided attention and absolute devotion. Small gentle hands lingered in her soft fur, and bright eyes that too frequently had been dulled with pain, sparkled in her presence.

Several times, Buffy was called upon to greet individual children flown to Washington by the foundation. When a child requested to be a "Dignitary for the Day" in the nation's capital, all stops were pulled out, and Hostess Buffy was called out to help with the festivities. For those golden hours after the child arrived, thoughts of pain and medical treatments were forgotten. From the moment the child stepped into the black limousine, escorted by police SUVS and motorcycles with all lights flashing, it was a day of wonder. Often the SWAT team made an appearance to "protect" their special charge and give out hats and stickers. Like a revered Head of State, the child watched enthusiastically as his motorcade ran red lights at intersections as the procession made its way to the Capitol building.

The arrival point at the Capitol was momentarily shut down to other visitors, and the young dignitary made his or her way from the limousine to the entrance into the Rotunda. And it was there that Buffy took over.

Jason and Buffy await visitors on the Capitol steps.
Courtesy Becki and John Johnston

AceK9.com

Young hands frequently fed her dog bones, and upon one occasion just for fun, a young boy held a bone in his own mouth and offered it to her. Ever so gently, she approached the young man, and displaying her most gentile manners, she retrieved it softly from his mouth. Buffy remained on hand for pictures and the tour of the Capitol, and once endeared herself to a young boy to the point that he insisted that she stay with him for the entire day. She did just that serving as his moral support and cheerful companion. No finer hostess could have been found for the joyful child benefactors of the Make-A-Wish Foundation, and smiles and laughter were always the order of the day.

In 2004 and 2005, Jason and Buffy were assigned to the COPS (Concerns of Police Survivors) picnic in Alexandria, Virginia. During Police Week, seminars were held for survivors of police officers killed in the line of duty, and at the conclusion, a picnic was held in their honor. Live bands and good food were enjoyed, and later the K-9 Association put on an entertaining demonstration where highly-trained dogs performed showing off their skills in obedience, agility and locating simulated explosives or narcotics. From the sidelines, Buffy watched her counterparts from other agencies who came to entertain the families. An apprehension drill with a chosen K-9 galloping after a "bad guy" in a padded suit was the perfect finale to the lively demonstration.

Buffy easily negotiates the A-frame with the same
expertise as her male counterparts.

Courtesy of Jason Conlon

Buffy was up next, doing what she did best with families being petted and spreading goodwill. Amid a sea of smiling faces, Buffy walked among family members and especially the children as Jason handed out junior officer stickers to eager hands. Answering all the questions about Buffy that were asked, Jason found much satisfaction in giving the grieving families a brief respite from their pain, and at the same time, watching Buffy benefit from all the attention and affection the families showered upon her.

For approximately three hours, Buffy visited with the families and children of the fallen officers. Many of the children were very young and didn't understand that dogs did not like to have their ears and tails pulled. Again, sensitively assessing the children's situations, Buffy took it all in stride and gave each of them a lick anyway. Because of her hard work and dedication working with the COPS Organization, she was awarded an Honorable Mention Award by the Capitol Police. She is one of only a handful of K-9s to receive such an honor and wears the red and blue pin proudly above the police badge on her collar. Buffy and two other Capitol Police dogs received the prestigious award, and each received a certificate issued in the dog's own name. Awarded at the annual awards ceremony, the certificates reflected the appreciation of the department for the dogs' contributions as members of the Capitol Police.

Buffy's training continued, and she easily passed the standard National Odor Recognition Test in 2007, given by the Bureau of Alcohol, Tobacco and Firearms. In 2007 and again in 2008, she became a Certified Explosive Detector through the United States Police Canine Association, and her increased skill levels qualified her for even more pressing assignments. Now highly-credentialed, she was qualified for the most demanding and important of assignments.

Between work assignments, Buffy posed in front of the Capitol to become a "Cover Girl" for the United States Police Canine Association's magazine, the Canine Courier, her broad "smile" reflecting her easy nature.

"Cover Girl," Buffy, keeping the Capitol building safe

Courtesy of the United State Police Canine Association - Photo by Jason Conlon

In addition to her own searching duties, Buffy was called upon as an already-certified dog to contaminate "hides" where uncertified dogs would search to find planted explosive material to gain their own accreditation. Explosive substances were planted in two of three rooms in a search area. To qualify, the tested dogs had to find them in both rooms. Then they went on to the hidden danger again, this time secreted in cars. Out of five cars, the dogs were required to determine which two held the explosives. They had to find all four locations to obtain a perfect score to be certified as an explosive detector dog.

With so many dogs being tested, the search area became more contaminated for the dogs that searched last. So K-9s already tested were called in to contaminate the search areas with scent to create a level playing field for all the dogs. Buffy had to find the explosives first to validate that the substance was placed where it should be, authenticating the results of the testing for the other dogs. Assisting with the testing kept her skills sharp and aided the other handlers and dogs in their quest towards certification, which would allow them to join the ranks of dogs expertly trained in bomb detection.

In 2007, Buffy was also called back to New York on another protective assignment near the United Nations. Her previous trip to New York had made her accustomed to the hustle and bustle of the dynamic and fast-paced city life there, and she worked with no distractions as she focused on the serious business of the day.

The Republican National Convention, in 2008, took her to Saint Paul, Minnesota, and as always, she handled the call with perseverance despite the long hours and numerous sweeps required of her. While on the protective details, Jason and Buffy constantly searched sensitive areas for the nation's leadership, once more providing the assurance of absolute safety.

Back at the Capitol, Buffy was selected to participate when students visited there. All eyes were on her as Jason spoke to the students. Bomb techs and SWAT team members spoke to them also as part of the program, but afterward the students routinely bypassed the human participants and headed straight for Buffy to meet and pet her. And as the hot summer days in Washington turned to fall, Buffy attended scheduled career days at local schools where Jason spoke of the benefits of studying hard and obeying teachers and parents. Buffy was the perfect symbol of obedience. Even the youngest students responded to Buffy's talents and gazed at her kind eyes and stunning beauty.

In late December of 2008, Buffy and Jason attended the National Canine Initiative hosted by the Bureau of Alcohol, Tobacco, Firearms and Explosives. The federally-administered course was rigorous, and the pair put in long hours increasing their knowledge of the safe handling of explosive training aids, how to properly store the training aids, legal issues and how to recognize IEDs (improvised explosive devices) when conducting searches. There were written tests to be passed as well as operational tests. The stringent National Odor Recognition Test was also administered during that time, and Buffy passed her recertification with flying colors. Their success was another example demonstrating the effectiveness of the Capitol Police Canine Training programs. Recognition by such a respected agency, well-known for expert training of detector dogs, was yet one more jewel in Buffy's shining crown.

The year 2009 brought the inauguration of a new president, and the occasion meant long days for Buffy and Jason. On Inauguration Day, they were hard at work long before anyone else attending the event had arisen. From the early morning throughout the entire day, Buffy's expertise was needed. She first conducted explosive detection sweeps of military personnel coming to the Capitol. Later, her duties included keeping watch over the first motorcade before moving on to other rendezvous points throughout the city to meet, sweep and then motorcade the VIPs to the Capitol and to the White House reviewing stand. On that extremely cold day, Buffy moved down the parade route in full view of all the Americans that lined the streets to catch glimpses of the new first family.

Inauguration Day, 2009 - a top honor for a top dog

Courtesy of James Davis

For such a high-society lady, Buffy's needs are few. Verbal praise, a run in the park with Jason, a throw of her favorite Kong toy and an ice-cold cup of Frosty Paws on a hot summer's day are all she requires. With her four furry paws planted firmly on Washington D.C.'s historic and hallowed ground, there is no air of arrogance about her. She parades the Capitol grounds with beauty and dignity, but at the same time she unmistakably performs her bomb detection duties with complete focus and ability. As the glamorous Belle of Washington, K-9 Buffy will continue to diligently perform her duties until her retirement with her proud and loving handler, Jason Conlon, at her side.

Sitting at her vantage point on the U.S. Capitol steps, K-9 Buffy has a clear view across the sparkling Reflecting Pool on the Mall as she gazes at the people below who come to visit daily in her impressive domain. In the shadows of the Washington Monument, she is one dog who found a life and job with the United States Capitol Police that so well-suited her personality, and it placed her exactly where she needed to be.

An impressive view for an impressive team
Courtesy of Becki and John Johnston–AceK9.com

14

MWD Rinny #681F

"Never Forget"

Tom Wilson, a Missouri farm boy assigned to the Air Force Security Police, arrived in Vietnam in 1966 at the ripe age of twenty. He had been married just two weeks. The foreign land shrouded by mystery and warfare became slowly visible when his plane broke through the clouds on final approach to the air base runway. Tom was struck by the lush green scenery below and wondered how a vicious war could be taking place in such a serene and verdant landscape. But as the plane's tires hummed down the runway to a gradual stop, reality tempered the moment. In a more austere moment, he wondered if he would ever see his parents and new bride again.

Tom had no thoughts of becoming a dog handler when he arrived at Ton Son Nuht Air Force Base near Saigon. Dressed in the typical tan shirt and slacks, with an Air Force blue cap hugging his head, he descended the steps of the Continental Airliner that had brought him that far. Blinking into the sun as he deplaned, he felt a rush of hot air hit him like a blast furnace. With each labored breath, he felt as though he was inhaling thick syrup. After walking just twenty-five yards into the terminal his shirt was soaked, and sweat dripped profusely in steady rivulets off his arms and legs. Tom thought he surely had descended into hell.

At the initial processing, his group was told by the briefing officer that they would see a lot of death during their tour of duty. The morgue at the base held over one-hundred-fifty bodies and numerous limbs, and the count rose daily. Although he could not hear gunfire, that macabre fact reminded him why he was there and forced the tragic reality of the war to come rushing back. Culturally and literally, he was a long way from home.

Tom processed in the next day and was instructed on the ways of survival while "in country." It was imperative not to leave the base alone, not to live downtown or not to buy souvenirs there, as reports of explosives planted in some of the beautiful oriental dolls sent home to loved ones had been reported. He was reminded to wear mosquito repellent and be sure to sleep under mosquito netting. Then the men were told how to exchange their American money for foreign currency. All of these warnings and instructions swirled in his head as he familiarized himself with his new and dangerous surroundings. Vigilance was the key to one feeling so vulnerable in this land.

The next day, Tom crowded onto a bus with other recruits heading towards Bien Hoa, where they would be stationed. Through the bus window, Tom could see the mass of humanity teeming in the streets of Saigon. Under a scorching sun, the bus wound its way like a slow slithering reptile through knots of congested traffic and honking horns. Military vehicles with an air of urgency raced along in both directions. Vietnamese peasants on bicycles and motor scooters and hundreds of people chattering in high-pitched unrecognizable tones walked in and along the fetid streets. Tom gazed at the shop windows as the bus crept forward. Rows and rows of beautiful wooden caskets were displayed in so many of the shop windows.

"One of those is for me," he thought as he passed them.

The ornate caskets were an ominous sign and a vivid reminder that all those who served "in country" did not return home.

The town was pungently alive with a mix of mold and sweat. Small clusters of natives cooked spicy food on the streets, and the resultant aroma mixed with distinctive barnyard odors filled Tom's nostrils. It was to be a smell he would never erase from his memory.

The next day, Tom would see more when he visited Bien Hoa City. After exchanging money, he and three others boarded a lambretta, the traditional motor scooter with an attached cab. Rows of hot wooden benches in the back seated all the passengers. The dark-skinned driver weaved in and out of traffic with terrifying abandon dodging the noisy Vietnamese and the sight-seeing Americans who walked there.

Tom was relieved when he arrived with his friends at a designated local "safe café," where the hungry men sat down and ordered steak. When it arrived, Tom found that it had a flavor totally unknown to him. His friends only smelled their food and would not touch it. When Tom realized that dog was served in the café, he felt he would be sick. It was a rude awakening and a most unpleasant introduction to the foreign culture of Vietnam.

In Bien Hoa the next day there were more briefings. Tom was taken to one of the Security Police "huts" and was advised it would be his home for the next twelve months. He swung open the hinged screen door, and his eyes slowly swept over the torrid hut. Steel-framed bunks sat side-by-side, double stacked. Each held a thin, uncomfortable mattress, and each bunk had its own mosquito net which kept mosquitoes at bay, but also locked in the smothering heat.

The forty-foot tin-roofed building had a concrete floor, and the outer walls slanted away from the building to channel the excessive rain away from the foundation. Stand-up lockers held clothes, weapons, pictures of distant wives or girlfriends and the ever-present "short-time calendars" to mark the days until each man would rotate back to "the world." Like everywhere else, the hot sweaty smell was pervasive despite heavy doses of talcum power generously applied by the men who lived there. Save for a few overhead fans, there was little ventilation, and the stagnant air hung like a low oppressive cloud that never dissipated.

Bien Hoa was an extremely busy Air Force base. F100 fighter jets whining and straining on take-off streaked through the azure skies like arrows eclipsing into silver crosses against the sky. The Vietnam Air Force's A1E propeller fighters sputtered and lifted upward, and whirring helicopters hovered over the tarmac in an un-ending drone, ferrying crews in and out of battle. Around the clock in sun or rain, aircraft took off and landed, and parachute flares dropped from hovering aircraft to light up the dangerous night. It was a constant show of sound and lights.

Tom spent his nights as a flight-line guard walking around aircraft and sometimes sitting in a flight-line observation tower for an eight-hour shift watching for intruders on the base. Perched ten feet up in the air, he had a clear view. A sandbag bunker surrounded the base of the tower in case of a sapper attack (Viet Cong ground soldiers), and sandbags strung like plump beads on a sagging necklace hung around the platform. Sentry dogs with their handlers patrolled the perimeter of the airport protecting the men and planes there.

Tom carried a mobile radio to call control if he spotted anything suspicious. From that radio crackled messages from dog units on the outer posts calling for back-up. He could not imagine what the dogs were seeing that he could not, but the handlers trusted their dogs' alerts and cautiously followed up on them.

From his vantage point, Tom watched lumbering C133 cargo/troop carriers land and take off among Australian Air Force Caribou Troop Carriers. With fascination, he watched the enormous C47s nicknamed, "Spooky." They were WWII vintage troop carriers used in Viet Nam as gun ships and for dropping parachute flares to illuminate the night as bright as day. On night shifts, Tom watched the red flames of Spooky's mini guns fire at VC positions on the ground. The tracer rounds fired so fast that the mini guns glowed red against the black sky from the heat of the firing.

Early one morning, after just finishing an 11 p.m.-7 a.m. shift, Tom watched a C130 unloading Army troops that had just come in from the field. He felt tremendous sadness watching the dead and wounded being unloaded. More mothers' sons would not be returning home.

From atop the tower, Tom had a bird's eye view of the lightning storms that struck on a regular basis. In the black of night, long fingers of white-hot lightning cracked with ear-splitting ferocity. Clawing the sky in a continual dazzling display, the electrically-charged strikes traced the image of reptilian predators it seemed to Tom, stretched out in blinding patterns against a black canvas. Over and over, the lightning cracked, and watching it, Tom could easily understand why the Vietnamese believed in dragons. During one particularly bad storm a young airman had been struck and killed by the beast's unpredictable and unrelenting fury.

The intensity of the sweltering heat was constant during the day, but when the orange Asian sun slipped below the purple horizon, Vietnam cooled off to the point of being almost cold at night. It was a constant adjustment for a newcomer to acclimate.

Tom remained a "ramp rat," for about a week, when an opening came up in kennel support. Feeding and watering the dogs and cleaning up their kennels seemed more appealing than his current job. Since he had always liked animals, and they liked him, he eagerly volunteered and was accepted.

But these dogs were not the pets he had played with on the farm. They were not dogs to run up to and playfully wrestle with. They were not even dogs that played with each other. And unlike police dogs, military sentry dogs at that time were not paired with just one handler. The dogs had a succession of handlers over the course of the war, making it hard for them to bond with just one. So feared and effective were that dogs that the Viet Cong placed bounties on them and their handlers. Trust from the dogs was elusive but could be earned. They were invaluable considering all the lives they had saved.

Back to day shift, Tom reported two miles from the airbase to the kennel office located in a tent and was taken down to the dogs with another worker. A chain link fence strung with razor wire at the top marked the compound.

Sentry Dog Compound – Bien Hoa, Vietnam
Courtesy of Tom Wilson

An old parachute supported by jagged chicken wire hung loosely over the kennel, which confined fifty dogs. The dogs were attached to their original shipping crates by chains clipped to each collar. The metal crates served as their daytime home. Large holes had been drilled in the sides of each crate for ventilation, but the crates were still too hot to enter. The dogs' individual yards were covered with sand, which was sometimes watered down before the dogs arrived back from night shift to keep them cool during the hot day that each sunrise brought. Four feet separated each dog's quarters.

Off from the kennel, there was a cemetery for the dogs that died on the flights over or that died from the extreme heat. It sat just behind a small rubber tree within the compound. En route to the sentry dog compound, the assistant kennel master indicated to Tom what a dog post would look like. In the distance was as an old French fort, a reminder of France's presence in Viet Nam from the 1800s to the early 1950s. No one was allowed to enter the structure, even if the dog alerted, as there could have been many explosive traps inside, as well as many large snakes.

Small cemetery for the dogs that died in Bien Hoa
Courtesy of Tom Wilson

Old fort left by the French from their earlier occupation
Courtesy of Tom Wilson

Once "in country," the dogs had excellent veterinary care, but disease ravaged the land, and dogs also fell victim to snakes and poison foliage.

The sergeant in charge of the kennel walked Tom and another man around in the blistering 100-plus-degree heat. The dogs began to bark wildly and looked at Tom curiously.

"How do the dogs take it?" Tom asked.

The sergeant told him that it was imperative that the dogs had plenty of water.

Tom warily eyed the chain on one of the dogs.

"Is that chain sufficient?" he asked with some trepidation.

"Better hope so," the sergeant laughed, "'cause he could tear you up if he got close to you and didn't know you."

Tom could not imagine how he would feed and water so many hostile barking dogs. The sergeant explained that one of the men would distract the dog, and the brave one of the pair would grab the food and water pans.

"Do you trust each other?" he asked with a smile.

The men, until then unknown to each other, stared at each other with some skepticism, but later found they worked very well together.

The dogs could detect the smell of fear and uncertainty in Tom. Three times over the course of his training period he came within a few inches of being bitten. A particularly aggressive dog named Rinny was one of the potential biters.

A month later, one of the K-9 handlers was removed from service for throwing a hot cup of coffee into the face of a dog he could not control. That dog was Rinny, and he was left with no handler. Rinny was worth $100.00 to the military, which had paid that for him when he was taken from his Indiana home in 1962. He had been just a year old. After his previous experience with his last handler, it would be especially hard to teach Rinny to trust.

Tom watched him from a distance to assess the dog. Despite his aggression, Rinny was a smart and observant dog. He had dutifully learned the basic K-9 commands so that he would sit, heel, come and stay. He knew hand signals as well. Somewhere along the line, one of his handlers had taught him tricks. He knew not only how to sit, but to "sit high," raising his front legs to paw at the air to beg. He could stand tall on his back feet, and if someone asked him what he thought of the enemy Viet Cong, he would emit a low growl.

K-9 Rinny "sits high."
Courtesy of Tom Wilson

"What do you do if an officer comes near?" the men would ask Rinny, and he would raise his paw and salute.

Tom was hesitant yet intrigued by the dog and decided to consider him later, when he was asked to become a handler. Rinny was a bit of an enigma and would present real challenges, but Tom could not take his eyes off the dog.

Rinny was not a dog who would easily allow anyone near him. First Tom had to establish a trusting bond. He needed Rinny to become accustomed to him and become familiar with his scent and mannerisms. Rinny and Tom would have to learn to communicate and read each other even with subtle gestures and expressions. Tom wondered if it would even be possible. If so, he realized it would take time.

Tom moved to the K-9 hut and lived with the fifty other handlers there. They all worked at night when it was cooler and tried their best to sleep during the stifling day. At night the Viet Cong chanced to come closer to the air base. If they mortared the base, it was from outside the perimeter, but if they came in as a sapper squad that is when the dogs sprang into action.

Eager to start with Rinny, Tom returned to the kennel area to begin the process. At the entrance, he could see an obstacle course at the back of the area. A huge sign sat in front of the kennel area warning all those who were unauthorized to keep out. An unlawful or unescorted entry the sign stated in both English and Vietnamese could result in potential damage from the dogs.

The kennel master, assistant and a third kennel worker were in the tent relaxing when Tom edged his way towards Rinny. The kennel master had strictly forbidden him from getting close to any dog while he was there by himself, so he sat on a small stool a foot beyond the dog's reach.

Tom began to read the Air Force manual to Rinny. He thumbed through the pages and found the section that pertained to the guidelines determining how dogs qualified for service.

"A dog needs clear eyes, a good bone structure, a passing dental exam and a good disposition," he read to the curious dog.

Rinny stared into his eyes as he read, totally absorbed by the calming spoken words. Tom continued reading the written paragraphs to soothe the dog. When he tired of reading, he simply talked to Rinny.

"You look like a wolf, Rinny," he said as he noted the dog's dark face and body coat. But you are just perfect."

Rinny seemed to love the flattery, yet he was still wary.

The kennel had just one female dog, Tammy, fairly docile unless she had to go after any Viet Cong. Then she was transformed into a terrorizing attacker that would not back down.

"I've got a new wife at home, Rinny," Tom told him, "How about you? Are you sweet on Tammy?"

Tom told Rinny about all the dogs he had owned growing up, and the dark head cocked to one side listening intently. The quizzical dark eyes followed Tom's every word and movement. Day after day, Tom read and talked to Rinny in the improvised version of canine school.

Finally, the kennel master said, "Today's the day for you to get up close and personal with Rinny."

Tom dripped with sweat at first thinking it was the jungle heat, but he noticed the kennel master was perfectly dry. It was time. The assistant kennel master strapped a muzzle over Rinny's nose and mouth and instructed Tom to walk up to the dog and pet him but to show no fear. Rinny evidently could not hear Tom's knees knocking as the potential human partner suspected he might.

Tom took a first hesitant step toward Rinny, and despite their previous friendly conversations, the massive dog growled and lunged at him. That stirred up all the other dogs in the kennel, and a chorus of guttural growls and sharp agitated barks echoed within the enclosure. It seemed to Tom the dogs were all saying, "Good job, Rinny, show him who's boss."

After several tries, Tom slowly put his hand on Rinny to pet him. The assistant kennel master held the dog very tightly, and Rinny was still growling.

"What have I gotten myself into?" Tom thought.

He had such a short time to make progress with the dog or be out of the program. The next day he would try again.

Just inside the kennel area, in close proximity to the dogs, sat an odd-looking piece of training equipment. It was a piece of pipe attached to a metal box. It represent "a dog" and was used to show the handler in training how far the dog should be held from his body when taking the dog to and from the kennel and to the waiting truck. It was also used to determine how the dogs, especially Rinny, would react to Tom giving loud commands to the non-compliant metal dog.

Rinny's "girlfriend," K-9 Tammy

Courtesy of Tom Wilson

Tom and his metal dog
Courtesy of Tom Wilson

Over time, it also became part of an initiation ritual. Tom's picture was taken next to the metal "dog." He was holding a leash attached to it, and the picture would be posted at each guard mount for the more experienced handlers' amusement until Tom was accepted by them. In the interim, Tom was eager to learn all the techniques of dog handling.

Rinny had been taught that when the choke chain and muzzle were on, he was off duty. The muzzles and chokes were used only to lead the dogs to and from the kennel on six-foot leashes. Tom, still tentative, was assured the dog would not hurt him.

Days passed and the routine continued with gradual progress on each successive day. Finally, the day came when Tom was to get close to Rinny with no kennel master holding the dog. Tom swallowed hard several times and felt like crying, "Mama!" but stepped gingerly into the dog's area. Rinny wore his muzzle, but he still lunged.

"Get him on your left side!" ordered the assistant kennel master, "That's how the dog knows where his place is when walking with the handler!"

Rinny was not ready to cooperate.

"Be forceful, tell him OUT!" Tell him heel, sit, stay!" ordered the kennel master sharply.

With authority in his voice, Tom called out the commands. He finally got Rinny on his left side and patted him several times on his left shoulder running his fingers through the amazingly hot fur coat.

Once again, Rinny growled. But then, most surprisingly, he stretched up on his bushy hind legs and placed his front paws on Tom's chest, and the dog was taller than Tom. With the full weight of the dog pressing against his chest, Tom peered into the dark eyes as the dog stared back intensely into his own. Then Tom stepped back. It was, indeed, a slow process bonding with a dog, but the first step had been taken. Tom knew the bond would last forever.

This same exercise continued for a week. In Tom's spare time, he continued to read to Rinny and talk to him. Finally, the day came for Tom to slip Rinny's muzzle over his long snout and sharp teeth, snap his leash on and take him for a walk. Tom was overjoyed but a bit apprehensive still, and he hoped Rinny did not remember the day that he almost bit Tom.

The muzzle slipped on easily. Rinny pranced outside the kennel area through the kennel master's tent and out to the training area to the obstacle course. The course was used to keep the dogs in shape should they ever have to be turned loose on the post, where they would have to jump over ditches, climb rough terrain or jump to attack the enemy.

The pair practiced some commands, and Tom walked the dog down the road and back. For the first time he "put Rinny up," returning him to his kennel after removing his choke chain and muzzle before ordering him to sit and shake hands. Sit and shake hands signaled finality. Their time for the shift was over. Then Tom backed away from him and told him, "Good boy."

Slowly, the connection started to form. Rinny's behavior became consistent. For the first time, Tom felt that he could trust Rinny. One day when they shook hands and Tom walked away, Rinny barked as if to say, "Let's work together." Rinny was finally Tom's. They would work together as a pair in a hostile foreign place always looking out for each other. That night, he would finally be "on post" with Rinny.

At 10 p.m., fellow handlers met the new dog handler for guard mount where they all fell out in formation for roll call. They were given any special information needed and told what to watch for while on post. The dogs were always happy to hear the kennel truck with their handlers coming in the cool evenings to get them for a shift, barking long before the truck was even in sight.

The handlers went down to the dogs to get them ready for the shift, and Tom hoped Rinny would remember him at night since they had always seen each other during the day. With renewed confidence upon seeing Rinny's face, Tom easily slipped the muzzle over the dog's nose. He clipped the leash on Rinny's choke collar and trotted the dog to the training area next to the kennel tent where the dogs ran the obstacle course before reporting to their designated posts. Tom had never put Rinny through the course before, and although Tom was nervous, he found that Rinny knew what to do and did it to perfection. The handlers ran the course with the leashed dogs, and it seemed effortless.

As a team, they boarded the truck and were dropped off to patrol the side of a long runway. As posts went, it was known by the more-experienced handlers to be fairly safe, and nearby was an open sandbag bunker where the handler and his dog could take cover in case of an attack. The handler could also sit on it and eat his C-rations given to him at guard mount. Once on post, each handler removed the muzzle and replaced the choke collar with the leather collar. That collar indicated to the dogs that they were on duty, and their demeanor changed accordingly.

Tom was glad to start out at a more secure post. The sounds of gunfire and Spooky firing stuttering mini guns and dropping brilliant flares surrounded the dog teams. The fear of the unknown erupting instantly and savagely weighed heavy on the lonely more isolated patrols. Large cats and tigers moved with stealth through the country side, and beyond the minefield fences Buddhist monks, incongruously, walked back and forth. It was as far from a Missouri farm as a man could get.

First night on post, Tom plopped down on the bunker and ate his C-rations as Rinny watched him closely. In the bright moonlight, Tom saw the sensitive eyes. Then Rinny put his front paws on each of Tom's legs and licked his cheek. It was the first kiss he had received from the dog, and it cemented their partnership. Tom patted him and told him what a good boy he was.

Out on post, Tom reviewed in his mind the standard operating procedures. Orders were to only fire or turn the dog loose if fired upon. Handlers were to call in for back-up when the dogs alerted to humans they might detect approaching the base.

Hour after hour, Tom watched for Rinny to alert. At Rinny's first alert, Tom, without hesitation, called for back-up. A jeep arrived with a driver, rifleman and a machine gunner. The men popped an illumination flare, but all they saw was a rabbit.

This scenario was repeated several times that night with a variety of animals being detected, and soon Tom could hear the other handlers on the radio laughing and making fun of him and his lack of experience was exposed as clearly as if it had been illuminated by a thousand flares.

Thankfully, a handler who later became one of Tom's best friends came to the post and instructed him on how to differentiate between the dog's alerts. The alert when Rinny scented an animal differed from when he scented a human. The two men walked the post together that night, and the handler explained that Rinny could scent an intruder from as far away as fifty yards and could also see in the dark for about that far. Having had no K-9 training did not deter Tom, and he learned a lot on post that night. The trainers had used a pouch scented with snake or cat when Rinny was first trained in order to instill the difference between a false animal alert and a potentially lethal alert to human danger. Sensing an animal, Rinny had learned to pull on the leash and whimper but to do no more. Tom was to take up the slack on the leash and in low tones say, "Good boy, Rinny, no," and pat him on his left shoulder and keep giving him praise.

The low growl was key. When Rinny sensed human danger, not only would he pull on his leash, but he emitted a low growl that would make the hair on Tom's neck stand up. Tom soon learned it was a far different response than an animal alert where the dog really seemed to just be begging to be let off the leash to go have fun chasing an unsuspecting animal. With time and experience, it would all fall into place.

When the truck arrived that first night to pick up all the teams, the other handlers tried to sit as far away from Tom and Rinny as possible. Once again, it was made clear to him that he had to earn their respect before he would be accepted.

Tom knew the second night would test him. When he arrived to go on post, much fun and harassment was directed towards him.

"It would be a lot more quiet tonight, Wilson, if you took your metal dog with you instead," laughed one of the handlers. Maybe you could read its alerts!"

Tom spent many a lonely night just he and Rinny side-by-side, but alone, as the handlers remained cool to them. But Tom would not give up. Soon, he became expert at reading the dog's alerts. They worked as one efficient unit. As he became more proficient and familiar with Rinny, the other handlers trusted him more. His dog became as loyal to him as the other handlers' dogs were to them. Finally, after a few weeks he was one of them.

On an isolated night, Tom and Rinny checked out the area and settled in for their watch. Tom sat down next to the bunker and called Rinny to him.

"Rinny, I'm gonna groom you," he said, and Rinny sat up and got very happy.

Tom proceeded to give the dog's massive body a rub down, loosening all the thick matted fur. That job done, Rinny would be cooler in the daytime heat.

Tom thought back to the day a visiting high-ranking officer came to Bien Hoa and wanted to see how the dogs worked. In the heat of the day, the muzzled dogs were paraded in front of the officer in the unbearable temperatures as the sun beat down on the over-heated dogs and handlers. He hoped nothing like that would happen again and was sorry he could not have protected Rinny from that experience.

Rinny continued to be an overly-aggressive dog, and unfortunately, liked to show that side when the dogs and handlers practiced together on the firing range. As Tom fired his gun, Rinny was supposed to lie at his side. But Rinny had too much energy and just didn't like to sit still, and his behavior did not go unnoticed by the kennel master.

Rinny on the left, not yet ready to lie by Tom's side when the guns were fired
Courtesy of Tom Wilson

29

"Wilson, make that dog stay down!" he yelled to Tom, "Who is handling whom?" "We are gonna talk about this when we get back to the kennel!"

While in the kennel area, Tom noticed the dogs dragging their chains would often knock over their water buckets, so he suggested the buckets be hung from the crates and that proved to be a much better arrangement for the dogs.

On post, in the cool of night, Tom enjoyed the relief as he opened his C-rations. The handlers carried a small duffel bag with a sterno stove to heat the rations. They carried a small flashlight, band aids and other medical supplies, but the dog was the most important provision they brought along.

Tom dug through the rations and noticed that some of the dates on the coffee, creamer, gum and matches were stamped 1945.

"Will you look at that, Rinny!" Tom said in disbelief showing the interested dog the WWII vintage contents he had found.

The men complained that the cigarettes were like cardboard, and the food was little better. Rinny sat in the moonlight and stared at the C-rations. Even if Rinny begged, he was not to be given any, and Tom felt after seeing them that it was a fortunate thing that Rinny was denied them. Tom picked through to find the waterproof matches and pulled out the contents and evaluated the quality for Rinny.

"Now sometimes we've got ham and lima beans, and that's good," he told the focused dog, "but sometimes, it's chicken salad, and that's awful. Looks like tonight it's beefsteak, and that's okay."

Then he found the fruitcake.

It was older vintage but when he showed it to the inquisitive dog, his ears seemed to perk up. "November, 1950," the wrapper said. But Tom figured it was a dessert, and after long stares from mournful eyes he decided to share a bite or two with the begging dog. Rinny eagerly gobbled up three bites of it hardly noticing the date of issue. With stomachs full, they both finished out their watch.

When Tom got to the kennel for duty the next night, the assistant kennel master drew him aside.

"Hey, Wilson," he called to Tom as he arrived at the kennel, "Rinny dimed you out," he said.

The kennel master held a plastic vial containing chunks of pineapple and cherries given to him by the kennel help who cleaned up after Rinny.

"I can't find any of this stuff in the dog food, can you?" he asked Tom.

"Snitched out by the dog," Tom thought.

Sheepishly, he admitted his role in the moonlit fruitcake party he had held with Rinny. The dogs were to have a daily vitamin and eat only dog food which contained a little lard. From then on that is all Rinny was fed, but he had tasted what passed for dessert and that was fine with him.

A new kennel with concrete floors was built in January, 1967. Each dog had his own roomy chain link cage. It was much easier to maintain sanitary conditions for the dogs and safer for the kennel support who could slide the food and water pans under the door while the dogs were out. The floors could be hosed down with water as they were cleaned and cooled. Tom was glad to see living conditions improve for Rinny and the others.

One night, five months later, Tom was assigned a more isolated post. Arriving at each post, Rinny routinely paused to sniff the air and look around to find the best route into the brushy area. Tom always relied on the dog's good judgment. Rinny's decision made, the two waded into the thick brush. A bright moon shone down on the eight-foot tall elephant grass casting it in bluish light. In the shadows, the native grass looked like a high wall standing as a stiff barricade. It was noisy to walk through, but it seldom blew in the wind. It was an excellent place for the enemy to hide.

Tom carried an M-16 rifle with bayonet fixed. Just as Tom sat down to eat his meal, Rinny alerted. What had he heard? Tom was convinced it could be just a snake so he told Rinny to sit and stay. Then he thought more about what could be slithering around him. In the dark, Tom hopped about wildly jabbing his bayonet into the grass and started to jab again when Rinny jumped just as Tom's bayonet accidentally poked the dog's foot, luckily doing no serious damage. Years later, Tom still remembered the look the dog gave him that night.

"You have got to be kidding! How stupid was that!" he had imagined Rinny saying.

Months slogged on through steamy days in the oppressive heat. The blazing sun continually bore down, and noisy planes continued to fly in and out on urgent missions. Tom soon lost track of the number of nights that he and Rinny had patrolled together, but there had been sufficient number that the two had become very familiar with all the posts. During the long hours there, he thought of his wife and his family back home. Rinny still seemed to be thinking of Tammy. Tom had noticed how each time he had Rinny muzzled and leashed at the kennel that Rinny walked a certain path in Tammy's direction. If she was working that night, the dog would sit or lay nearby until she was ready to head for the truck with him.

"I think Rinny had a thing for her. It was as if Rinny had manners. And if we were on an adjoining post, he always seemed to mysteriously get an alert in that area. After duty when we got on the relief truck, he always seemed to try to sit next to her."

One day, a big chocolate cake packed in popcorn arrived in perfect condition for Tom's twenty-first birthday. How much older he seemed than his twenty-one years. Tom shared it with his fellow handlers in the hut but knew better than to save a piece for Rinny. It was inconceivable that Tom had been so long "in country," and his birthday cake was a true reminder of the passage of time.

On the nights Tom and Rinny were posted at the runway post, Tom watched for a spectacular sight. At first light, as they waited for the relief truck to pick them up, they could look upward to see the highly-secret SR-71 Blackbird spy plane soar almost noiselessly through the sky on take off. Few people stationed on base ever saw it. Like a black bat emerging from its cave before dawn, the plane, capable of flying Mach III, climbed high into the sky to complete a secret mission. At twilight, it returned to be once again hidden in its tightly-guarded hanger. Tom remained in awe of it each time he saw it fly.

Sometimes Tom and Rinny were assigned to a post near the Vietnam Air Force officers' housing. One night while they were on post, the wife of a Vietnamese officer crept up within twenty-five to thirty feet of the post. Rinny immediately alerted with a low growl. Tom was getting ready to call in an alert and prepared to set Rinny loose when he saw her. He was greatly relieved when he saw she was not Viet Cong. Then she called to him.

"Number one chop, chop, G.I." she called enthusiastically motioning toward Rinny.

Tom understood immediately. Number one meant good, and chop-chop meant food. The woman was shopping for her family's meal!

"Di' di' mau, Mama San, NO CHOP, CHOP," Tom called back to the disappointed woman, which loosely translated meant, "He ain't for sale!!"

Tom sent her away. His dog was not going to be on any Vietnamese table for dinner. Tom and Rinny returned to the post many nights but never saw her again.

The posts were most often very brushy, and it was good to have an extra pair of canine eyes scouring the dense surroundings. Rinny's nose could indicate what was out there, and Tom watched him carefully as they approached a post at night. Without the dog, a handler could walk into trouble, and the expertise of the dog precluded the men from relying on flares to illuminate the posts, which would give their position away to the enemy. Stealth was always the guard's best friend.

Only fifty yards from the Vietnamese Air Force housing, Tom was sitting on the bunker eating as Rinny sniffed around on the other side. Suddenly, Tom felt something tapping on his foot. Taking a risk, he turned on his flashlight and saw that he had stepped on the tail of a dreaded "seven stepper." It was a small snake unable to strike but capable of chewing on the webs of fingers or whatever it could get hold of. Once the skin was broken, it was said that the victim could take only seven steps before collapsing and dying. He had taken the risk of turning on his flashlight, possibly subjecting himself to sniper fire, but at least he and the dog could see which way to go to get away from the deadly snake. Cobras, pythons and anacondas all posed a lethal danger to dogs and handlers working in Vietnam. He made sure that he and his dog were not victims.

Late one May evening, while working kennel support for a soldier who went to town and had too much "fire water," Tom and Tammy's handler, who was to return home the next day, discussed the possibility of a pending attack after they got off duty.

Tom glanced at his watch. It was around 12:15, and the heat of the day was long behind them. He walked with Tammy's handler to get late chow and to check his mail before returning to the K-9 hut for bedtime, and he speculated that in about an hour they would get hit by the Viet Cong. As he had predicted, in the next hour a rocket/mortar attack erupted. Just as Tom was coming out of the K-9 barracks to enter a bunker, a mortar took a direct hit on the hut across from his. The shattering sound of the explosion was of such magnitude that Tom's hearing was partially damaged. Later in life, he would require hearing aides as a result of the Viet Cong attack. One man was killed in that hut, and fifteen others in the area were killed or injured. Tom and his dog would have to be even more vigilant. It was a time of high alert.

Tammy's handler finished his tour of duty the next day, and Tom witnessed his parting with Tammy. The young handler who had been so brave on post cried like a baby leaving Tammy behind. It was difficult to watch, and Tom tried to put the image out of his mind.

The next night, Tom and his unit were advised by their commander at guard mount that intelligence and forward observers had heard of a pending attack by the hardcore Vietcong. They were to be hit that night. The most aggressive dogs, of which Rinny was the most aggressive, were to be placed strategically around the base. Tom took Rinny to a post farthest from the base at the end of a runway, a most vulnerable position that experienced teams were tapped for. Closer in, Tom had the noise of the continual take-offs of the planes for company, but the posts farther out were eerily quiet. The profound silence was deafening, and in such solitude the pair was even closer than usual. They were each other's only protection and company.

Tom listened in the darkness for each sound. The crack of a twig, the rustle of high grass or the slightest shadowed movement could all prove deadly. All was quiet, and for a short time he felt he could relax. As Tom stood by the bunker to light a cigarette, he felt something he had never felt before exerting pressure on his leg. He looked down and saw Rinny's warm body leaning with full force and bracing against his leg. The dog was sound asleep! Thankfully, the Viet Cong did not decide to strike that night.

During their months of service together, Tom saw handlers come and go. On countless patrols, Rinny alerted several times to Viet Cong creeping through the underbrush. Most anything could creep towards the isolated posts presenting a variety of dangers, and Rinny had heard them all.

Soon, a year was up, and Tom was to be rotated back to the States. In that time he and Rinny had become inseparable. Rinny had once broken a tooth during training, and it was replaced with a steel one. Tom cut out the article from the military newspaper, Stars and Stripes, that had reported Rinny's dental mishap. It would be carefully packed and go home with him for remembrance. Together the duo had survived the Viet Cong, the insufferable climate, the incessant insects and the deadly "seven steppers." The ornate caskets he had seen on display the day he arrived had thankfully not been for him. He and his dog had survived the year.

Now only one would go home.

In his last days in Vietnam, in August of 1967, Tom took Rinny to some of the posts out beyond the bomb dump where bombs, the Spooky-bird flares, Spooky's ammo and ammo for the troops was stored. It was far from the base, and in the day time Tom played with the dog he knew so well. Despite the heavy armament there, it was a peaceful place with a Buddhist temple just a few yards away. They would be safe there.

Tom smiled as Rinny performed all the tricks he had learned to perfection. The last command was to stand tall with his paws on Tom's chest, and he gave the dog a big hug. Rinny gave him a lick on the cheek. Then it was time to take him back to the kennel and say good-bye.

Tom and another handler and his dog boarded the truck. Tom patted Rinny on his left shoulder constantly. He never wanted to forget the feel of the dog's warm fur.

When they arrived at the kennel where he would put Rinny up for the last time, Tom led Rinny to his cage for a few last pictures. He knelt down and shook Rinny's paw as he told the faithful dog how very proud he was of him and what a wonderful friend he had been. Tom pulled a picture of his wife out of his pocket and showed it to Rinny explaining why he had to go home as Rinny softly licked the picture. Then Tom scooped the heavy dog up in his arms and quickly pressed his head again the warm fur before the sheer weight of the dog made him put him back down.

On the night before Tom's departure from Vietnam,
he scooped up Rinny in his arms.

Courtesy of Richard Ingler

He told Rinny to "stand tall" and gave him one last big hug. Once again, Rinny licked his cheek.

Tears streamed from Tom's eyes as he tried to explain to Rinny that they would not see each other again. The dog had been such a loyal companion, and his questioning dark eyes stared into Tom's as they had the first time he had placed his paws on Tom's shoulders when they first met.

"You are just perfect, Rinny."

Sit, shake hands, and back away. That's what Tom had been taught. The commands signaled finality.

...obediently sitting as Tom had taught him

...one last shake

...sitting tall one last time for his beloved master

Courtesy of Richard Ingler

That was the training. But it had never been a harder exercise to execute than on that night. Tom closed the kennel door and walked away. As he left, he heard the kennel master laughing at him for being such a big baby over a dog.

Years later, Tom could still see the silhouette of the dog's pointed ears as the ruffed neck turned to follow Tom's departure. He could still hear the dog's bark as he boarded the truck alone to return to the hut. One last bark, as if to say, "Good-bye friend."

A "freedom bird" awaited Tom at the airport. Safely aboard the commercial airliner, his mind could not dismiss his friend. The memories were too fresh. Tom could still feel the massive body asleep against his leg. He could see the eager eyes focusing on an old piece of fruitcake. And the memory of the dark expressive eyes would forever haunt his soul. The jet-liner lifted off the runway at Bien Hoa, and Tom knew he would never return to the war-torn land. A loyal dog named Rinny had gotten him through it all.

As the steamy jungle landscape land slipped away from his blurry view, shrinking into a brownish yellow patch on the ground, and with only memories to bring home, Tom knew that a part of his heart would always remain in that forbidding place where not all veterans of the war, human or canine, came home. The men were told to change into civilian clothes just before the plane arrived home so that protestors would not recognize them and harass them stateside.

After his return to the States, Tom, haunted by the loss of his Rinny, bought a white German shepherd dog, but it reminded him too much of the dog he had known and loved, and he had to give it up.

Many years later, Tom located Rinny's military records. He found that on Dec. 20, 1970, Rinny was euthanized in Vietnam. The records simply stated that the dog had bilateral cataracts and was "ineffective." Tom knew that the dog would not have been "ineffective" for him. The dog had been worth $100 to the military but far more than that monetary value to Tom.

Black, wolf-like K-9 Rinny, had the number 681F tattooed inside his ear, which identified him as a piece of impersonal military equipment. He was an American dog caught up in a foreign war and had become an expendable commodity to be utilized and then left behind. Tom Wilson and other Vietnam dog handlers knew better. Their dogs were never expendable.

"Rinny 681F was my pal. I wish I could have brought him home," Tom would say forty years later. I have never loved an animal like I did Rinny."

K-9 Rinny is representative of the nearly four thousand dogs that never came home from Vietnam after saving untold numbers of lives. They are dogs never to be forgotten.

Tom Wilson was proven correct— Rinny was just perfect, and the bond did last forever.

K-9 Cinder

"Canadian Cinderella"

Prior to 1994, the Winnipeg Police K-9 Unit in Manitoba, Canada, was comprised of all German shepherd dogs and had been since its inception in 1971. In 1994, the unit acquired a Belgian Malinois, "Buddy," from the Royal Canadian Mounted Police. Buddy was unique in his tracking ability, but he was not a particularly social dog. Constable David Bessason teamed up with Buddy and had much success on the street in comparison to the other handlers in the unit. In fact, he had more arrests with Buddy than all the other handlers combined in the unit so the quality of the dog was well-tested and proven.

For years, frigid Winnipeg was known to have the highest number of homicides and stolen vehicles per capita in Canada so good dogs were essential. In 1995, the Winnipeg Police K-9 Unit started its own breeding program to offset the cost of buying dogs at a price ranging from $5,000 to $8,000 each. Buddy sired all the litters with a female Malinois named Cinder that the Winnipeg Unit had purchased. They used several of the pups from each litter and sold some to other law enforcement agencies.

After five litters and over thirty-five pups, the unit decided to use only the Malinois breed for general purpose dogs. One of the litters produced two promising dogs, a robust male and a small female. The bright little female was named Cinder after her mother. It was thought that she, too, would work out well for the breeding program, but the little dog had ideas of her own.

Constable Bessason, who did all the breeding and raising of the pups, was in charge of training the K-9 teams. Almost immediately, he noticed Cinder's drive to track early when he was testing and imprinting the dogs.

In 2003, two canine teams were chosen for training. One of the dogs included was young Cinder's male litter mate. Although she was not considered for the program, Bessason allowed Cinder to tag along to classes to observe the big boys as they trained. Like a small child on the side-lines who wanted desperately to get into the game, Cinder watched intently. In a world of male police dogs, she was completely mesmerized by the training process. Throughout the gaps in time during the eight-hour day, when the other dogs were not training, Bessason began some initial training with her. Those who watched the eager little dog could not help but notice her strong tracking drive. This was, indeed, Buddy's daughter.

One of the dogs in training had completed a one-and-one-half mile track. At the conclusion of the track, Cinder was let out of the truck to relieve herself and to stretch near the vicinity of the track's end. Suddenly, she hit the track and started off on her own. There was no calling her back. The trainer went to the opposite end of the track and placed a tug toy there and waited. Ten minutes later, Cinder came back on the dead run having completed the track on her own figuring out all the corners and double backs the previous dog had run. After that demonstration, the department was more convinced than ever that female or not, they had to make the best of her abilities.

Because of Cinder's tracking drive, she went on to complete a sixteen-week training course with Constable Eric Luke. She sailed right through the training, and Eric started to work with her on the streets. The department had never used a female dog before, and there was a good degree of skepticism about the little dog's abilities. At just fifty-eight pounds, she weighed thirty-percent less than her male counterparts. "Cinderella" and "Gopher on a Rope" were nicknames given to her by the more-experienced officers who doubted her strength, fearlessness and her abilities compared to their large male dogs. She was a small dog, even for a Malinois, so her nicknames stuck, and she would have a lot to prove.

Still a bit unseasoned, at first Cinder appeared nervous in the buildings and was reluctant to search on certain kinds of floors. The team worked together for awhile, but some doubts lingered regarding her usefulness, so with other dogs available to him, Constable Luke felt it best to change partners.

A controversial decision by a supervising sergeant at that time, protested by many in the K-9 unit whom the dog had finally won over, removed her from the denizens of working K-9s. The sergeant preferred to use her for search and rescue, as he was starting to assist in organizing a search and rescue program for another agency.

But there was a problem. Cinder could search just fine as that was her passion. But when she found her quarry, she did not want to be rewarded with the typical ball or toy. What she wanted to do was bite the quarry she had just found. Many a decoy "victim" had to scramble fast from a hiding place to avoid her snapping teeth. Her days in search and rescue were numbered, and once more she remained in limbo.

After conducting another training class, Trainer Bessason found himself without a dog since Buddy, Cinder's father, had just retired. So for six months the trainer worked Cinder with the stipulation that she could not search any buildings. Bessason later transferred to the Homicide Department leaving Cinder once again without a partner.

K-9 Cinder--alone again

Courtesy of Rob Tighe

Officer Rob Tighe with K-9 Cinder

Courtesy of Rob Tighe

Shortly thereafter, Constable Rob Tighe trained two dogs in the program that were both eliminated due to their tracking inconsistencies. There were no dogs left to draw from. Dismayed, he convinced his sergeant to partner him with Cinder and give her one more chance. The sergeant granted his wish, and she joined Rob for the sixteen-week training class.

Around week ten, Rob and Cinder approached a training track that had aged for nearly an hour in a nearby park. The day was dry and very hot for both dogs and handlers. Since Cinder was blessed with a high-tracking ability, she knew to dig in nose to the ground, and she pulled hard to find her prey. The grass was short and held the heat making it a good bit hotter at nose level than the actual air temperature. Cinder was so driven that Rob had to constantly put tension on her line to slow her down to a jog on the track so as not to over shoot any corners or turns. Her digging into the track and his constant pulling on the harness put extra strain on her causing her to exert even more effort.

Rob and Cinder completed the track, had a short play session and then he kenneled her in the air-conditioned training van. After about ten minutes, Cinder began to make a wheezing sound which was completely unfamiliar to him. He stopped the van immediately along the park road and let Cinder out. As soon as she jumped out of her kennel, she collapsed on the ground and could not stand up. The dog was disoriented and was unable to put any weight on her hips. Recognizing the signs of heat exhaustion, Rob scooped up the wheezing dog and carried her to a water faucet that he had spotted along the road. He continually doused her with cool water to bring down her internal temperature. Another trainer contacted the vet who instructed Rob to continue the water bath for fifteen minutes and then bring her immediately to the clinic.

The fifteen minutes felt like days, and Rob feared the worst. His instinct was to get her to the vet as soon as possible, but the vet was half-an-hour's drive away, and without the cooling, he did not know if she would survive that long.

Upon arrival, the vet immediately examined the dripping wet dog. Her temperature was high, and the doctor was glad she had been cooled down in the park. Cinder was admitted to the veterinary hospital and stayed for three days before returning home to rest for a few more.

The Malinois breed performed much better in cold weather but was more prone to heat exhaustion in warmer temperatures than its German shepherd dog counterparts. Cinder's drive and intensity probably blocked out any pain she had been experiencing. Rob learned that he would have to take precautions with her and in the future would need to stop to hose her down in someone's back yard if necessary to keep her cool on a long track in hot and humid weather.

Cinder and Rob finished the sixteen weeks successfully, as she had already worked the streets and had numerous arrests/bites. Soon she was back to work, and being finally vindicated, she was able once more to search anywhere that the other dogs could.

K-9 Cinder--always in close proximity to Rob for a good ear scratch

Courtesy of Rob Tighe

Loaded up and ready to go
Courtesy of Rob Tighe

A bullet-proof vest for the most dangerous jobs
Courtesy of Rob Tighe

The howling northern winds blew winter into Winnipeg, and a solid blanket of snow would remain on the ground for months. Rob and Cinder patrolled the cold dark Canadian streets in some of the most dangerous areas of Winnipeg. The pristine mantle of snow sculpted in high and graceful drifts was picturesque at first glance, but it deceptively hid the gritty underbelly of the desolate crime-ridden streets.

In the early morning hours, K-9 Lacy, Rob's black Lab bomb-sniffing dog, rode along nestled next to Cinder in the Tahoe 4X4 wagon ready to search for explosives if necessary. Looking for attention during the long less-exciting hours, patrol dog, Cinder, periodically raised her front leg to paw the door of the shield to let Rob know she needed a scratch behind her ear.

Rob routinely searched two buildings a night shift with her including schools, crawl spaces and commercial business. She was flawless. Nose to the floor of any buildings she entered, Rob could always tell where a suspect had spent the most time. Completely focused, Cinder methodically searched back and forth and high and low, missing nothing. Cinder's reputation for success was gaining ground, and her confidence was growing. Around the male dogs of the unit, Cinder could hold her own and proved to be just as dominant.

At home, she still maintained an alpha dog presence respected by Rob's fourteen-year-old Golden retriever, Tango. Although Cinder was very dominant around other dogs, she always enjoyed Tango's company and constantly tried to entice him to play. Tango, knowing his role in the pack hierarchy, allowed Cinder to climb on top of him and jump over him but wanted no part in her playful games. He was the submissive dog and took whatever Cinder dished out.

But Tango's days were short-lived, and while Cinder was still young and playful, her old buddy passed away. When Cinder lost her geriatric companion, she no longer pranced with joy waiting for him to come out the back door each day. She mourned in her own way, sun bathing in the yard mouthing her ball like a baby's pacifier.

Cinder beside her old pal, Tango, watching and waiting for Rob
Courtesy of Rob Tighe

Cinder took comfort in her favorite ball after the loss of her friend, Tango.
Courtesy of Rob Tighe

Another Golden lived next door, but it was not HER Golden. Cinder raced to the fence when she saw the dog and gnawed menacingly on the metal wanting to fight. All it took was a look from Rob, and she slunk to her open kennel door, tail down and hair up knowing she had misbehaved badly. Thereafter, when she caught herself charging her canine neighbor, she retreated to her kennel and dog house even before Rob could reprimand her. It was her own self-imposed exile. She missed her friend, and sometimes she just had to be a dog.

Back at work, Cinder's professional skills paid off one cold Canadian morning at 5:30. Rob and Cinder eased into the parking lot at the local Tim Horton's for Rob's usual medium black coffee. As hot steam arose from the hand-warming paper cup, and the rich essence of coffee filled the vehicle, he heard the call.

"Commercial alarm," the dispatcher's robotic voice called over Rob's radio as he quickly downed the last of his coffee with quick swallows.

Just four minutes from the location of the crime scene, Rob rode in silence, using no sirens or lights to tip off the suspect who might still be hiding inside. The element of surprise was essential.

For two weeks, Rob had been called to "break and enters" during the early morning hours. This one would no doubt be no different. A rock or piece of cement was always thrown through the glass window to gain entrance.

As his car negotiated the slippery snowy roads, he soon approached the scene of the crime and parked in the curbside slush. An alarm continued to wail through the pre-dawn air signaling the recent break in. Through a veil of fluttering snowflakes, Rob could see the stark building with dirty snow packed around its foundation. Motion detectors on the main floor, basement and back door of the Chinese restaurant had all been activated, and one unit had already arrived at the scene.

The collective condensed breath of the policemen who huddled together stomping their feet to stay warm drifted into the Arctic air in wispy puffs as they speculated about what they had found. The chilled officers told Rob that they believed the suspect was gone. Together, the police inspected the damaged front door. It was a typical glass door, and the bottom half of the glass was smashed out. A heavy piece of concrete located inside the business about ten feet from the door told them that this was the work of the same suspect. Rob tapped out the top half of the glass with his baton so it would not fall out when the door was opened, and the cold glass came tinkling to the ground. The officers requested the usual building search with Cinder, as it was quicker and safer than searching without the dog's nose.

In the moonlight, jagged broken glass from the front door lay scattered and shimmering at the entrance. Flashlight beams bounced off the sidewalk illuminating a few footwear impressions around the building indicating that the suspect had checked the rear of the business to possibly gain entrance there. Six feet from the front door there were partial impressions of a man's shoes molded into the disturbed snow.

As Rob brought Cinder from the car, the blustery Canadian wind ruffled her fur, and snow fell lightly on her tan back. Neither dampened her enthusiasm to track. Rob hooked a six-foot leash onto Cinder's leather collar and brought her to the front door of the building, careful to keep her paws from the sharp glass that glittered in the moonlight like diamonds at her feet.

With a blanket of crusty snow covering the ground that twenty-five degree night, Rob stood squarely near the restaurant's entrance and called out his usual warning.

"Winnipeg Police! You are in this building illegally. Come out now or a trained police dog will be sent it, and you will get bit!" Rob called.

Then he waited five seconds.

Once again, he gave his loud warning. Cinder stood ready at his side panting rapidly but lightly into the frigid air remaining alert but calm. Without so much as a whimper, she listened attentively and watched to see if her master's words would generate any action from within the building.

Her long pointed ears, braced against the rising wind, stood straight up, and her lean muscled body stood tense as she readied herself to spring forward at the next command. Already, thin shards of ice coated her whiskers that protruded from her frosted muzzle, and her small paws began to sporadically crunch on the crust of the snow where she stood patiently waiting.

When taken off leash, she would probe the building's interior to clear the immediate area. Once an area was cleared, Rob would advance with his back-up officer to continue to work until all the rooms were cleared. Cinder knew the routine well. If she tended to get out of Rob's sight, he would call her back to ensure she cleared every door and room before the men moved up. If she didn't come right back when called, Rob knew she was still carefully working an area. He knew how focused the dog could be when she gravitated to an area where there was a high degree of human scent left behind. Trained to "find and bite," Rob would let her work undistracted. He would listen carefully for a scream. If he heard it, he'd know she found what she was looking for.

Time seemed to pass slowly as everyone involved waited for a response to Rob's warning. When there was no response at the front door, Cinder finally received the command she had anticipated.

"Search!" called Rob, and off Cinder raced released like a well-aimed rocket, paws scrabbling across the glacial ice.

Searching for a scent with Rob following closely behind, Cinder tried to pick up a track inside the building. The restaurant smelled faintly of the lingering odor of Chinese food, but that was not what Cinder was interested in. Instead, she charged down to the basement where the restaurant office was located, only to find the suspect had ransacked the office looking for money.

"Where is he?" Rob whispered excitedly and continually to the searching dog, but her enthusiasm needed little encouragement.

After fifteen minutes, the premises were cleared. As Rob exited the door, he noticed Cinder's nose remained scouring the ground, and she was pulling hard to the northwest side of the building. It was obvious she was on the track of the suspect. Rob quickly pulled her off the track, brought her back to the cruiser and harnessed her up with the twenty-foot tracking harness. Crunching back again in the snow, he made note one more time of the partial footwear impression left at the scene. Cinder once again indicated on the same track, so the two were off to see what she could find.

The track started north in the alley behind the restaurant and continued for about a block and a half. Cinder cut back west to the rear of a yard and out to the front of a one-and-a-half-story dwelling. She showed some interest at the front step and then left it as there was no one there to bite. She continued to search for a track in the front yard, but there was nothing there either. Rob took her back to the rear alley in case the suspect back-tracked and continued to run. There was no other track leaving the rear alley, so the suspect had to have taken refuge inside the house. It was nearly 6 a.m., and soon the sun would rise, illuminating the stark surroundings as the team continued its work.

By process of elimination, the scope of the search had narrowed dramatically. The residence Cinder had found was not unknown to the police. An officer checked the address from his laptop computer to confirm that it was the home of a person who had been known to commit commercial burglaries in the past. Officers converged on the residence and waited.

Rob trudged through the deep snow to approach the front of the house and knocked on the door. There was no response. The other officers joined him and banged on the door loudly with their batons. Cinder barked and paced in excitement straining against her harness and leash to get to the door, her prey drive increasing by the minute. With no response after ten minutes of knocking, the street supervisor drew back his snowy boot and kicked the door in with a loud crack. No warrant was needed. Cinder's indication was cause enough.

A startled, middle-aged woman of aboriginal descent stood in the kitchen. She said she had been sleeping, but Rob could see she was wide awake, and he knew she had been standing there the whole time they were knocking. He was determined to find the suspect's shoes to make a match to the impressions he saw at the scene, and the woman did not attempt to stop him.

As Rob spoke to the woman, the other officers went upstairs to find her thirty-year-old son in bed pretending to sleep. He was covered by a simple sheet. Sweat dripped off his head and face, and the back of his shirt was soaked. The front of his hair was bathed in sweat and melted snow. In addition, the bottoms of his pants were wet and icy cold. He had reached the end of the line, and the game was over. After he was arrested, he was hurried downstairs.

"Ah," said Rob to him, "where's your shoes?"

The man did not reply but instead reached for a pair of shoes that Rob noticed were completely dry. Rob was convinced someone in the house had hidden his wet shoes probably when the officers were knocking. Soon, the suspect's mother just wanted it all to be over and for the police to leave her home, so she pulled out the sofa from the wall, and there were the suspect's wet running shoes with the matching tread impression that Rob remembered in the snow at the scene.

As the burglar was taken away, Rob and Cinder returned to the warm car, exhausted but elated. Rob praised the successful dog and rewarded her with plenty of scratches all over. She wiggled with delight and wagged her tail happily knowing that she had done well. The heat in the car warmed her, and she settled in for a well-earned rest. Soon they would be home.

For a wintry Canadian night, the weather could have been much harsher Rob thought as he drove home. Staked out with an Emergency Response Team stuck stationed at the back of a home waiting for a suspect to surrender would have been far worse. Cinder had had such nights where she hunkered down with wind swirling white around her as she lay in the snow perfectly still except for the occasional shiver.

Sub-zero night in Winnipeg
Courtesy of Rob Tighe

Thankfully, this had not been one of those nights. Before winter melted into spring there would be more of those long stake-outs for sure, and as difficult as they were, Cinder would still be up to the task.

The current suspect was turned over to detectives, and a Crown Brief was written listing the offenses the accused had committed. There was a documented chronological narrative of what he had done to be read before the judge at the suspect's first court appearance. He was accused of fifty commercial "break and enters" with the same method of entry. He was believed to be responsible for all, but he was charged with just fifteen of them. Of special interest to the Winnipeg police was a note that the suspect had a twin brother with an equally-long criminal record, so it was likely Cinder would more than likely meet the family again.

Between November, 2007, and January, 2008, various commercial businesses located within Winnipeg were being illegally entered by persons unknown. The havoc the burglars wreaked throughout the city was tremendous and becoming more and more routine. Their main target was cash and/or computer equipment, and many times two suspects were caught by surveillance cameras at the establishments they robbed. One man wore a black, three-quarter length, wool Tommy Hilfiger jacket making him easily recognizable and demonstrating his love for fine attire. Later, the two were tracked by purchases on a stolen credit card, but still they continued to hide out within the confines of Winnipeg remaining elusive to the police.

Once again, the main method of entry was the same. Smashing the front door glass and/or windows of each business allowed them easy access. In just over three months, the pair had racked up over $70,000 in stolen property and damages, and now they were getting even bolder. At the end of January, they decided to steal a 2007 Chevy Tahoe, the property of a car dealership. The vehicle was valued at approximately $30, 000. Not missing a trick, they also stole a Manitoba dealer license plate from the lot and placed it on the stolen Tahoe. Now they were back in business and riding in style.

On January 30th, 2008, at approximately 1:30 a.m., they struck again causing $1500 damage to a window at a rent-a-car business after smashing it to pieces to gain entry. Working quickly, they stole a cash box containing $350.

Forty-five minutes later the suspects set off alarms at another commercial business after they gained entry by shattering a front door window with a car-jack. Once inside, they caused more damage, the total value of which was approximately $10, 000.00. This time, they stole an unknown quantity of clothing, no doubt as a complement to their growing wardrobe that would serve to perfect their image as high-fashion aficionados on future surveillance camera shots.

But they were not done yet. As Rob navigated the icy streets in his car, the weather hampered his visibility. Straining to see above the glowing colored lights of his dashboard through a perpetually-frosted windshield, Rob monitored the reports over his radio. He did not have long to wait to hear another. At 2:25 a.m., the duo hit a third commercial business by breaking in the door's window. They left with $600.00 in cash and caused another $1,000 in damage.

The attending unit on the scene requested that Rob search the premises with Cinder. So at 2:33 as the city slept, he turned his car towards the crime scene. Slapping wipers working in rhythmic unison pushed the heavily falling snow from Rob's windshield. While he was on his way, the radio reported that the pair had struck again. Neither snow, nor ice, nor cold seemed to slow the burglars down.

At 2:37, they smashed another window. This time, they stole two cash register drawers valued at approximately $600 and which contained various denominations of store gift cards. As they continued their rampage, the two had just caused another $2,300.00 in damage.

Cinder and Lacy panted in anticipation of a surge in speed as the messages continued to break through. That bitter night, the wind chill factor registered at almost forty below zero. It was not a night fit for the proverbial man or beast, but it was not a major concern for the two furry beasts in the car as they waited for some action.

As Rob was making his way to the crime scene, he noticed a new silver, very clean four-door SUV in the parking lot of a music store. The occupants of the vehicle observed his marked police vehicle and sped away from the parking lot at a high rate of speed. Based on its speed and the driver's demeanor, he knew the car was stolen.

The vehicle was picking up speed sliding through slush and snow as it continued north moving from a business area to a residential one. Rob drove his Tahoe as fast as he could, but with the two dogs in the back, he could not drive as fast as the typical police Crown Victoria for fear of tossing the dogs back and forth as he careened around corners. Slowing down on the corners cost him time and soon the stolen vehicle was out of sight.

About five minutes later, police were alerted to a single-vehicle accident involving an SUV. The caller related that the SUV, newer model and light in color, had ploughed into a snow bank. The two males had fled on foot into a back alley. Both, the caller reported, were carrying something close to their chests.

Rob arrived at the snow bank and recognized the car as the same vehicle he had seen only minutes before. As he stepped out of the warmth of his car to observe it, he felt the full brunt of the cold blast of Canadian winter in his face. The wind whistling around him had picked up, and he was grateful for the heavy gloves and balaclava he wore that night. The black headgear covered his whole head exposing only his eyes.

Before starting the track Rob had a brief look into the vehicle, spotting clothes, cameras and two or three laptop computers. He adjusted his ski mask and harnessed up Cinder for the track through two-to-three feet of snow.

Predictably, Cinder found a scent immediately. She briefly deviated from the track and quickly sniffed between a nearby garage and fence. The two empty cash drawers were discarded there. Rob would have never seen them in the dark. As he and a back-up officer running along with him continued the track, Rob reported over his radio the location of the cash drawers to be seized and dusted for fingerprints.

They continued down ice-packed back alleys until Cinder hit the track where snow blew sideways across the sidewalk in wavy swirls. Just up ahead in the bluish haze, Rob observed a taxi cab without a fare driving very slowly, almost at a crawl, as the driver looked for his pick-up. It was not uncommon for fleeing criminals to use a cell phone to call for a taxi to get them out of a hot area.

On the run, Rob immediately and breathlessly radioed to have a unit check the cab to see where he was picking up his fare and whom that person might be. Around the next turn, Rob spotted a male standing about one hundred feet in front of him slouched down against the relentless wind. Cinder tracked right towards the shadowy man. Rob had his back-up officer detain the snow-covered man and waited for a unit to come and speak with the detainee. At that point, there was no reliable description of the suspects.

While the back-up officer stayed with the man, Rob slogged on through the snow continuing tracking to the next intersection. Cinder remained bright and alert showing no signs of stopping. He cast her all around the intersection, but it seemed the track had ended. Either the suspect was picked up in a vehicle or fled on a bicycle. It could be that the suspect doubled-backed the same way he had come, or Cinder simply could have missed a part of the track but that was unlikely. Rob spent a minute at the intersection determining his next move and decided to return to meet his back-up officer who was still detaining the man on the street.

Rob held Cinder on the leash and maintained a safe distance from the detained man who said he had just been coming out of the residence where he now stood as it was his aunt's house, and he had called a taxi to take him home. Nothing suspicious about him stood out. He was dressed for the weather in average clothes, and he didn't appear to be out of breath like he had been running. Rob checked to see if the suspect's chest was rising and falling rapidly, as a suspect wouldn't give himself away by visibly sweating in the extreme cold. Everything seemed in order.

Bright headlights shone down the hazy street and penetrated the darkness growing into two bigger and brighter spheres as a car with two officers pulled up and got out to interview the man. Just as they were pulling up, another unit transmitted news that crackled loudly over the radio. A unit had just observed a male running north through a yard.

Rob, Cinder and the back-up officer raced on foot to where the unit had last seen the male running. They sprinted for four blocks feeling the sting of blowing snow, and just as they were within a block of where the man had been seen, the winded back-up officer spotted him. This time, he was running south through some yards. It was the lucky break they needed, as it lessened the gap the suspect was trying to create.

Based on the new information, they headed west ten-to-fifteen houses, and Rob cast Cinder along the front of the houses. Nose down, Cinder took a sharp left turn, an obvious track indication, and started pulling hard into the harness. There was no doubt she was on a fresh track that headed back towards where the stolen vehicle had been dumped. The confused suspect had no idea how many units were in the area, and in his panic, he changed direction each time he saw one. With such quick changes of direction, it would take an accomplished dog to keep up with him.

The winter parade of Cinder, the officers and the suspect continued running through deep snow until Cinder suddenly raised her head up at the rear of a yard transitioning from tracking to wind/air scenting. She jumped up and over the deep snow as sprightly as a leaping lamb and trotted up onto a slick wooden deck about three feet off the ground. Rob's first reaction was to shine his light under the deck since he knew that scent would rise. Dancing beams of bright light from his flashlight panned beneath the deck. Then the white light stopped on the face of a snow-covered man who squinted his eyes at the sudden brilliance.

Rob pulled Cinder off the deck before she had time to dash under and bite the dismayed suspect. From twenty-feet back, Rob shouted his warning.

"Come out from under the deck with your hands up!"

Cinder barked non-stop. Rob shone the light directly into the man's eyes so he could not see them. The man did not come out so Rob shouted out again emphasizing that Cinder would come under and drag him out.

Cinder continued to strain against her harness. She momentarily gave some slack and then with renewed force and enthusiasm lunged again just waiting for her prey to make a false move. As Rob tried to maintain a safe distance, the suspect still chose not to comply. After a third warning, the frosted felon, crouched tightly under the deck, crawled out. No stylish hat covered his head this time, and his cheeks and ears were bright red, having been exposed to the frigid sub-zero Canadian wind.

Get on the ground!" ordered Rob.

The stiffened form fell forward into the snow where he was handcuffed and arrested. He was then taken back to the cruiser and searched, and he was found to have some of the stolen money in his possession. Accordingly, he was read his Charter Rights and taken back to the station.

Two hours later, he was being treated in a hospital for a frost-bitten ear. The game was over, and Cinder was victorious.

Back at the home where the taxi had prowled the street, officers checked the identity of the man they held. He was identified and found to have been arrested before for break-ins. But the officers failed to verify his story by checking the address he said he had just come from. With no reason to hold him, they had let him go.

Only when detectives arrived and found out who he was did they realize the man was the second suspect. After another day of detective work, they were able to locate him at his mother's home the next evening, where he was promptly arrested.

The brazen pair had terrorized Winnipeg for months but would soon be off the streets. In court, a report from the detectives was posted to the Crown Brief.

"Both accused in this matter have extremely lengthy and continuous records for property offences. It is clear that these two individuals have earned the title 'serial and habitual offenders,' and that they have no intention of ascending to anything but a criminal lifestyle. Police strongly believe that if released, the accused will both continue to prey on commercial establishments in the city of Winnipeg. As a result, police are vigorously opposed to their release."

It was Cinder's good nose and scenting ability that stopped them in their tracks. Businesses in the area would be safer as a result when the career criminals were finally locked away. If they ever were released, chances are Buddy's daughter would remember them well.

Cinder was the only female dog in the history of the Winnipeg unit since 1971. The scrappy dog had outshone her own littermate in tracking ability, and her tenacity and determination allowed her to remain in a program when other fine tracking dogs of lesser ability were washed out. So successful was the former "Gopher on a Rope" that she was once featured on the television program, "Dogs with Jobs."

K-9 Buddy's daughter—as talented as her accomplished father
Courtesy of Rob Tighe

This "Cinderella's" world was not one of glass slippers and fairy godmothers. She was the feisty daughter of a top police dog and proved her worth following in his snowy paw prints. The stroke of midnight found her not riding in a pumpkin coach, but riding in a speeding police Tahoe and tracking the numerous treads of criminals' running shoes. Yet, her nickname was aptly applied. With the canine equivalent of waving a magic wand, she easily turned criminals into wards of the Province and created safe and peaceful streets for the Canadian citizens she served. And more importantly, in Constable Rob Tighe, her third and final handler, she finally found her story book Prince Charming.

K-9 Conan

"Portrait in White"

Many a white dog has been passed over when it came to selecting a K-9 partner. When a pure white German shepherd dog was born in 1988, he could not have known he was destined to be an inductee into the prestigious White German Shepherd Dog Hall of Fame. In fact, when he joined the Saint Louis, Missouri, Police Department at age two, he was a real novice embarking on a career that could have taken any direction. But he was lucky enough to be partnered with Officer Edward Meyer, who was given the dog as his fifth partner and instructed to train the unseasoned animal. The alabaster dog and runt of the litter had been donated by a breeder in Illinois, and the young fellow arrived already named with the interesting appellation of "Kaiser the Role." (sic)

Having served five years with another dog named Kaiser, Ed's ex-partner's dog, the name left a bitter taste in Ed's mouth.

"The first Kaiser was ill-mannered and continually used the police car as a restroom," Ed remembered, "I decided to pick a new name for the dog, a name to match appropriately what I was determined would be my best dog."

New partners, Ed and Conan
Courtesy of Ed Meyer

A pure white dog was not every officer's first choice. Many looked at a white dog as an albino or they worried that the frosted snow-white coat would be hard to keep clean. And more importantly, some officers felt that the glowing-white coat would be easier for the bad guys to spot at night at a time when the handler would prefer his dog to be less visible. But Ed was instantly attracted to the dog because of its appearance and temperament. The new recruit was the first white German shepherd dog that Ed had come in contact with, and from day one he felt that it was strikingly beautiful. Despite any drawbacks concerning visibility and cleanliness, Ed decided to keep the unique dog and felt confident that the animal would have no problems that giving a few extra baths would not take care of. Such a dog would add a new challenge, and where others rejected a white dog outright, Ed felt that he had a real "jewel."

For the first few weeks of training, the dog with the milk-white coat had no real name. He was simply "white dog." Ed settled back one night and watched an episode of Conan the Barbarian and marveled at the strength of the courageous gladiator who put his trust only in a mighty sword presented by his father, after being warned by his father that he should not trust men, woman or beasts.

"But this you can trust," the father had advised giving him the sword that would always be by his side.

The new dog would always be at Ed's side fighting many a battle. "White dog" had a name. He would proudly carry the name, K-9 Conan.

Conan quickly became a family favorite, lovable, playful and just fun to be around. He was a young dog who liked to climb on the kid's playground equipment in Ed's yard and did not tire of ascending the tower, balancing across the wooden bridge or joyously whooshing down the slick slide.

"My wife was a misguided person who had to have a cat," said Ed with a smile.

But even the cat warmed to the white dog curling up against Conan's belly when the dog would lie down for a lazy nap. And Conan never seemed to mind.

In his training, Conan showed that he had the courage to do well in his new responsibilities. In the first week of tracking classes, he was doing tracks as difficult as dogs are required to do in order to graduate. He loved to track, but he loved to jump more. He seemed to be a natural acrobat, and perhaps all his "training" on the children's playground equipment was conducive to a bright future in agility work. His best "trick" was his own version of a gymnastic back flip. When Conan was in his kennel, he lunged at the metal gate and sprang backwards into a perfect back flip and astonishingly landed on his feet. Where he learned his trick, no one knew, but his ability to jump and leap was entertaining to all who saw it. It also assisted him greatly in his agility training, climbing the tall A-frames and balancing on a variety of wooden platforms. The dog was as agile as a circus performer and never intimidated by training equipment he encountered. That earned him a second place medal in agility during his very first United States Police Canine Association (USPCA) dog trial.

A very young Conan poses on the children's play equipment.
Courtesy of Ed Meyer

Agility Training

Conan starts the climb up the ladder of the catwalk.

almost there

Upon reaching the top, Conan views the ramp from the 19-inch wide walkway.

scrambling up the wall climb

white lightening over the eight-foot broad jump

sniffing for human scent in the box
Courtesy of Ed Meyer

Evidently curious about the neighborhood where he resided, Conan once jumped over the backyard fence and took off down the street. By the time Ed got around to the front of the house trying to catch him, the quick dog was out of sight. Ed ran to his police car and followed down the street trying to find the wandering dog. Such a distinguished-looking animal should be easy to find. But Conan was not to be found. After about twenty minutes, as Ed was cruising a street a few blocks from the house, looking in all directions for some flash of white, he heard a jingling sound coming from outside. He drove a little further and then he heard it again. A quick look into the rear view mirror revealed a white dog loping along after the familiar police car, dog tags jingling at his neck. Ed screeched to a stop, opened the door and the now well-exercised dog having explored his neighborhood, jumped right in as though nothing was amiss to settle back and enjoy the ride home. It was as if he had hailed a passing cab and climbed in to direct the driver homeward.

On his first week on the street with Conan, Ed received a call about a woman who had been robbed at knife point of her purse as she stood at a parking lot in a low-rise housing project. Conan started to track from the point of robbery where a man in his mid-twenties had started to run. The track continued down a sidewalk and outside the housing project before turning to cross a lawn. Conan continued on for about two city blocks and then picked his way through some pedestrian traffic, which could have easily contaminated the track. Just ahead was the suspect. Trained to follow a single track even if someone else crosses that track, Conan did not miss a beat. The panicked man turned and saw Ed and Conan and started to run faster. Conan pulled the lead taut having spotted his prey and charged ahead with full intent. At that, the man knew his escape was futile. The best course of action was realized and that was to surrender. The purse, contents and knife were found with the suspect, and he was arrested and led away.

"Good boy, good boy!" Ed said, patting Conan's head.

The words of praise, for Conan, were the best reward for a job well done. He required nothing else.

Conan was a good patrol dog, and he had an extremely keen nose, so much so that was singled out to train for explosive detection, and he graduated in 1990. His skills impressed the trainer at the Saint Louis Airport who was experienced with military bomb dogs and Federal Aviation Administration certified dogs, and as the white dog's reputation grew, he was soon serving

Presidents George H.W. Bush, George W. Bush and Bill Clinton along with their vice presidents and their wives when they visited Saint Louis or the immediate areas. Before their arrivals, Conan cleared their way after determining no explosive devices were present any place those he protected would visit. Conan, nose to the ground, eagerly sniffed hotel rooms, corridors, shopping areas, vehicles and any packages to be delivered in the area. When he determined that nothing dangerous caused a threat to his visitors, the guests of Saint Louis were allowed to enter the premises.

Since Saint Louis was the heart of the country, it was a favorite meeting place. Frequently, Army generals held enclaves in Saint Louis, and it was Conan who swept the areas where they stayed and visited as well. His expertise earned him letters from the military experts for his good work, and many high-ranking generals stopped to comment on how beautiful the white dog was, and how they had never seen a white police dog before. At those times, Ed's "jewel" of a dog really did shine.

Although most calls were routine, occasionally there was reason to exercise more caution. During the Gulf War, a package wrapped in plastic appeared at the door of a four-star general. It was found hanging on the door handle of the general's hotel room, and he was surprised to find it there. The plastic bag became the subject of much concern. As the general was expecting no packages, an Army demolition expert called on Conan to check it out.

Reporting for duty as any good solider in the war against crime would do, Conan attended to the general's mysterious package. The dog tipped his nose upward towards the mysterious bag and sniffed it carefully. Then he came to a quick sit, indicating that he had detected the odor of an explosive. With full concentration, he stared directly at the source of the odor and remained steadfast. His reaction caused great alarm, and it was the signal to call for the bomb and arson squad. Upon their arrival, they quickly cleared the entire floor in the area in case of an explosion, and Ed and Conan watched from a distance to observe what had been found. Long minutes ticked slowly by as the Army demolition experts, dressed in camouflage carefully x-rayed the package. The atmosphere was tense as no one knew if whatever the bag held had a timer or fuse. If that was so, it could detonate in just seconds.

Upon closer examination and with x-rays to identify the object, the experts determined that the package was a gun-cleaning kit. Everyone was relieved, but Ed was very puzzled. Conan did not make such mistakes when it came to detecting explosives. Ed had great faith in the dog's expertise and had not had a bad indication before. At first, he was embarrassed that Conan had misjudged the package, causing such a furor, but he still could not doubt his dog. He went over to question the demolition expert who told him that the brand of gun-cleaning solvent in the package contained a nitrate base, which was, indeed, highly explosive. Conan's powerful sense of smell, over a-thousand times more sensitive than a human's, had detected the minute traces of nitrate. It was impossible to fool him. He knew the odor of nitrate well, whether it was in a bomb or gun-cleaning solvent. He had been right when others doubted him. If Conan indicated there was explosive material, there WAS explosive material, and no one that day was more worthy of a sharp military salute.

"Hang on to that dog," the Army demolition expert told Ed, "He's good."

Conan sniffs for bomb scent around the police car.

Courtesy of Ed Meyer

75

The Gulf War also brought heightened security to the Saint Louis airport, and Ed and Conan spent hours searching thousands of bags and packages that came through there and searching the airplanes that brought them. At times, Conan was called upon to stand along side of the conveyer belt where hundreds of checked bags passed along before him. The bags were about nose high at the point where he searched, and he carefully waited for each one to pass as he determined if it had a suspicious odor. If he showed even the slightest interest in any bag, the line of moving bags was stopped so that he could take a "closer sniff." At other times, the luggage would be placed in a group in a certain area, and Conan walked through the bags at his leisure and just sniffed them individually. When he searched aircraft, Conan had full run of the interior strolling down the middle aisle searching for anything between the seats. Then he was taken to the baggage area of the plane where he continued his search. Only when he completed his work and cleared the entire plane of any explosive threat was the plane allowed to take off.

Side-by-side, Ed and Conan walked through the airport terminals. If they found any bags or packages that were left unattended, Conan went to investigate. He carefully sniffed the bag with his long sensitive nose as Ed waited for the familiar alert. Sometimes a small crowd in the terminal gathered to watch him work. They were relieved to find that the bags usually contained clothing or personal items left behind. If a bag contained food, Conan knew he was not to consume it. So often, his efforts brought praise from the waiting passengers who stopped to tell Ed how much they appreciated the white dog there helping to make their flight a safe one, and many times, Ed heard the familiar phrase, "Thank you for being here."

When Conan was not searching, he mingled with the passengers who scurried through the airport. Passengers stopped to smile at the friendly white dog that diligently made his rounds. He became one of the best public relations tools the airport had, offering a bright spot in the lives of many harried and frustrated travelers, and he was a reassuring presence calming the fear of those who flew in an increasingly-troubled world. The youngest passengers were drawn to Conan like a magnet because of his beauty and his good nature. One unintended consequence resulted. Conan became somewhat of an airport Pied Piper delighted to have children tag along behind him. When he came into sight, small children left their parents' sides and ran to greet him. The dog's tail wagged happily as he welcomed their pats and words, and the children took much pleasure in playing with the gentle dog. More than once, Ed and Conan served as escorts taking a lost child who had become enamored with Conan to the lost person area where parents came to be reunited with their children.

In 1995, Conan won the German Shepherd Dog Club of Saint Louis award for explosive detection when he found explosives in two forty-foot interstate trailers that were carrying souvenirs. The merchandise was from Russia, and the dog was called in to check the load. The trucks were backed up to a loading dock, and nothing about them seemed unusual. That afternoon when Conan and Ed arrived, Conan readily leaped up into the open trailer while Ed waited outside watching. Before the dog was an array of sloppily-packed boxes that appeared to have been just thrown into the trailer. Slowly, he wound around through the mess to explore the truck contents. When he came upon a certain box, he stopped and went into a sit. At that, Ed leaped up into the trailer to join him knowing Conan had picked up the scent of an explosive. Other officers that were there followed and looked to see what was in the box. Mixed in with the clothing in the box were rocket launchers and gun parts, both illegal to bring into the country. The box was removed, and Conan went to work again ferreting out everything that should not have been there.

The find brought Conan congratulatory letters from the Secret Service who later presented him with a Secret Service identification pin. The pins were normally given only to human police officers working with the Secret Service, but on that day the furry white officer earned the prestigious honor.

For all his successes with bomb detection, Conan was first and foremost a patrol dog. In that position, he commanded the respect of the officers with whom he came in contact, and many frequently requested him by name when they required a good dog. Conan was a multi-faceted dog who did equally well whether he was tracking, searching for evidence, searching buildings, doing suspect apprehension or handler protection. The versatility of the dog seemed unmatched confirming what Ed had always thought.

One afternoon, a burglar alarm screamed out signaling the break-in of a building in a distribution yard which was part of a trucking company. Officers on the scene called for a K-9 to conduct a building search there and see if the burglar was still inside. When Ed arrived, he put Conan on his lead, entered the fenced-in lot and walked towards the building. But Conan was not interested in the building. He stopped and looked towards a high tower with a broad tank sitting upon it that sat adjacent to the building. While Ed wanted to proceed to the building, Conan insisted upon staring at the tower.

Ed was fifty feet from the tank when Conan's head suddenly lifted upward to the top of the ninety-foot tower. Immediately, Conan let out a sharp bark. Ed looked up in the direction the dog was looking, and he could see something on the top of the tank. That something moved, and the shape of the figure made Ed think it very well could be a person. With much care, the officers at the scene climbed to the top of the tank and made the arrest of a man evidently unafraid of heights. Down below, Conan watched the men capture his quarry. Conan had been trained to search for human odor, and all it took was a breeze to bring that odor from the top of the tower down to ground level, something a fleeing suspect would never have imagined. The officers at the scene were all known to Ed, and they took his word when it came to interpreting his dog's signals. No command had been given to the dog. He just knew his job. It would not have occurred to the officers to search on top of the tower first, and Conan's quick discovery saved them much time and effort.

Ed knew better than to ever question the dog's instincts. Once when Ed and Conan were tracking a burglary suspect, a witness told Ed that the suspect had run north in the alley. When he tried to get Conan to head north, the dog insisted on going south. Conan won the argument, and Ed opted to follow his lead and ignore any other advice. Within fifty feet, Conan found the suspect hiding, holed up in the corner of a garage still in possession of his loot. The suspect played dumb and said he could not understand why they were looking for him. Just because he had some of the loot on him didn't mean he was guilty, he protested. At such times, Ed was convinced that his dog had more intelligence than most of the people he chased. It was phenomenal how Conan could track an elusive scent.

In responding to a burglar alarm in a trucking terminal, once, Ed found that upon entering the shipping area it was filled with stacks of car tires. Conan went to the corner of the building and began barking his head off. No person could be seen. The barking continued until Ed climbed up the tall stack of tires on the right and found the suspect in the bottom of the stack. The man's odor had chimneyed up to the ceiling then over to the wall and finally drifted downward where Conan picked it up.

So many suspects thought they could hide evidence from, run faster than or outwit Conan. A young man was wanted in questioning for a shooting, and a report came in that officers were involved in a foot chase trying to apprehend the man. As he fled from pursing officers, K-9 back-up was requested, and Ed and Conan sped to the scene to join the chase. In the car, Conan knew a chase would ensue, and he barked and paced waiting to be let loose. Ed released the dog, and Conan burst onto the scene. When officers were gaining ground on the suspect, the man stopped abruptly and turned. Then he fired a shot to slow down the pursuit. After the shot was fired, he ran down an alley. In minutes, a streak of white galloped past the pursuing officers, and soon Conan was closing in on the suspect. The man tossed his gun over a fence and tried to climb another fence to get away from an imminent bite from Conan's sharp teeth, but he was no match for the dog's speed. As the man tried desperately to reach the safety of the fence, Conan tackled him and grabbed him by the ankle tripping him up so that he could run no further. The man went down, and Conan held him firmly.

"Get the dog off me!" the man screamed.

Only when Ed released Conan, did he relax his hold. When the other officers caught up and made the arrest, Conan stood by watching. The suspect had never seen a white police dog before, but the shiny badge on Conan's collar proved to the astonished man that he had been caught by not only one of Saint Louis's finest but one its prettiest.

In Saint Louis when a child under ten years of age is reported missing, police officers are required to call for a K-9 to help search. Such was the case one day when a call came in that a young boy, just one-year-old, was reported missing and was considered a "serious missing" by the department. Officers had already checked the apartment where he lived, and he was not there. The distraught mother was sitting in a juvenile detective's police car when the dog arrived, and Ed proposed that he and Conan search the house again. Some of the officers told him that was unnecessary and a waste of time repeating a job they had already done.

But Ed was insistent upon doing what he and Conan always did in such cases search the house that second time. The statistics backed up Ed. Many of the younger missing were often found at home. Conan did not need to sniff a piece of the child's clothing to get a scent. He knew the human scent too well and that was all he needed to proceed. So the two partners searched the apartment going room-to-room. Finding no trace, they entered the child's bedroom. Conan stood looking around the room, and then he walked over to a closet. The floor of the closet was filled with piles of clothing. The curious dog stuck his nose into the pile and then backed away and barked. Ed recognized the bark as an indication that he had found a person. Conan knew the difference between his indications well. Just as he would sit for a bomb, a simple bark and back away was reserved for the location of a human. Ed pulled some of the clothes away, and there sound asleep on the floor was the missing boy. All the officers thanked Conan for making their job a lot easier, and the mother was reunited with her son.

Any person who works with dogs knows the pride and wonderful feeling that goes with a successful dog. The abilities and success of the dog can have tremendous impact on the lives with whom the dog interacts. For one Saint Louis woman, brutalized by the criminal element, Conan's intervention definitely saved her life.

In 1996, the woman was abducted from a street by three men and taken to their home in a burned-out two-and-a-half-story house. The suspects, armed with a meat cleaver and two butcher knives, viciously terrorized and assaulted the woman. Then they invited ten to fifteen of their street friends in to do the same. The frightened woman was threatened with death if she told or resisted. After fourteen hours of terror, the suspects fell asleep. Not being tied up, the woman took that opportunity to sneak out the door. She called the police who sped to the scene, and she was immediately taken to the hospital. Officers at the scene arrested two of the men who were still sleeping. But one was gone.

Conan was called to the shabby home to try to round up the third subject. The cruiser eased through the decaying neighborhood past peeling paint and broken sidewalks where the veil of crime hung over each worn block like a heavy mantle. The house where Ed stopped stood in a dilapidated condition, broken-down on the outside and an absolute mess on the inside. It was located across the street from a housing project in a well-known drug area where crime thrived and where police made continual visits. Discarded furniture and items of clothing were scattered throughout the house, and Conan stepped over and around piles of debris to start his search. Holes pockmarked the walls, ceilings and floors in a structure hardly fit for habitation.

Besides human odor, Conan was trained to find blood odor. After some initial searching, he approached a dirty stuffed chair and sniffed around the seat and the armrest. Reading the dog's signals, Ed then reached his hand down into the stained cushion and pulled out the hidden meat cleaver the woman had described. The knives were then easily found on a table in the living room. But the third man still was nowhere to be seen.

With the weapons found, Conan went to search the building. He picked up the odor of a person and responded as trained, by barking. When only half-way up the steps to the second floor, he began to bark again while looking up toward the ceiling. An arrest was imminent. But the man who cautiously climbed out from the beams turned out to be a homeless man who had taken refuge in the house, and detectives there determined he was not their man. The search continued.

The police returned to the stairway to continue the search, but Conan stubbornly continued barking upward towards the second floor where some of the ceiling was missing. With flashlights in hand, the police climbed up to that area. They shone their beams around to illuminate the space, but they were unable to see much at all and found no one. The third man had gotten away.

But after combing the rest of the house with no result, Conan led Ed back to the stairway and began barking wildly again. The dog was insistent that someone was there. Ed wasn't satisfied to walk away at that point even after the area had been checked twice. He knew his dog too well.

Ed obtained a ladder from the evidence van that had responded to the call, and he climbed upward his feet creaking on each rung until he reached the ceiling. He climbed up through some missing ceiling tiles, carefully poked his head through the opening and shone his flashlight into the dark recesses of the building. At the far point of the crawl space where the ceiling and roof met, he noticed a large ball of insulation material. Other than that he did not find much. Disappointed again, he turned to leave, but suddenly the ball of insulation moved slightly.

Ed called for the man to come out.

"That dog woke me up!" the man complained. I was sleeping up here to get out of the cold."

"Come out!" Ed yelled again at the ball of insulation, "or I'll put the dog up to get you out!"

The man slowly emerged from his hiding place. Detectives determined him to be the meat-cleaver-wielding felon, and the police were more than happy to take him from his hiding place and off the city streets.

With the trio safely behind bars, over thirty-five felony warrants were issued against them thanks to the keen nose and determination of Ed's special white dog. They would terrorize the public no more.

In the midst of Conan's heroics, he still found time to be the favorite dog at public K-9 demonstrations and fell easily and comfortably into the role of favorite dog with Ed's grandchildren as they played with a most successful and recognized playmate. But even though playful, uppermost in the dog's mind was always the protection of Ed.

Saint Louis's older police cars had a little door between the kennel in the back seat area and the driver's compartment. Ed always left the door open so that he could scratch Conan's soft ears or just in case he might need the dog to get out to help him. One night he stopped a car for a traffic violation after noticing that the car had bad license plates. Upon checking them, he found they were not the plates issued to that particular car. The car had dark tinted windows, and Ed strained his eyes to see only two occupants inside. He got the driver out of the car to "discuss his sinful ways," and before he knew it, another, then another, and yet still another occupant got out of the car. With one purpose in mind, they started to surround him. When he could only see the driver due to the dark windows, Ed had no fear. But when the others got out of the car, Ed wished he had Conan with him.

Soon, the multitude of occupants started closing in even closer on him menacingly asking why he was stopping them. Ed eased his hand on his gun, but the crowed of men did not seem intimidated. Before he could answer them or react to them, with great relief Ed saw a familiar white sight. The dog did not bark. He just appeared. And he stood quietly close to Ed's left leg surveying the crowd. He was an ephemeral ghost that materialized before Ed's eyes, and his timing was perfect. In the nick of time, Conan and squeezed through the little door, uncalled, and he emerged from the car to protect his master. Ed was never happier to see him. Conan's presence changed the whole tenor of the discussion. Suddenly, the occupants backed away from Ed a bit.

"Sir, ...," one of the men nervously stammered, " ....is that dog supposed to be out here?"

Once more, Ed observed how the sight of a dog could change one's attitude. The driver was ticketed, and the car pulled away. Tragedy was averted.

What could have been a deadly consequence of a traffic stop for Ed turned out to be further proof that his safety so often was left to four white paws with the ability to slip quietly to wherever they were needed. For twelve years those white paws stayed close by Ed's side never straying from him whether in active service or retirement. At twelve, long after the paws had slowed their pace, Conan succumbed to cancer, and the white knight, the trusted sword by Ed's side, was just a memory.

As Ed had originally thought, during Conan's career his white coat never really presented a problem, except once when they searched an undeveloped area behind an old trucking company. Ed found out the hard way that the owners had discarded much of their used motor oil in the woods behind their lot. After sending the dog to search there, Conan emerged from the oil field a black dog. The burglars Ed was chasing found out the same way. They ran from the woods darker and slicker than they had entered, and after climbing a fence, they got away. But their dark, newly-oiled appearance was hard to hide, and it allowed them to be caught just a few blocks away.

Conan was getting a bath, but they were going to jail. Ed transported the black Conan to the police garage car wash area and gave him several baths with dog shampoo that Ed had in his police car. Using a bucket of water and a stiff wheel brush, Ed went to work. Conan did not like it a bit and made sure that Ed got as wet as he did as the handler scrubbed and rinsed to restore the unrecognizable dog to his gleaming white self. Most of the oil came off, but it did take several weeks for all the black to disappear.

Over the years Conan had received citations and certificates of merit from the USPCA, and in Ed's thirty-three years working with canines, five of his seven dogs won the German Shepherd Dog Club of Saint Louis award with several Honorable Mentions to the credit of each dog. Ed received the Meritorious Service Citation, ten letters of commendation from the Chief of Police and fifteen Awards of Excellence. He was named an Honorary State Trooper during his service when his dog at that time tracked a suspect that had shot and stabbed a Missouri State Trooper. In 1979, Ed was named the Parade Magazine International Association of Chiefs of Police, Officer of the Year.

"The dogs made me look good," Ed said humbly, thinking back on not only Conan, but Caesar, Willie, Luke and Bear, who came before the memorable Conan, and Nando and Pablo who came after.

Conan sits proudly by his awards.

A "jewel" of a dog—K-9 Conan

Courtesy of Ed Meyer

Now retired, Ed still enjoys the company of dogs as he works as an expert trainer of police dogs teaching from years of accumulated knowledge. His own dogs were his best teachers. For the dogs he has loved, Ed keeps a box of awards and trophies. Each dog held a special place in Ed's heart, but one that will always remain a bright spot is the dog who loved to jump—the acrobat with the coat of ivory that gallantly took on the dark crime-ridden streets and proved that despite his snowy beauty, he was as tough a street cop as any. He had the strength and courage of his name, and as the movie had long ago foretold, Ed put his trust in that "familiar sword" that was always by his side.

K-9 Senga

"Scotland's Highland Lass"

Far to the north on the eastern side of Scotland in the heart of the Grampian Mountains lies a sparsely-populated area of vast terrain. The mountain ranges bloom with purple heather in the spring, and as late summer days stretch into the early days of fall, the hillsides fade into muted reds and browns ushering in the cold days of winter. Then the mighty peaks wear a silvery mantle of snow atop the dusky lavender hue that forms a natural barrier between the scenic highlands and southern Scotland's lowland bogs.

The heart of the Grampian Mountains
Courtesy of Victoria Stables

The rocky mountain contour laced with patches of highland grass has changed little since the Roman defeat of the native Caledonians in 83 A.D., and even today, the rugged topography presents a challenge for modern-day police to patrol. The local police jurisdiction is also responsible for an area called the Royal Deeside where Queen Elizabeth and her royal family stay when they return to enjoy the beauty of Scotland.

Nearby, is the city of Aberdeen, the oil capital of Europe, and home to the largest oil companies whose offshore rigs dot the expanse of the cold North Sea. Oil workers and native Scots alike populate this northernmost section of the United Kingdom, and it is there that a young policewoman named Victoria Stables patrols.

Together with her policeman husband, Tommy, and a houseful of canines, she lives nestled in the stunning hills in a small village just outside of Aberdeen. Centrally situated, just fifteen minutes drive from beaches on the east coast of Scotland, Victoria and Tommy traverse a territory anywhere from the City of Aberdeen proper to the widely-scattered quaint towns and villages at the foot of the ancient Grampians. To drive from one side of the jurisdiction area to the other would take two to three hours.

Victoria moved to Aberdeen when she was eighteen-years-old to work in the oil industry but later joined the Grampian Police Force in 2000, when she was just twenty-one. After serving six years on the beat as a constable, she applied to become a dog handler.

In 2005, Senga, a coal-black German shepherd dog, struggled through training at the Guide Dogs for the Blind Association. Born to the "S" litter of pups at the Association, like her siblings she was given an "S" name. Senga, which is Agnes spelled backwards, was a common traditional name in southern Scotland.

"Many folks in Scotland," Victoria explained, "choose to give themselves the nickname Senga, but I'm not sure why."

Playful Senga was more concerned with running and chasing and had found it difficult to acquire the calm demeanor necessary to become a successful guide dog. As expected, she failed to pass her testing. The trainers for the guide dogs finally determined Senga was too high-spirited to remain in their ranks, and she was dropped from the program.

With nowhere to go, Senga was donated to the Grampian Police when she was just a year-and-a-half old. The strong drive she showed at the Guide

Dog Association served her much better with the police department so that in the fall of 2006, her paws first tread the dominion of the glorious Grampian range.

The department had acquired three new dogs, and they tested them with interested officers. The first week Victoria worked with each of the dogs, and she was rated on how well she interacted with each. By the end of the week, each applicant was asked which dog he/she would choose. Victoria picked Senga as the two of them just seemed to click from the first time they met, and Victoria found Senga to be extremely attentive and eager to please.

When a dog handler position opened up three months later, Victoria was permanently assigned Senga as her general purpose police dog. They completed eight weeks of intensive training together, and Senga was duly licensed.

K-9 Senga on duty at Public Order Training Day
Courtesy of Victoria Stables

The guide dog washout had a new job and a new "Mum." The Stables already had a fine complement of dogs when Senga moved into Victoria's home as the newest member of the family. The household came equipped with a yellow Labrador retriever named Jodi and a chocolate Lab named Kali. From the very start Senga took her place as top dog in the household when after a few "arguments," Kali relinquished her cherished title, and the dogs got the pecking order sorted out.

Senga lived outside in a kennel provided by the department and warm summer days found her playing out in the garden with the other dogs and her new owners. The welcoming garden provided Senga a safe haven from the crime-ridden streets and became a family place where all of the Stables' dogs could romp with abandon. The Stables' large garden was well-stocked with crisp green lettuce, tatties (potatoes) and neeps (turnips). The well-cultivated plot burst with succulent raspberries and sweet juicy strawberries during the glorious Scottish summers, and a fence surrounded the bountiful garden to keep the family dogs from helping themselves. Senga was a dog who loved vegetables, and her "Mum" often brought her a carrot or a neep to chew on in her kennel after she was put in for the night. Senga remained one hundred percent police, but at home she was a big lovable pet.

"What I could never get over was the fact that Senga was like an on/off switch. She would switch on when going to work and was always so alert and vigilant, and when home she loved to chill out in the garden or at my feet. Wherever I would be, she would never be far away."

The Stables often worked different shifts and shared the care of all their dogs.

"When Tommy worked days, he let Senga out of the kennel in the morning, and the first thing she did was run past him and come into the house looking for me. If I was still in bed after a night shift, she would lie at the bottom of the stairs and wait for me. She was always the first thing I saw when I came downstairs in the morning and was always greeted with a big hug."

As brand new partners on the street, Senga and Victoria worked the nightshift and investigated a break-in and burglary where a suspect escaped through a rear garden. The theft was so new that it was not yet determined how much or what had been stolen. Senga tried to pick up a track from the rear garden out onto the street, but it was difficult for her as she had almost no experience tracking on a hard surface. But despite the newness of the situation,

Senga persevered as Victoria used her own instinct determining where she would have gone had she been the suspect.

Senga took her down a side street where just up ahead Victoria saw some objects on the street. As she and Senga drew closer, she could see two jackets obviously thrown down there. She radioed the officers still at the robbed home, and they confirmed that jackets had been stolen. After taking possession of them, Victoria continued the search.

Senga remained focused and took her farther along the street which crossed the main road. Then Senga turned into a dark lane, which ran in between some houses. In the lane, the dog indicated on a series of scattered items lying discarded on the ground. Next, she found a purse with its emptied contents and also a "beanie" style hat, which Victoria picked up. The home owner confirmed that her purse had been stolen but not the hat so Victoria suspected that it belonged to the thief and sent it on for DNA testing by forensic scientists. Senga's timely discovery of that hat later led to a conviction.

Days off for Senga meant playing in the snow in winter or initiating her favorite chase game in the springtime garden with the other dogs. Above all, Senga loved to swim. On hot summer days, she paddled along in a local river or pond after a walk with her "Mum," and she never tired of jumping in with a loud splash to retrieve the ball that Victoria threw out into the water for her.

Despite the fact Senga spent hours riding in the police car, she never missed the opportunity to ride along on days off with Victoria and Tommy, when they took leisurely drives in the Scottish Highlands. Her big pointy ears appeared to be a permanent fixture reflected in the rear view mirror, and Victoria always smiled seeing the soft black silhouette of them that stood upright like two goal posts as Senga alertly watched the world go by through the car's back window.

Back at work, she accompanied Victoria one day when a call came that an elderly lady had her handbag snatched in the Aberdeen City Center. The male suspect was being chased along the streets by an irate member of the public, but, unfortunately, the thief was soon lost in the crowd. Before he disappeared, the man dropped the handbag but not before he had taken the money out and stuffed it in his pocket.

Not long afterward, he was spotted on the CCTV surveillance cameras, and Victoria would need to find his face in the crowd. When she and Senga arrived, they were the first on the scene. Slowly and carefully, as a boat trolls in still water, Victoria drove along turning onto the street where the camera had captured the man's picture. She studied each passing face in the crowd to

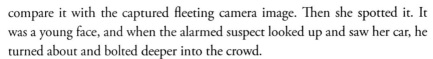

compare it with the captured fleeting camera image. Then she spotted it. It was a young face, and when the alarmed suspect looked up and saw her car, he turned about and bolted deeper into the crowd.

Victoria jammed her car into park, jumped out and raced to the back to release Senga. Adrenalin surged for both handler and dog. For the first time, they were on their own to make the arrest. It was the first time she would have to confront a potentially-dangerous suspect, who for all she knew could be very heavily armed. Since the level of crime in Scotland did not require all police to carry guns, only a few select officers were permitted to carry them. Victoria was not one of them. She had to put her implicit trust in rookie, Senga, for her protection and possible survival.

Abandoning the car in the middle of the street with its bright blue lights still flashing, Victoria pursued the man on foot. Crowds of curious pedestrians slowed her progress, and as she tried to weave through them, she found it difficult to find an opening where she could successfully deploy Senga.

But, suddenly, she saw the man up ahead and got close enough to call out her challenge.

"Stop! Police with a dog! Stop! Stop or I will release the dog!" she screamed.

The suspect, a drug addict in his early twenties, darted into the alleyway and tried unsuccessfully to hide. Terrified when Senga caught up with him, he began to cry and expressed regret for what he had done.

"Please, please," he begged through his tears, "Don't let that dog near me!"

Seeing he was cornered, the frightened thief gave himself up.

Victoria and Senga detained him as the victorious dog emitted a series of warning barks to hold him until back-up police arrived. When the man was taken into custody, Victoria lavished Senga with praise realizing how different the outcome could have been. She gave the excited dog her favorite ball on a rope as a reward, and at dinner time that evening Senga discovered another of her favorites— delectable pieces of chicken given with thanks for a job well done.

As fluttering snowflakes showered the Grampians, and the lights of Christmas began to twinkle throughout the highlands at dusk, Victoria shopped for bones for all the dogs. They were not the kind of bones that disappeared in a matter of minutes. They were the kind of bones prized by any good dog that made that dog delirious with joy. Gnawed on happily for hours before a warm fire on a cold winter's day, the treats were the ideal canine Christmas gift.

Senga receives a tasty Christmas bone from her Mum's soft hand.

Courtesy of Victoria Stables

The frosty days before Christmas brought other elation to the growing household. Kali gave birth to seven cuddly black babies the second week of December, filling the air with squeals of tiny helpless pups singing their own style of Christmas carols. Kali was a great "Mum" to the pups, but Victoria was concerned that Senga might harm them given her status of top dog in the household.

Victoria watched with some trepidation as curious Senga first approached the helpless creatures one day. After a few exploratory sniffs, the police dog showed her tender motherly side and proved to be extremely gentle and caring with them. When Kali was not around, surrogate mom, Senga, grasped the little bodies between her paws and washed them with great determination, and as they grew, she took them out into the garden to tumble in the grass. Only when they disturbed her sleep would she turn grumpy with them, but when bright and awake Senga once more accepted them into her care.

With the sparkle of Christmas just a memory, weeks later the puppies were found new homes. Senga missed her charges, but one male named Bosco remained, and he formed a close bond with Senga. Wherever she wandered in the garden, Bosco wasn't far behind. His short stubby legs could not keep up with her at first, but the little legs grew, and he then became a formidable opponent in the chasing game in the Stables' seldom quiet garden.

The following spring brought a roommate for Senga in the backyard kennel, when explosive detection dog, Bonzo, was given to Victoria by another handler who retired in 2008. The dog was a big friendly boy, a Lab crossed with a Springer spaniel. One of Bonzo's primary jobs was to search Queen Elizabeth's royal residences and any other places in the area where her family visited. Often that meant searching the royal cabins and lodges where Prince Charles liked to fish or hold barbeques during the summer, and after a thorough search Bonzo was rewarded with a cool refreshing dip in the crystal-clear water of the nearby loch.

Bonzo on duty in Deeside

*Bonzo sits dripping wet after a cool dip in the loch
at Deeside while working for the Royals.*

Courtesy of Victoria Stables

If the queen visited Balmoral Castle and attended church there or visited the Highland Games, it was Bonzo that preceded her making sure every step she took was on safe ground. Once Bonzo was called upon to search at Fyvie Castle, one of the most haunted castles in Scotland. But far more frightening than ghosts was Bonzo's close proximity to the priceless treasures the castle held. On that occasion, Victoria stepped lively to keep up with him as his waggy tail came excruciatingly close to expensive lamps and priceless antiques.

"It can be quite scary sometimes," said Victoria, "as Bonzo has so much drive when he is searching. He can sometimes be like a bull in a china shop."

Bonzo had to search all areas of the castles he visited before the queen and her favorite corgis arrived.

"I think his favorite room was definitely the kitchen and the dog room where he could scrounge anything he could sniff out. The dog room, used by the queen's corgis and also staff dogs, is located at the back of the castle near to the housekeeping/staff quarters. The lady of the house/housekeeper gave Bonzo a "Bonio" for his hard work the last time we searched."

Serving the Royals was a good life for a Scotch dog. It afforded Bonzo a comfortable spot in the Stables' growing menagerie of dogs, and Senga always enjoyed his company in the kennel.

Five months later, Victoria received a radio call that a man had been found lying stabbed in the chest in Aberdeen. Upon her arrival, she saw ambulance workers hovering over the victim administering emergency aid in order to save his life. He lay in a pool of blood, and a gruesome red trail marked a path from him to a nearby lane. As the man appeared to lie dying, Senga was deployed and already on the trail of his potential killer.

The aging tenement where she searched was a large granite building consisting of six-to-eight residential flats sharing a communal back garden. In the lane that adjoined the building, Senga showed special interest in a seven-foot-tall locked wooden gate. It was too high for dog or handler to scale, so they carried out their search elsewhere but were unable to pick up a track of any person due to the number of passers by in the area contaminating the track.

After leaving the area, Victoria was haunted by her dog's particular interest in that gate. There was no reason to think the killer went through it or over it, yet Senga was very intrigued by the old gate. Not being able to shake the feeling that Senga's interest was not random, Victoria decided to return to explore that area more thoroughly.

This time, she was able to gain access to the area by going around to the front of the building. Finally entering the area through a communal door, Victoria momentarily gazed about the quiet enclosed garden. Senga immediately started to scour the area for whatever scent had first drawn her there. Sniffing along the ground, she carefully searched the area. Victoria stood patiently at the edge of the garden so as not to disturb the ground. She watched her dog explore everywhere and then Senga turned toward a weathered shed near the west side wall tucked in among other communal sheds and outbuildings. When Senga got closer, she lay down and would not leave until Victoria went to her. It was the classic indication of a find. Beside her was the object of her hunt. There beside the shed lay a knife. It was at the far side of the garden far from the locked gate, but Senga had always known it was there.

In the suspect's panic he had thrown the knife over the gate as he fled. It was taken for forensic evidence, and its discovery saved the police search team much time looking for the missing weapon. Due to Senga's miraculous find, two people were later arrested and charged with attempted murder.

Friendly and intelligent, Senga was the ideal dog. Her guarding tendencies never left her, and she allowed no one to come into the house or garden without her knowing about it. Her personality appealed to everyone she came in contact with from veterinarians and their assistants to Victoria's kennel maid who cared for Senga in the police kennel on the few occasions Victoria had to be away. Even victims of crimes took the time to write thank you letters to Victoria after Senga had come to their aid.

As the sun rose over the Grampians, melting the snows of winter, heather again bloomed in the warming valley. Spring days turned into summer, and one balmy day Victoria and Senga worked the day shift waiting to see what would come their way. When they got a call that a male suspect had been breaking into houses along the banks of the River Don, they sped in that direction. The river was one of two main rivers flowing through Aberdeen, and the region was half a mile from the sea. The urgent pull of strong sea tides forced the water in and out with great rapidity.

By the time Victoria arrived at the scene, an off-duty officer had caught the tall, thin twenty-year-old suspect, but the belligerent man put up a spirited fight and escaped onto an island in the middle of the river. At that time, the tide was going out to sea so the river was relatively low leaving the silt-covered river bed slippery and hard to negotiate. Faced with such a difficult impediment, Victoria estimated the distance between the island and where she stood. She would need a plan to catch up to the man and make the apprehension.

Senga was deployed down the steep river bank and scrabbled along over the slick uneven terrain, and Victoria struggled behind to maintain her own footing on the slimy stones that lined the river bed. The island sat one hundred feet out into the river, and as they moved closer, Senga and Victoria waded through ankle-deep water. Splashing along and finally stepping onto the island, they pursued the man and immediately flushed him out into the open. The returning incoming tide would not give him long to make a decision. Not knowing where to turn, he decided to try and make his escape by wading out into the river bed again.

Victoria challenged the man, threatening to send her dog, but he refused to stop and waded farther out into the river before swimming away under a bridge in the direction of the sea.

"Follow him!" Victoria called to Senga, and the dog complied with no hesitation.

Once again, the shallow river bed slowed Senga's progress until she managed to move deeper into the rising water and start to swim.

"My heart was racing, as I knew she was not trained to deal with this scenario."

The man soon realized the folly of his ways finding himself in much deeper water than he had anticipated. It was then that he began to flounder and flail. Senga watched him constantly and paddled out to approach him. But she had never been exposed to such a situation, and it was hard for her to know what to do when she finally swam up beside him.

In order to save himself, the sinking man grabbed onto her collar. In noisy splashes of water, Senga began to flounder as well trying desperately to keep her head above water when his weight continually pulled her downward. Struggling to free herself, she tried to swim back to Victoria, but the panicked suspect clung to her tightly and time after time, he pulled her under water.

"I must admit I was very angry with the man for grabbing her collar like that, because I could see she was distressed."

Chest-deep in water, Victoria shouted to the man to let Senga go, but he could not hear her. Fighting the strong incoming tide, Victoria swam under the bridge and came out the other side, but she was dressed in full police uniform and wore two large heavy boots that impeded her progress. The river was quite deep in parts, and the weight of her full body armor made it impossible to swim out to her dog. She fought to keep her head and shoulders above water in the swift tide and finally found a large stone in the river bed to stand upon, but that was as far as she dared go.

On the banks of the River Don, Senga and Victoria entered from the left as the man escaped to the island on the right. Eventually, he went under the bridge's second arch from the left out towards the sea. Just through the second arch, the small protrusion is the top of the tree that the man clung to while holding Senga until Victoria could swim out to him with a life ring.

Courtesy of Victoria Stables

Victoria strained to watch the situation unfold in the distance. As Senga's panic escalated, Victoria knew time was short if her dog was to survive. Recalling her seemed to be the only thing to do. Victoria shouted for the tiring dog to come back, and when Senga turned and looked at her Victoria could see in her eyes that she was not at all comfortable. The worried policewoman pointed in one direction towards the branch of a tree standing in the river, and Senga turned to swim as best she could in that direction. The man still held tight to Senga's collar slowing her like a heavy anchor when she started to swim the other way. As hard as she could paddle, Senga slowly pulled the man along with her.

Getting her head above water again after several submersions, the weakening dog dragged the sinking man towards the tree branch sticking out of the river bed. She was able to assist him in grabbing onto the branch, and finally he let her go. Once more, Victoria shouted the challenge to the suspect and then she called Senga to her again. Given more freedom to move, exhausted Senga clumsily paddled her way back to relieved Victoria who waited for her with open arms.

A fellow officer standing on the bridge lowered a life ring down to Victoria, and she swam out toward the man with it. Although Senga was extremely tired from her ordeal, she was alert, and she turned again and swam right next to Victoria the entire way out and back as Victoria dragged the man back to the river bank.

As they neared shore, another police sergeant waded into the waist-deep water to assist in pulling the man out of the water. Victoria was very weary, but she had to keep Senga under control. The dog was quite angry with the man at that point and remained highly agitated.

Although the river had been unusually warm for that time of year, the man claimed hypothermia and was unable to move too much. With the help of the sergeant and another officer, he was helped to his feet and walked back along the river bank to the beach to meet the arriving ambulance. The river bank was too steep to climb, so Victoria followed with Senga behind in the event that the man tried to run off again.

When the man was taken away, Victoria had time to reflect upon and assess the situation. Senga had always been a dog that loved to swim, yet she had no training in river rescues. Many police dogs would never have gone into the water as she had done. It was a sobering thought to think that being weighted down with cumbersome body armor could have easily caused Victoria to drown trying to save her dog. And the loss of the brave dog performing such an heroic act she had never been trained for would have been devastating.

Many members of the public had watched the whole suspenseful incident, and some took pictures. The story was broadcast on the local news and was splashed across local and national Scottish newspapers. Senga had won the public's hearts for her self-sacrificing bravery, and they continued to follow the whole case as it went to trial. The police department recognized the valiant efforts of Senga and Victoria at the river and applauded them for their good work.

Weeks later, Senga took part in the competitive Callander Police Dog Trials for novice dogs and handlers who had never competed before.

"Let's give it a go," Victoria said enthusiastically to Senga as she patted the "smiling" dog's head.

The experience would do them good Victoria thought. She was not concerned about how Senga would perform there. After the river rescue, Senga would always be a bright shining star in her eyes, but she felt the experience would make them grow as a team.

Eager canines barked on the sidelines as the competition began that day, and Victoria took Senga gingerly through a round of obedience with agility. Then they finished up with some criminal apprehension work. All dog handlers started with the same number of points and had them subtracted for each extra verbal command or hand signal they gave their dogs. Senga performed well, and Victoria was reasonably pleased with her performance.

Smiling and self-assured after the display, Victoria stood proudly. Then she saw the judge walking her way.

"Your dog was good and showed potential, but you were rubbish!" he said. "You need to keep your mouth closed and keep your hands to yourself. Why give ten commands when one would have done?"

Victoria felt as if she could have slunk away in her embarrassment. She was so afraid she had let Senga down. But faithful Senga happily wagged her tail, prancing at Victoria's feet and felt nonetheless for wear. Her true happiness was not in gaining competition points, but with the sheer fun of being with her "Mum." Victoria promised her they would practice and re-enter the following year at the Police Dog Trials for Scotland, which Grampian Police would host in 2009. Still smiling, Victoria left with Senga and her participation certificate. There would always be next year.

Victoria shows off Senga's "Certificate of
Participation" after the Callander Trials.

Courtesy of Victoria Stables

With the trials behind them, Victoria and Senga went back to working the day shift and breathing in the first crisp woodsy scent of fall after an unusually hot summer in Scotland. Cooler breezes blew through the Grampians, and trees were just starting to show their brilliant colors when Victoria took Senga for a walk in a very large field at the edge of Aberdeen.

It was a large plain grass field fenced on all sides, and it had been used for dog training and exercising purposes for many years.

Victoria and Senga ready for their off-duty walk.
Courtesy of Victoria Stables

They had walked the field together many times before, finding peace and solitude there. Wild animals sometimes visited the field, and as Victoria and Senga leisurely strolled along, a very young and timid deer stepped out from the bushes and stood like a statue. Senga, knowing great fun when she saw it immediately gave chase. She had seen deer there before early in the morning or late in the day, and the big ones had easily escaped her, but she knew she stood a good chance of catching such a little one. Victoria had never seen her more focused. When the deer saw the black dog charging forward, it bounded away finding a gap in the fence at the very edge of the field. Instead of turning away from the road, the frightened deer headed right towards it. Within seconds, it leapt out onto the open road. Not to be deterred, Senga galloped closely behind, all four feet hitting the ground in a hard rhythm as she gained on the deer as it entered the roadway. Then both animals disappeared from Victoria's line of sight.

Victoria was so far behind the rapidly-running animals that she could only imagine what was transpiring ahead. Her instincts told her that whatever it was could not be good. Her blood ran cold as she ran as fast as she could across the huge field. As she approached the road, Victoria could see cars slowing down. The horrific scene played out in an eerie slow motion before the reality of it all registered. Victoria screamed and ran to the edge of the roadway.

"I knew in my gut that something was wrong. I was hoping she was just running about on the road and cars were stopping for her, but as soon as I got across the fence, I could see her lying on the road. I could hardly move my legs I was so devastated."

With leaden legs and heavy heart, Victoria stumbled out onto the road where she could see two cars stopped. A car had hit Senga with full force and killed her instantly. The shaken driver of the car that hit Senga was directing traffic along with another passer-by motioning cars around Senga who lay perfectly still on the road.

After making sure that the driver was not injured, Victoria collapsed beside her dog. She tenderly surrounded her beloved Senga and buried her face in the thick black fur.

"I was no longer a police officer. I was an owner who had lost her best friend."

Victoria, inconsolable, sat in the middle of the road sobbing her heart out as the sympathetic woman passer-by tried to comfort her. The driver directed traffic around Victoria so she could momentarily mourn the loss of her friend. Then he approached Victoria and gently told her she had to get off the road for her own safety. He helped lift limp Senga to the side to allow oncoming cars to pass.

Nearly paralyzed with grief, Victoria radioed in and quietly asked for further assistance. It felt like an eternity for help to arrive, and while she waited, Victoria stroked and cuddled her dead friend.

The tiny deer lay dead beside Senga. She had come so close to catching it, and she had been so focused that she never saw the car coming.

"I was pleading with her to wake up, but she wouldn't. She didn't have a mark on her except a bit of blood from her nose. Her eyes were still wide open and focused on the deer. I just couldn't believe it. She was still warm."

Finally, two colleagues and a fellow dog handler arrived at the scene.

"My colleagues dealt with the driver and passer by, and the dog handler comforted me."

The other dog handler placed Senga in his car as Victoria's car was still at the other end of the field. With fingers that could barely dial the phone, Victoria made the painful phone call to Tommy who was working that day, and he came to drive her and Senga the sad ten miles home. A glance in the rear view mirror gave a clear view, no longer offering the image of two familiar alert black ears. The void was breathtaking.

No amount of stroking the deep black coat or pleading or sobbing would bring Senga back. In all the years the field was used by dogs and handlers, there had never been an incident there.

Once home, Victoria placed Senga in her kennel where for years she had enjoyed so many carrots and neeps and the company of her fellow police dog, Bonzo. Victoria sat with her beautiful dog, still tasting the salt of so many tears to weep alone before letting the other dogs come in so they could see that their friend was gone.

"They knew straight away. Bosco, the pup, was very gentle and tried to clean Senga's eyes and ears. He just sat next to me and whined now and again. It was heartbreaking seeing him like that. Jodi was also very sad. She sat next to me and comforted me."

"Kali and Bonzo, who were the least closest to Senga came in and had a sniff and look and then left. It was so strange how they all seemed to know that she was gone."

Bosco, Jodi and Kali
Courtesy of Victoria Stables

Later that day, Victoria took Senga to the crematorium. The following day Kali started to reclaim her "top dog" status and was very possessive over her food at dinner time, which was unusual for her. The primitive drive to maintain alpha status drove her.

"She had a go at Jodi and started fighting. I had to intervene, and Kali was so angry she bit me on the arm. She didn't mean it and let go straight away, but she was so intent on showing who was boss. She is now top dog."

Victoria later gently placed Senga's ashes contained in a small wooden casket in the hall where in happier days the dog always lay at the bottom of the stairs waiting for her. Senga would continue to be the first thing Victoria saw in the morning and the last thing she would see before bed at night.

"I loved her so much, and I miss her every day."

For a year-and-a-half Senga served Scotland with honor, and her department called her a tremendous credit to the Force. Sometime after Senga's death, a Belgian Malinois named Lux joined the family and like so many lucky dogs, he found his way into the Stables' family garden bringing the number of dogs back up to five.

Lux was a young dog with a lot to learn, but he gained in confidence every day. He soon became best friends with Senga's favorite pup, and once more Bosco romped with a friend in the garden in the shadows of Senga's favorite ball on a rope.

"He gets on well with Bonzo too, as they have not had any cross words yet whilst sharing the kennel outside."

New friends, Bonzo and Lux
Courtesy of Victoria Stables

Tucked into the kennel for the night, curious Lux softly took his first carrots and neeps from Victoria's offering hand and when the river water warmed in the spring, Victoria would take him for his first swim. Lux would carry on filling the void left in the Stables' home by Senga's passing, but never, never would any dog truly replace the endearing and unique Senga.

Senga set the bar high for the long line of police dogs that would likely come into Victoria's life during her future career. Scotland will long remember the daring river rescue when untrained Senga not only saved the life of the suspect she chased, but returned to protect her beloved "Mum."

Victoria's prophetic words came to pass and forever will be true.

"Wherever I would be, she would never be far away."

In the years to come in the purple shadows of the majestic Grampian Mountains, when the awakening petals of sweet heather once more splash the ancient hills in brilliant color, memories will linger of Victoria's perpetual "shining star." Regardless of the years that pass, the spirit of K-9 Senga, Scotland's always remembered Highland Lass, will just as before, always remain at her "Mum's" side.

K-9 Senga – Scotland's Highland Lass

Courtesy of Victoria Stables

107

MWD Duke

"Jaws, Paws and Claws"

No one would touch him. The staff at the local pound never entered his kennel at all for the three weeks he was there. Born in the spring of 2004, he had lived on an unknown property and became too much of a handful for the owner. And now the nameless dog, only ten-months-old, was scheduled to die.

LACW (Leading Aircraftswoman) Tricia Reynolds of the RAAF (Royal Australian Air Force) was looking for a military working dog (MWD). She had joined the Air Force in 1999 and worked as a supplier in a warehouse. Her love of dogs knew no bounds, and she always felt compelled to work with them. Tricia couldn't imagine her life without a dog being an integral part of it, and her military career gravitated in that direction. In 2003, she worked with a dog named Bullet, and she later took on a dog named Rudi, but a bad case of hip dysplasia in the dog was diagnosed and that ended his career. For several months, Tricia was without a dog at all, and she was anxious to find one that could serve well with her. In April of 2005, the possibility of a new dog came her way.

The wait had been overbearing, but one day a call came in from a pound in New South Wales, Australia's oldest state, to the RAAF base where Tricia was assigned. The caller said that the pound held a German shepherd dog, but the staff could not get him out of the kennel and re-home him, as he was too aggressive. Barking wildly, baring his teeth and defensively lashing out at whomever tried to approach him, he was an unlikely adoptive candidate for anyone. So for his three weeks at the pound he kept to himself, growling and snapping when necessary to preserve his image, and in his loneliness he simply chased his tail. The uncontrollable dog was due be euthanized the next day if the Air Force did not want to take him. Despite the reluctance on the pound's part to keep the unruly dog any longer, he was granted just a one-day reprieve if Air Force personnel would promise to come the next day. Losing no time, Tricia and her sergeant drove for three hours to the pound to take a look at the beast.

When they arrived, they found the pure-bred German shepherd dog who greeted them from within his enclosure with much hostility. He was identified simply as "mersewayvagrant," sadly fitting. He was by far the most unapproachable dog at the kennel. The dog was missing a huge chunk of fur from his tail, where he had bitten it in an endless round of tail chasing, as he continually spun in circles in the cage. Unfortunately, he had developed the neurotic behavior in reaction to being enclosed in the kennel. The scruffy dog was unreceptive when the sergeant opened the cage door, and the animal showed its displeasure by inflicting a few bites upon his hesitant greeter. The sergeant continued to coax him out of the cage, but the dog remained very fearful, and it could only be imagined what he had endured in his relatively-short life to create such behavior. Not understanding the difference between friend and foe, he fought them off, barking, snarling and snapping at the only people who could save him. Defensively, he paced and growled, defying anyone to get near him.

After thirty minutes of trying, Tricia and her sergeant were about to give up on him. They had tried everything. Calming words, friendly gestures and bribery with food, but they still couldn't get him so much as an inch out of the kennel. The sergeant finally gave up and was prepared to leave the facility empty-handed so he and Tricia started to walk away. Just then, the hostile dog stuck his head outside of the kennel door, not far, but just enough to feel freedom on the other side. He really wanted to get out and experience that freedom, but he just didn't know how. One small part of him wanted to cower in the cage, yet another conflicting emotion begged for freedom.

"His whole body language has changed," Tricia said, "He can sense freedom!"

The sergeant slowly cracked the cage door just a little bit more, so the dog's head could stick out. When the insecure dog ventured close enough to poke his head out a bit further, they tried throwing the leash around his neck like a lasso, but it didn't work. As soon as the fearful dog felt the leash around his neck, he backed into the security of the dreaded cage and slipped the leash.

After half an hour of trying to get him all the way out of the kennel without losing a limb, patience and perseverance won the day. Using food to coax him out of the cage finally worked. Showing a minute bit of trust, he allowed the leash to be put around his neck, and he took a few steps outside of the door. Then fully out of the cage, he was a completely different dog. He calmed himself and allowed Tricia to inspect him more closely. He was a very skinny and unhealthy-looking dog covered in ticks, and hundreds of fleas crawled over his thin frame. The pound was across the road from the local dump, and the dog appeared to be yet just one more piece of refuse that had been thrown away.

The sergeant held the dog as Tricia assessed the pitiful animal for suitability as a working dog. It was Tricia whom he would belong to, and she wanted to see if he "had the goods." Even in his sorry condition, he passed the initial assessment, so they decided to give him another chance at life. The flea-bitten waif was put in the dog truck to leave the place that caused him so much distress. The personnel at the pound could provide little information on him so he had no real history to speak of. Tricia noticed a breeder's tattoo in the dog's ear, which piqued her curiosity. At one time there must have been great hope for the dog to fulfill his potential. Later, locating Duke's breeder to gain more information about him only led to the comment that he had been a "very defensive puppy," but with renewed hope, Tricia knew that the trait could lend itself well for his future training.

Despite the challenging state of the dog, Tricia was ecstatic on the drive home. She finally had a new dog to work with, and as she rode along she pondered a good name for him. She decided to call him Duke, as he had been such a "hazard" as they tried to get him out of the kennel. So reminiscent of the American television program, The Dukes of Hazzard, the dog had an inspired name.

Getting Duke out of the truck at the end of the trip was the first hurdle. Who knew if he had ever even ridden in a vehicle at all? He reacted to unknown experiences the only way he knew how, with aggression. Fear was all he knew. As Tricia tried to unload him from the truck, he returned to the same aggressive behavior he displayed at the pound. This time, her approach was different. After a few stern words, he learned that she was the boss and with that fact established, it was the start of a great relationship. Having someone assert authority over him seemed to give him some measure of security.

Duke fully understood the hierarchy then, and he became more docile. Tricia took him to one of her mentors, who was a prison dog handler in Fiji before coming to Australia and joining the Air Force, and together they worked with the dog. Then she took him on a four-week re-team course, and after completion the former vagabond dog came off the course as a MWD, Military Working Dog. Everything he did was to please Tricia. His former aggression eclipsed into the drive he needed to become a working dog, and his absolute love for Tricia was the catalyst that made it all happen. Now a member of the Royal Australian Air Force, untold adventures awaited Duke that he could hardly have imagined.

Tricia and MWD Duke
Courtesy of Kirk Peacock

Free from the confines of the pound and on the way to becoming a MWD

Courtesy Judith Watts

Beauty in motion
Courtesy of Tricia Reynolds

Once a year, there was an exchange between the Royal Australian Air Force and the New Zealand Air Force. Tricia applied for the program but was not optimistic since no MWDs had been accepted before. Not only was she later hand-picked and accepted, but for the first time the Air Force allowed her to take a dog along. Far from the confining walls of a common pound, Duke was on his way to New Zealand where he would spend the next three months.

A shiny NZ Air Force Boeing 747 landed in Australia to fly Tricia and Duke to their next point of adventure. Duke, secured in his dog box, was stored in the cargo hold for the flight to Ohakea that fall day and when he emerged, he was met by Quarantine. He was closely inspected to make sure he wasn't carrying any diseases or ticks, and as Tricia expected, he was given a clean bill of health. They jumped back on the plane destined for Auckland.

Once at their destination at RNZAF Whenuapai, close to Auckland, Tricia lived in the barracks on base, and Duke stayed in the kennel bank at the dog section. When they were together, they explored all that the area had to offer. As they strolled along in beautiful Christchurch on the South Island, it was like nothing Tricia had ever seen. The golden leaves of the autumn trees showcased the rugged beauty of New Zealand's muted amber mountains. Alternatively, the North Island featured a starker landscape with a stunning vista of rolling hills where a good dog could run.

On duty, Tricia trained two junior dog handlers as Duke served as the well-seasoned "demo" dog. She was able to locate a recruit dog at a house near Auckland for the small Military Working Dog unit there, and the dog later became a full-scale MWD under her training and guidance.

Days in New Zealand provided Duke and Tricia with many hours walking together to enjoy the quiet solitude of such a mysterious and unusual locale. Their time together there only served to make Duke love her all the more, so much so that when she left him in the kennel at the Air Force base to visit with friends on the South Island, Duke made his feelings known. Harkening back to his days in the pound, some of his kennel aggression returned and after a brief run in the yard with his keepers there, he refused to get back in his kennel. Four other dogs staying there watched the drama play out as the "demo dog" demonstrated his displeasure without Tricia.

He would allow no one to take his leash off. For two days he kept it on perhaps thinking if it was on, he would be all ready to go when Tricia returned. So he sat, leash on neck, in the immaculate quarantine-approved kennel gazing at its oddly-colored green walls until it was time to go.

When Duke was back in Tricia's caring hands, they set off for a careers expo in Auckland. Duke was on constant display there, on his best behavior and did his part to promote good public relations. After a few demos, Tricia decided to coax him into the huge LAV (Light Armored Vehicle) there. Duke had always done anything Tricia asked of him, but he eyed the vehicle warily.

After a challenging entry, MWD Duke poses proudly beside Tricia.
Courtesy of Glenn Blay

After strapping a muzzle to Duke's long nose, Tricia then jumped up onto the front of the LAV. A second dog handler lifted Duke up while Tricia gave the "up" command. So far, so good, especially since Duke was not enthused by another handler touching him. In a flurry of fur, Tricia maneuvered the dog over to the driver's hole in the vehicle, but it was so small that she had to make him go down head first. Muzzle and snout first, he worked his way down into the tiny hole next to where she was standing. That left his huge back legs and long tail swishing above the hole. Working his legs around, he managed to turn around down in the hole and with a big push jump his front paws back up onto the front of the LAV. Soon, he was successfully standing upright in the hole poking his proud military head outward for photos. No other LAV occupant had ever had such trouble just getting into the vehicle. It was not the easiest maneuver he had ever tried, but he trusted Tricia so much that, as always, he did what she asked of him without even thinking.

When their time in New Zealand ended, the team returned once more to Australia to guard planes and assets at the Air Force base. The scenery there was quite a change from the haunting beauty of New Zealand, but not without its own character. Patrolling the base, Tricia could often see koalas lazily sleeping in the surrounding eucalyptus trees or crossing the road. Sometimes kangaroos with springs for legs jumped about, and it was not unusual to slow down or stop traffic to assure that the furry creatures that roamed the area could make it across the road safely.

Tricia and Duke on patrol.
Courtesy of Scott Woodward

A dog to be reckoned with, MWD Duke in New Zealand

Courtesy of Daniel Hall

Two of the Royal Australian Air Force's finest

Courtesy of Andrew Eddie

Duke demonstrates his intimidating "smile."
Courtesy of Judith Watts

"We have plenty of 'roos that jump around on base at night, but luckily, Duke has never tried getting close enough to one to see what would happen. If he sees them, he gets very excited, but I always have him on leash or in the truck."

Amidst the roar of the intimidating planes scattered about the airfield, grey wallabies, the smaller version of kangaroos, went on their way paying no mind to the air power there. Many times, Tricia had to swerve as she drove along in order to avoid hitting a kangaroo or the small wallabies that continually jumped in front of moving vehicles. While most of the dogs barked out a warning, Duke found the indigenous animals to be curious creatures and mostly just stared at them never making a noise.

Surrounded by kangaroos, Duke keeps his distance.

Courtesy of Tricia Reynolds

Spring of 2008 brought more adventure for Duke and Tricia when they were called from their home in Australia across international waters to the troubled land of East Timor in Indonesia, where they would spend the next six months. Tricia was only the second female handler to be deployed on operations with her MWD. Along with three fellow RAAF MWD handlers sent to guard Blackhawk helicopters belonging to the Australian Army, the new assignment would create an interesting chapter in her military career. Tricia's husband, Harvey, was also in the Air Force and had been deployed in Afghanistan and during their time apart, Duke was always welcome company.

Before her deployment, Tricia took some leave to return to South Australia to visit her parents. She was due to fly out in the morning, and she could hardly sleep as she anticipated the exciting days ahead. Duke had been kept on base during her leave, and he was extremely happy to see her when she returned, prancing about and wagging his tail. He could scarcely control his enthusiasm.

The trip started from RAAF Base Williamtown, New South Wales. Next, they flew to their staging area, which was at Darwin, the capital city of NT (Northern Territory) and the gateway to Asia. The dogs were loaded into their traveling boxes and carried to the rear of the plane. Everyone aboard, they were off to Dili, East Timor, flying across the Timor Sea.

Ever since she joined the Air Force, Tricia had dreamed of being deployed overseas and serving her country and to be able to do it with her best friend, Duke, was a dream come true. The flight over on the small chartered plane was just short of two hours, but anticipation made it seem forever. Throughout the flight, the dogs seemed in high spirits.

"They know they are going somewhere exciting," said Tricia, "so they behave themselves!"

As the plane approached East Timor, it dropped through a bank of clouds, and Tricia could make out the forms of mountains. Some lay directly in front of the plane, and as the cloud cover re-emerged, it appeared that the plane could easily fly right into one of them. Through swirls of misty clouds, the view reappeared and beyond the mountain ridges the land below then opened up into a beautiful splash of green.

As the plane descended further over the troubled island country, Tricia could see the brilliant blue waters below and more of the green island coming into view. The small country in Southeast Asia had been a 14th century stop on the Indian and Chinese trade routes, exporting aromatic sandalwood, slaves, honey and wax. After years of harsh and oppressive Indonesian rule in more recent years, it was a hot spot of extreme violence and brutality resulting in thousands of deaths of its inhabitants. The crystal clarity of the waters and the serene landscape was deceptive, and it was not a safe assumption that the new visitors would be completely safe there.

Timor was a land of immense beauty filled with impoverished but gentle people. The brilliant hue of indigenous feathered birds flying through the sweeping vistas of a rain forest was stunning, but on the horizon the ever-constant presence of the violent gangs posed a real threat. The political instability of Indonesia had spread to the island and hopefully the Australian presence would calm the precarious situation there.

When Tricia and the three other handlers stepped off the plane, the heat of the island hit them squarely in the face. But far worse was the humidity. It was nearly 92 degrees Fahrenheit and before they could collect the dogs, they were already starting to sweat. The airport was very small, and all the buildings were shabby and run down. East Timor had a distinct smell of burning rubbish, and Tricia was overwhelmed by it as soon as she stepped off the plane.

Standing on the tarmac, Tricia anxiously watched for Duke to be loaded off the plane. The dog boxes had been offloaded onto a device that looked somewhat like an escalator and slowly the boxes made their descent. Tricia walked straight over to make sure all four dogs had survived the trip in good shape. She was a bit worried about them being in their boxes in the heat, but they were all fine. As soon as he caught a glimpse of her, Duke started to whine and started scratching at the door to get out. The dogs were loaded onto a truck for the short ride to their new home, and Tricia and the other handlers walked across the airport hardstand, filled with the Blackhawk helicopters, to locate their new quarters.

How run down and poor the country looked! Sparse grass surrounded worn structures, and many places looked as if they sat in the middle of a war zone. In the remote areas, rubbish filled the streets. Australia had been involved in assisting East Timor since 1999, but the infrastructure was still deplorable, and the unsettled island country was still classified as a Third World Country. But the countryside itself was beautiful, and the teams on the ground were lucky enough to be situated just two-tenths of a mile from the beach.

Up ahead, the handlers saw a cluster of portable huts and some hand-made shelters the locals had erected. The structures were very impressive topped by thatched roofs that managed to keep out the heavy rains during the torrential downpours of wet season extremely well. East Timor's wet season meant that the rain could bucket down for days on end, and that was to be expected in such a tropical climate.

Tricia couldn't wait to get Duke out of his box so he could see his new home. Out he bounded when she opened the door, and he was happy to see her as always and looked to be as excited about his new surroundings as she was.

Duke and the other three dogs had temporary kennels, which the last dog handlers that were there had built. The structure had concrete floors which helped with cooling and helped prevent an infestation of the ticks and fleas that were rampant there. The dogs had further protection from them as the handlers applied a liquid to their coats every two weeks. The kennels sat very close to the women's toilets and shower block, and Tricia would find later that Duke kept track of all the comings and goings there barking to alert everyone to the activity throughout the night, which did not make him the most popular dog at those times.

Whenever the handlers walked with the dogs, the locals' greeting was the same. Timor's inhabitants remained wary of the dogs, understanding that the military dogs were trained to bite if anyone dared do anything wrong.

"Botarde, asu tata?" the natives always asked, meaning, "Good afternoon, dog bite?"

The village people were not used to seeing such large dogs as German shepherds, let alone well-trained dogs that were trained to attack on command. The locals kept an array of dogs as pets, but dog was also considered a food there, which took the team a little getting used to. Strays ran loose on the island, and the teams had to make sure the stray dogs did not bite their dogs, since rabies was still prevalent in East Timor, and Australia was rabies free. When he encountered the strays, thankfully, Duke just looked at them and minded his own business.

East Timor natives eye Duke warily.
Courtesy of Tricia Reynolds

Tricia's main role on the island was to provide aircraft security, and for the most part, she and Duke worked at night. In the cooler nighttime temperatures, they walked a perimeter around the airfield there. An IDP (Internally Displaced Person) camp sat adjacent to the airfield, and Tricia could see the tent-style encampment there. The people were close enough to the airfield that Tricia could often hear the inhabitants of the camp rummaging around the field, but they never dared to come near her, her dog or the aircraft.

On their first night on patrol, Duke and Tricia walked around the airfield to familiarize themselves with the new area. In the dark, she saw someone walking across the runway less than a mile in front of her. It seemed illusionary, but Duke saw the figure too. There were gangs there that caused a fair amount of trouble, and she was glad to have Duke at her side. Tricia's heart almost jumped out of her chest wondering who the person was and what he was up to. Suddenly, the figure ran off into the bushes on the side of the runway. There was no point following it up as the locals would cross the runway all the time walking to their villages, but she never knew if it was a pig, a large dog or a human. It could have been a gang member having a look around, but sometimes the enemy was hard to identify. Given the level of violence in the country, she learned that first night that she would need to remain vigilant and question all she saw and always remain close to Duke, her tail-chasing, but always-protective presence.

For the remainder of their shift, Tricia fastened Duke on his stake-out ten-foot chain. It was a twelve-hour shift, which made it difficult for a handler to hold the leash that long. Duke was content to wander very close to where Tricia sat and could more easily view the entire flight line. The rest of the shift was quiet, and at his leisure, Duke did some exuberant tail chasing when he saw nothing in particular at the airfield to be alarmed about. After catching up on sleep the next day, the two would have a good run around the airfield to keep in shape and to see the base in the light of day.

To see more of their new island home when they were off duty, Tricia took Duke into the town of Dili, the capital of East Timor, but he always rode in the back of the dog truck. It was obvious it would be impossible to walk the dogs around in town, as there were too many people, and there was always the risk that one of the locals may have gotten bitten, but the teams continually patrolled the nearby village greeting the friendly inhabitants there and hopefully providing some security for the people due to potential threats the island faced.

Away from the potential dangers in their new surroundings, there was always the countryside. Tricia and the other handlers loved taking the dogs down to the beach, which was about a ten-minute walk from the huts, to go for a swim in the crystal ocean. Duke remembered his swims in Australia, and as soon as he first saw the ocean in East Timor he started pulling like a freight train. Tricia ran happily into the waves with him as he led the way. The water was just what they needed to cool hot, tired bodies, whether human or canine, and as the bright sun reflected off the tranquil water, Duke and Tricia splashed playfully in the refreshing sea.

Once floundering around in the surf, the first thing that occurred to Duke to do was chase his tail. Round and round he went in giant splashes trying to keep a sure footing in the shifting sands and among the shallow waves that rushed up on the shore. But too soon, he felt the sting of salt water in his eyes, which caused him to spring from the waves to rush to the shore and rub his face in the warm sand to try to get the salt off. But then he realized that he had sand in his eyes and ran back into the water and dipped his head in the surf to try and wash the sand out. That led to more salt water in his eyes and another trip to the sand. If Tricia did not put a stop to it, the wave-to-shore trips would have gone on forever. Grabbing Duke, whose furry head was covered in golden sand, she diverted his interests. Soon, he was digging huge holes in the wet sand. The deeper he dug, the more he found that the wet sand was nice and cool on his paws. He didn't care to lie in the holes, he just liked to dig them. Duke was content to frolic in the waves with the person he loved the most, sometimes swimming out to deeper water with her, but he much preferred playing in the shallow water where he could simply chase his tail.

Wet from the surf, Duke relaxes in the sun in East Timor.

A scenic view of Duke's beach at East Timor

Courtesy of Tricia Reynolds

After a refreshing swim in the evening, in a place so close to the equator, Tricia and Duke watched the beautiful sunsets, the most beautiful Tricia had ever seen. A giant deep crimson sun hung low over the evening ocean horizon casting a rosy glow over the distant waves. At those times, Tricia forgot she was in a Third World Country beset with violence. Caught in the beauty and peacefulness, Tricia could drift away, and Duke understood and sat contently close by her.

Duke's time in East Timor was not always on the sandy shores or in the peasant villages or walking the airfield's perimeter. Sometimes he was flying through the air. In case of violence or war, the Air Force realized that the dogs could not be deployed into hostile and formidable territory easily and quickly. They would need to be inserted into action in such places in a timely manner, and the only way to accomplish that would be through the use of helicopters. So Tricia and Duke became well versed in the art of "helicopter winching," which the dog came to love.

Duke had flown on helicopters a few times in Australia, but he had never been lowered out of one. Now in East Timor, he ran out to the running helicopter with great interest. He pulled Tricia through the strong prop wash from the whirring propellers as he couldn't wait to go for a ride.

"Nothing seems to really scare him, and I think that may have to do with his earlier life before I got him. He will even walk over a cattle grid, whereas any normal dog would jump over it."

But familiarizing himself with a new experience still tested his limits until he was assured he could perform the task asked of him. Riding in a helicopter was one thing but being lowered out of one would require a new frame of mind even for an adventurous canine. This was made clear to the helicopter crew upon one of the initial jumps.

Due to space limitations on the aircraft, Tricia attached the dog's harness before they got aboard the chopper. The harness connected them both to the winching wire that would raise or lower them from the chopper by the loadmaster who would control their descent. As wind roared through the doorway, Tricia sat calmly in the open door of the helicopter holding Duke on her lap as she waited patiently for the loadmaster to push them both out. She and Duke were connected to the same cable, but Duke's connection on the cable was somewhat higher than Tricia's so he would hang a bit higher than she when they were initially lowered over the side.

With a hard push, Tricia flew out the door as momentarily Duke hung just slightly above her. But he showed some trepidation and anchored himself to the edge of the helicopter door. He hung on only by one claw, and that was enough to give him the security he still needed, touching just that one anchoring paw to the aircraft.

While normally the descent was quite rapid, Tricia sensed that her trip down was somehow slower than normal, but she could not figure out why. Unable to see the drama being played out just above her, she dangled helplessly just below the door not knowing quite what to think.

After sizing up the situation, Duke had had a change of heart about jumping. He clung with his paw to the helicopter door for dear life preserving the option to hop back aboard if he deemed it necessary. With his boot, the loadmaster tried to carefully nudge Duke's paw off the edge so that Tricia would not continue to dangle there, held up by a hesitant dog having second thoughts. But Duke was adamant that the paw would stay right where it was. Under no circumstances would he allow it to become dislodged.

Soon it became a stand off between Duke and the loadmaster. As the drama played out in the East Timor skies, the loadmaster, taking a hard look at his sizable boot, realized he had some leverage being on the pushing end of the arrangement. Getting into an all-out scrap high above the ground with an enormous stubborn dog who flailed about was not advisable, but the loadmaster had the upper hand. However, Duke had the advantage of sharp teeth and a long memory when it came to those that opposed him, and the loadmaster was reluctant to make an enemy of him. And if Duke had a mind to do it, he possibly could have attached his other paw and lifted himself up in a most cranky state of mind to deal with the loadmaster directly.

Wind continued to whip through the open door riffling Duke's fur and making it harder for him to hang on. Yet, with every ounce of strength he had, he clung tenaciously to the only solid ground he could find and defied the loadmaster to loosen his paw. Further canine diplomacy ensued, characterized by a firmer nudging with the loadmaster's boot, and suddenly the clinging foot slipped from the door frame. At long last, Duke was lowered with Tricia to the ground and upon touching he seemed totally delighted with the experience.

Duke is photographed near the helicopter with the use of a night vision scope.

Courtesy of Ben Geurts

Tricia adjusts Duke's harness.

Courtesy of Chris Moore

Helicopter Winching
Courtesy of Louise Morton

Further jumps followed, and Duke no longer showed any fear of the descent. It became routine. Having proved to himself he could do it, he became eager to jump once more. Once the chopper was in position, time after time, Duke and Tricia were slowly lowered out the open door with no problems. The loud roar of the mighty rotor blades was deafening. As the rotary blades cut through the warm air above them, the pair slowly made their descent. Swinging through the air with a huge dog strapped to her presented some challenges. She hugged him tightly the entire way down to the ground.

"It's alright, Duke," she said soothingly, "Are you having fun?"

On the way down, Duke seemed to enjoy the view around him and remained calm. Anything could have awaited them below. Far above the overgrown areas that were inaccessible by road, Duke and Tricia hovered in the chopper. She could see from above there was virtually no place for a helicopter or plane to land.

"Sometimes you start to spin a bit whilst going up or down, but if you just stick your legs out, this usually stops you. Duke sits there "happy as Larry," and I just hold him close to my chest to let him know he is safe."

As they neared the ground, Tricia could not help but wonder what slithering or brilliantly-colored but deadly creatures lived in the high grass below. But winching with a dog presented other dangers.

"There are snakes in Timor, but the rotor wash pretty much scares away anything that is below. The worst thing is hitting the ground a bit too fast and falling over to have a dog land on top of you!"

Edging closer to the ground, Tricia could see long grass and shrubs. Just after they touched the ground, Tricia unhooked herself and Duke from the winch and moved off to the side. Duke tried to run out from the "wash" of the aircraft rotors, but because he was on leash, he couldn't go far. If he got away, he came right back, not liking to venture too far from Tricia.

"The wash from the rotor is very intense, so you have a bunch of dust and stones being thrown at you. It's not a pleasant experience."

Partially removed from the prop wash, Duke watched intently when the other handler and dog touched ground.

"I reckon he was thinking, 'Is that what I was just doing?'"

Sometimes the two got even more adventurous when they did some winching at night. Tricia wore night vision goggles to see into the pitch black abyss below, but Duke had no more concern about night winching than he did for winching during the day. Quiet and content, he just rested in her arms seemingly enjoying the breeze blowing his fur on warm nights, as he observed the rugged view around him.

"I think he thought the helicopter was just some sort of strange car that flew in the air, as he would often stick his head out the door and let the wind blow in his face. If the helicopter doors were closed, he would just stand there looking out the window taking in the countryside wondering what strange smells he could find down below."

One smell that Duke learned early on was not in the air but on the ground. Feral pigs roamed the airport flight line area, and Duke and Tricia often watched a family of six of them make their nightly rounds.

"Mum, Dad and four piglets roamed there," Tricia remembered. "By the time we left, the piglets had all found somewhere else to live, and it was just Mum and Dad again. It was fun to watch them grow up though. We would see them quite often and even made up names for them. They would only be there at night when there was no aircraft noise."

As Tricia and Duke sat on the quiet flight line at night, the pigs became their entertainment. The animals would often come within five yards of them but didn't seemed to be fazed at all by a dog of over seventy pounds staring back at them waiting for them to come within striking distance.

"The Daddy pig was white with black spots, and Duke would alert me to the pigs nearby way before I had any idea they were there."

Duke's alert for animals was different from his alert for humans. When he saw the pigs, Duke was trained to sit and stare at them. He was trained to bark only when he saw a human. If the pigs got extremely close, Duke took a run at them on the end of chain and tried to scare them away. But they were smart pigs and managed to stay out of harm's way.

Six months went by very quickly, and it was time for Tricia and Duke to return to Australia. Wet season had begun on the island ushering in torrential downpours. Staked out at the airfield at night, Duke enjoyed the driving rain, stopping occasionally throughout his shift to give a hard shake to splatter it off his furry back. The dog would miss his frequent swims in the ocean and would not likely find a future scenario where he could utilize his pig alert that he had mastered so well on the island. Brilliant red sunsets would be just a memory for Tricia. Her time in East Timor had sadly come to an end. Having the night off on her last full day there, she enjoyed a giant lobster dinner and hot tea in Dili with the other handlers. Getting up the next morning, she felt sad to leave the remote island and its gentle people. The dogs were all loaded into their familiar dog boxes for their long journey home.

"Duke seemed to be pretty excited about leaving," said Tricia "He was straight into the dog box wondering where his next adventure was going to take him."

Arriving back in Australia, Tricia got the dogs out to stretch their legs and to be watered in Darwin. Tricia was finally able to see her husband, once she got back to New South Wales, but, unfortunately, as was customary, Duke and the other dogs had to go into quarantine to make sure they had not picked up any disease, especially rabies, and brought it back to Australia.

Tricia left Duke at the Australian Quarantine Inspection Service facility in Sydney where there were a few hundred kennels where dogs, including pets, were kept if they came in from overseas. Duke had his own kennel run, and Tricia got to visit him once, but the dogs did not get any human interaction, since the staff that worked there was not allowed to go into the MWD kennels in case the dogs were aggressive to people they did not know. After the month was over, Duke could not wait to see Tricia again and come home to Newcastle with her where he had many old friends in the kennels at the RAAF base.

Tricia would never forget the experience of East Timor. Spending long days with Duke every day for six months as they experienced a new country was an enjoyable memory. Back in Australia, Duke lived in the kennel on base, and their time together was less frequent. Tricia and her husband had two border collies at home, Calvin and Bailey, and Duke was possessive enough of Tricia that he could never be on friendly terms with them. After working with Duke, her two pets quickly picked up the dog's scent, but they never saw him. Duke continued to be a very aggressive dog, especially in the kennels. He permitted no one at work on the base or in the kennel to remove him from his run there or even to take him for a walk.

"He puts on a very good show when he is in his kennel with his teeth bared barking and asserting his authority. But he turns into a big puppy when he sees me. Every single person that sees him in his kennel cannot believe he is the same dog when I am around. He loves his Mum, and that's about it."

Duke and Tricia returned to guarding aircraft week in and week out. An abundance of kangaroos still hopped about the edge of the base at night where they patrolled, and Duke strained at his leash getting very excited when he saw them. Far more animated than the sedate East Timor pig family, the large animals never ceased to pique his curiosity.

It is not uncommon for Tricia and Duke to spend hours by themselves each night training and playing games. The gruff dog becomes like a small child playing hide and seek with Tricia. The game begins when Duke walks around off leash. As soon as he isn't looking, Tricia ducks behind an object to see how long it takes for him to find her.

"The best part is when he finally uses his nose to figure out where I'm hiding, and the pure joy on his face when he finds me makes me realize how much he loves me."

If Duke ever does something that makes Tricia angry, like jumping up on her with full force when she gets him out of the kennel, she only has to remember the joy on his face when he finds her during their games to forgive him very quickly. In his enthusiasm to greet her, he has hit her in the mouth with his muzzle instantly producing a fat lip, and at times he seems more content to chase his tail than play with her, but the majority of the time, she enjoys his full attention and devotion.

The team's spirit of adventure has no end. When the ADFTWDA (Australian Defence Force Trackers and War Dog Association) conducted their annual biathlons, Duke and Tricia won in 2005. Each year, the Police and Services Canine Association Queensland (PASCAQ) also runs a dog biathlon. Duke and Tricia participated in three of them winning the women's event in 2007. With much enthusiasm and competitive spirit, both handler and dog ran around a track just over three miles and jumped a series of obstacles. Then fully clothed, Tricia swam a few laps in a swimming pool before continuing on. At other times in other biathlons, Duke swam right along beside her through a river. There was no end to the variety of experiences Duke was provided, and with each new one, he thrived.

In 2007, the team participated in ANZAC Day, the Australia New Zealand Army Corps celebration of Australia's WW1 landing at Gallipoli. Ever since that landing, Australia and New Zealand celebrate ANZAC Day on the 25th of April. Every capital city in Australia and plenty of the smaller towns celebrate with a march through the city. Duke and Tricia march with the rest of her unit, impressing the spectators as fifteen handlers and dogs march in sync, and not one of the proud dogs marching stops to chase his tail.

Also in 2007, Duke and Tricia took the Top Dog award at the RAAF Base in Townsville, Queensland, one of the states on the eastern coast. Every quarter, all handlers and their dogs complete an assessment to make sure the team is proficient in all aspects of being a Military Working Dog Team. Duke and Tricia performed best out of their whole section, besting fourteen other teams. Tricia was bursting with pride for the dog who had such a shaky start and most likely would not have lived another day.

"Duke has a great work ethic and will do anything to make me happy" she beamed.

But in one respect, Duke was slow to give up his old ways.

On the base in Queensland, Duke and Tricia were requested to give a demonstration for some pre-school children. She put Duke through his paces, jumping him over obstacles and showing how he would heel and obey his normal commands. The children marveled at his obedience. If Tricia gave him a command, he complied immediately. When she gave him a command to cease what he was doing, once again, he obeyed instantly. The children saw how he listened to her every word.

Knowing that Duke had the strong tendency to chase his tail when he got excited and after he finished working, Tricia utilized his odd quirk to her advantage.

"Break!" she loudly commanded him.

The command allowed him to do whatever he wanted to do on his own, and she knew what that "something" would be.

Amidst loud laughs and hilarity from the pre-schoolers, Duke excitedly chased his tail until he caught it and flipped himself over to complete a full somersault. But true to his former self, he grabbed his tail again and kept going. Thinking that Tricia had taught the dog a wonderful trick, one little boy raised his hand.

"You forgot to tell him to stop chasing his tail!" he insisted.

Tricia knew that command would be useless, and she knew he would finally tire himself out and stop on his own terms. She learned to abide his idiosyncrasy and turned it into a positive they both could live with.

Proud members of the Royal Australian Air Force

Courtesy of Judith Watts

Partnered with Tricia, MWD Duke will show the gruffness needed to do his job. He will bark with ferocity at an intruder who tries to get near his planes, and he will run on fleet feet, far from the confinement of the city pound. The former "vagrant" will dig holes when he feels inclined with sharp nails that help him complete the task. With jaws, paws and claws, MWD Duke, spinning with abandon in the land down under, will remain an asset to the Royal Australian Air Force and more importantly, a companion and body guard wrapped in one furry package for the woman who had the faith and courage to save him.

K-9 Leon

"International House of Dogs"

The arid desert climate of Arizona made the hot streets a formidable place to patrol for both man and dog. The often unbearable heat never seemed to slow the desire of criminals to pursue their illegal activities. It was all the police could do to keep up with them.

John La Fontaine had been with the Mesa, Arizona, Police Department for six years when members of the K-9 unit asked him to put in for an open position. Once on the unit, it was customary for a new handler to go to Riverside, California, and help pick out a dog.

Within the confines of the closed kennel, dozens of dogs loudly barked and growled making their presence known as John entered the premises. He and his fellow officers would test several dogs judging their bites, attack potential and temperament trying to find the best fit for their department. Once a dog was selected, it fell to John to go into the dog's enclosure and bring him out.

After considering several prospective dogs, John was finally drawn to one named Ully, a big German shepherd dog that had been "black flagged" by the supplier for attacking his owner and the owner's son. The dog was a "Schutzhund I" import from Germany, indicating the highest levels of training. John was strangely taken with Ully and walked confidently towards the kennel to meet him. With great ferocity and speed, Ully leaped menacingly

138

toward the gate. Snarling and snapping, he slammed his black and tan body into the rattling metal barricade, his guttural growls symbolic of his strong Teutonic heritage. The hair on the dog's back stood straight up, and visually he presented a threatening force to be reckoned with. But when John opened the gate and calmly called the dog by name, Ully's bluff was challenged, and he immediately started wagging his brush-like tail. Ully trotted right up to John, and they were immediate friends.

Officer John La Fontaine and K-9 Ully

Courtesy of Tony Cerimele

www.acerimelephotography.com

K-9's ULLY
LEON
KINO
SPIKE

Ully, cross-trained for patrol and narcotics, instantly obeyed John's German commands, and he worked the streets successfully for several years locating hundreds of suspects. The pair had fought together when violent suspects refused arrest as Ully routinely watched John's back. John, unquestionably, did the same for Ully. The former "black flagged" dog proved to be very sociable and loved attention from the public, especially from children. Due to several injuries to his rear legs, Ully was retired at age eight. After thousands of calls for service, and after winning dozens of trophies in K-9 competitions, it was time for the tired old gentleman to remain at home. Ully was used only as a narcotics dog as his workload eased just before full retirement, and in January, 2006, John found himself back at the kennel in Riverside to find Ully's replacement.

As he strolled along the enclosed kennels slowly looking for that special and often intangible quality that made a dog appealing to him, John inspected each dog from a distance sizing up the dog's potential. Sadly, each dog needed a home, and only one dog would be taken that day. After pausing to look at several dogs, none really stood out. Then John saw a little guy named Leon standing in his kennel quietly looking out at him. Leon was all muscle. The tan, solidly-built import appeared very friendly so John went up to the office and asked about him.

The kennel owner told John that Leon was a French Ring dog he purchased in Holland and said he did not think the French-speaking Belgian Malinois was what the department was looking for. Leon had participated in the competitive ring sport that involved jumping, obedience, protection and attacks, and his scores had been high in Germany and France, but somehow he found himself there at the California kennel. There was a big trade in the ring dogs from Europe and for that reason they never felt the love of a true owner.

The kennel owner said he thought the dog was a little too soft for the street, but John took Leon out of the kennel and did some testing with him. After only about an hour, he told the department's lead trainer and his sergeant that he liked Leon. They both tried to talk John out of his decision reiterating the kennel owner's admonitions, but John remained adamant that he wanted to work with Leon and thought he would make a good street dog. Perhaps it was a soft spot in his heart for the underdog. Or maybe it was the dog's knowledge of French commands, since John was of French extraction that won him over. It was hard to ignore the small dog's expressive eyes that followed John's every move. In the end, John triumphed, and the small but proud dog pranced out past the larger dogs that he was measured against. He would finally have a home.

Leon and John trained together for one month. French commands would now be substituted for German ones. The German "Aus," that ordered Ully to stop would now become the French equivalent, "Alt," for Leon. Changing dogs and languages, John became master of his international brood. When he brought the little Frenchman home to meet German Ully, the retired dog was not at first taken with the new addition to the family. Ully growled at Leon a few times and became very clingy to John, but that was understandable. It was Ully's house first.

"Leon was not a dog fighter," John noted. "He was a lover as the French would say."

Leon gave Ully plenty of ground and did not bother his toys. It only took a few weeks for them to get used to each other. Ully never really played with Leon, but he tolerated him. Once outside, Ully hogged all the toys and just lay on the grass surrounded by them. Like a mother hen with its chicks Ully kept watch over four or five balls positioned all around him making sure poor Leon wouldn't have any. But if Ully turned his back, the alert Leon would dart forward to sneak one away. It was a canine version of "keep away" they both seemed to enjoy. Ully finally accepted Leon as a friend but remained the alpha dog of the La Fontaine pack. With some international canine diplomacy, a good balance was maintained in the household between Ully and his French-speaking counterpart.

Leon enjoying his new home
Courtesy of John La Fontaine

At first, Ully did not understand that he would be left at home on work nights. When John got ready for work, Ully happily wagged his tail and repeated his old routines getting ready to leave and then waited anxiously in the kitchen. The dog paced back and forth and spun in circles like a top. But it was Leon who was now in his place at the master's side. John had to firmly order Ully to STAY as he took Leon out to the waiting patrol car. The excited spinning stopped and dejected Ully stared sadly at his handler.

"Did I do something wrong, Dad?" the mournful eyes seemed to say.

John hid his own tearful eyes as he left the house and could not bear to look back. The glum dog slowly moped out to the back gate and stared after the departing car. Then he lay on the ground by the gate for several hours anticipating John's return. Ully waited in the same spot every day until he was finally put down for medical reasons. His decline was very fast. John had wanted the retired dog to live for a few more years to enjoy the good life of just being a dog, going camping and being pampered as a pet at home. But fate intervened and before Ully could enjoy those peaceful days, he was gone.

All too quickly, the dog could barely walk and was not responding. He could no longer faithfully monitor the gate, and in his weakness one day Ully stumbled into the swimming pool. John jumped in and pulled him out and carried the dripping dog into the house to dry him off. No one had to tell John. He knew it was time and called the vet. The day had come for their last ride together.

As they drove to the vet, John talked constantly to Ully and tried to explain what had to happen knowing full well the dog did not understand. John choked up as he drove stumbling through a progression of futile explanations to listless Ully, and he caught himself driving slower than the other traffic not wanting to complete the sorrowful trip he had started.

When he arrived at the vet's office, John sat in the car and continued to cry as he spoke softly to Ully. Finally, he opened Ully's door, the door he had opened for the loyal dog a thousand times. This would be the last time. Ully just lay there, no energy, no smile, no wagging of the dark brush-like tail. The fearsome Prussian bravado he had displayed that day of their initial meeting at the kennel had long since faded.

John tried to gently pick up the limp fellow, but Ully was a big dog lying in the center of the car. John called Ully to come to him and with much effort Ully, forever obedient, got up and stumbled to his waiting arms. Ully still wanted to obey his master—his beloved Dad. John carried Ully into the vet's and into a room they had been placed in numerous times over the years for regular check ups. Ully was well known at the office, because he was so vocal. When the doctors tried to work on him in the past, Ully growled like a grumpy bear rudely awakened from its hibernation and could be heard complaining throughout the entire building. This day, Ully did not utter a sound. John laid him on the cool metal table where the tired old eyes just stared blankly. Ully did not respond as John hugged him and spoke quietly. Then the nurse came in and gave the dog a sedative to relax him. At that, Ully emitted a weak little growl audible only to John who held the dog's head tightly to his own. The weak attempt was nothing like the impressive lion's roar Ully was known for, but in the twilight of his years it was the best he could muster. John held and petted his faithful companion for half an hour when the vet asked if he was ready.

"No, I am not ready," he said mutely, "but I won't let my friend suffer any longer."

As the fatal injection was given, John hugged the warm furry dog and felt the weight of the head in his supporting arms get heavier and heavier. In just seconds, Ully died peacefully in John's arms. The long-time partner and friend was gone, and in great despondency John left the clinic and started the lonely drive home.

K-9 Ully—partner and friend
Courtesy of Tony Cerimele

The little French Ring dog waited at home and helped ease the pain. Taking time off work to recover from his loss, John's bond with Leon grew and working with the little dog made the empty days of grief pass more quickly. Progressively, John became very proud of the dog he had taken a chance on. He and his dogs had a reputation for resolutely finding whatever they were looking for. They would not stop searching until a suspect was found. Leon would be no different.

K-9 Leon, following in Ully's footsteps

Desert Dog Trials - 2006

Expert agility

Desert Dog Trials – 2006

Dutch dog handler, Dick Van Leenen, feeling the full force of Leon

Courtesy of John La Fontaine

Leon was a fast learner and seemed to have a knack for police work. Reflecting back on their first month together, John remembered Leon locating several suspects, tracking two of them right to the front door of the house where they had run. The dog, less than two-years-old, had not gained John's full trust so early in the game, and John had pulled him off the track thinking he was unsure and confused. But Leon had proved him wrong. Leon knew what they were there for, and John began to trust him implicitly. Ully had been, and now Leon was the department's best SWAT dog working with the Tactical Team and responding to their calls. One call would prove to be most memorable.

Leon and John were on standby one sizzling-hot August day. They had worked together only eight months, and John knew that it usually took a full year to learn from each other and bond before they could expect big achievements together. At 12:50 p.m., John got the call to assist patrol officers with a hostage situation. He dressed quickly and then loaded up Leon and left for the call. En route, John listened attentively to the calls and could tell the first responders were desperate for help. As he sped across the city, he heard the startling news that the suspect was holding a three-month-old infant hostage. The man did not want to go to jail for his outstanding felony warrants and would use any means he could think of to stay out of jail.

In the Phoenix valley, where sun-drenched Saguaro cacti stand like sentinels, August temperatures could rise to 122 degrees, and it was already 110. In those conditions, the asphalt could get as hot as 130 or more degrees. John knew the difficulties he would face ahead on such a sweltering day.

The incident had started with a simple traffic stop for expired tags. The officer working the east side of Mesa ran a records check on the driver, and it located multiple warrants for his arrest. One warrant was for felony child abuse.

As the first officers tried to take the man into custody, he jumped into his car and drove off. The two officers on the scene Tased the driver, but he was so obese that the Taser had no effect on him. The officers, one weighing 190 pounds and the other at 155, were no match for the 400-pound man when he jumped back into the car. The suspect drove off westbound with his wife and infant in the car, and the department's air unit followed the suspect as he drove west and then stopped and forced his wife out of the car.

The driver kept the infant with him and again drove west on the highway at a high rate of speed. Soon, he approached the on ramp at the Mesa-Tempe border where he lost control of the vehicle. As the horrified officers watched, the speeding car crashed into the embankment. Scraping metal screeched against concrete, and after a deafening bang the car came to a sudden stop sustaining serious damage. The front end was smashed, and the radiator was torn open allowing the coolant to drain out. That meant no more air conditioning to cool the endangered infant. A red car in the scorching sun on a 110-degree day would simulate an oven. The dazed driver regained his senses quickly and threw open the door. As he emerged, he dangled the endangered infant carelessly in front of him.

"Stay back! I've got a gun!" the man threatened, his eyes darting wildly as he confronted the officers.

No one knew if what he said was true. There were numerous officers on the scene, and Mesa and Highway Patrol units blocked all traffic westbound. Thousands of gradually-slowing cars backed up for miles in the intense heat unaware of the drama being played out ahead. John raced in the emergency lane, and when he arrived on scene, the driver was standing outside of the car holding a black bag. Officers had been there for an hour negotiating with him. He had put the baby in the car placing it face down between the two hot front seats after a request from the negotiating officer. But he defensively held his right hand in the bag and repeated that he had a gun. The officers were desperate for a solution knowing the infant would not survive much longer in the suffocating heat. They were just about to fire fatal shots at him to save the baby when John showed up with Leon.

One SWAT team member ran up to John desperately hoping for some help. The officer fully realized the futility of the situation the officers found themselves in, and there was no question that time was running out.

"We're all out of options," he said in frustration, "We need to act."

About that time, John's sergeant and lieutenant, both of whom commanded the SWAT team, arrived. They put a small team together, and the sergeant asked if John could deploy Leon, given that the baby was seemingly in such a precarious position in such close proximity to the raving man. John never once questioned Leon's ability and told them absolutely he could do it. The more skeptical men there were fearful that Leon might become confused and bite the child instead of the driver.

"Once Leon identifies the suspect," John assured them, "he won't go after the child as long as the suspect is not holding the baby in front of him as a shield."

John knew Leon would stay with the suspect.

Within five minutes of John and Leon's arrival, the plan was in place. Heart pounding, John quickly slipped Leon into his leather harness and hooked sixty feet of leash on the eager little dog. John's sergeant and two other sergeant/SWAT team leaders set up on the left side of the vehicle where the suspect was standing at the open driver's door. John could not see the baby but knew it was in the front seat somewhere. When John, tightly holding Leon, was about fifty feet from the suspect, he began to talk the driver into giving up.

"There's no need for anyone to get hurt today," he calmly said. "Think about your wife and child."

The man did not move, nor did he answer.

"Look around," John reasoned, "where do you think you can go?"

John could see the paralyzing fear in the man's face when Leon edged closer. Leon was barking fiercely, and there was no doubt the man knew what was about to happen. The stubborn man would not cooperate and held his ground still holding his right hand in the black bag. The sergeant asked if John was ready.

"Let's do it," John sternly replied.

The SWAT team members deployed a "flash bang" device at the rear of the car creating a diversion. The device went off with a very high-decimal bang creating bright light and intense smoke. Through the translucent haze, two men raced to the passenger side of the vehicle, ripped open the door and grabbed the limp over-heated baby from the scorching front seat. Their daring action meant the quickly-dehydrating child would survive.

With the baby in safe arms, one of the sergeants instantly shot the suspect with a large bean bag gun, and the disoriented man dropped downward as the team approached the car. John could feel the nylon leash slide through his hand like an uncoiling rope as Leon shot like a rocket through the smoke towards the car. He thundered directly toward the suspect and made a ferocious leap towards the astonished man. As Leon made contact with the suspect, biting him on the inside of his left forearm just below the elbow, the man swung crazily with the black bag trying to hit the attacking dog.

In the smoky mantle that surrounded the car, John caught glimpses of Leon being tossed around by the suspect like a rag doll. Continually flung left to right, yet still attached to the suspect's corpulent arm, the brave dog hung on tenaciously as he sensed he was fighting for his own life. As trained by John, he would not let go. He had dealt with vicious suspects on the street before. He knew the routine well.

John grew understandably angry when he saw the suspect violently fighting with his buddy and partner. Just then, the SWAT team ran up to the suspect and Tased him utilizing the form of non-lethal pain compliance. Once again, the Taser did not seem to faze him, and with no more options remaining the sergeant gave the order to shoot the suspect dead. But the suspect had jumped back into the car with Leon still attached to him. He grasped desperately and futilely for the small baby already removed to use as a shield. At the same time, a third SWAT team member reached in front of another member's line of fire and Tased the suspect again unwittingly preventing the instant death of the suspect by the fellow team member.

With renewed determination, John lunged forward and grabbed the suspect's leg trying to yank him out of the car, but the morbidly-obese man wedged himself between the front seat and the steering wheel clinging tightly to it. John asked his sergeant if he wanted Leon removed from the bite, but the sergeant waved him off with his left hand indicating the dog should be left on. The group of officers struggled to get control of the suspect, but he was too heavy, and they could not move him. With a last concerted effort, the sergeant and John finally pulled the suspect out of the car after another SWAT officer had punched him several times from the passenger side trying to break the suspect's hold on the steering wheel.

The fighting suspect was successfully dragged out of the car and landed a few feet out on the hot asphalt.

"Alt!" John commanded the small French dog.

John removed Leon who was frenzied from the fight and led him off to calm him down. The dog's snout had been completely buried in the man's fat tissue. When released, Leon's furry face was covered in blood and fat tissue, and he looked like a lion that had been lying next to a kill having plunged his face into the carcass for his dinner. The team was no different. They all had blood and fat tissue splattered on their shoes, pants, gloves and equipment. Had the suspect stood still as ordered, he would only have suffered a few puncture wounds. Instead, he tried to shake off a dog with an alligator grip causing all the ripping and damage to his forearm. Had he complied in the first place, he would have the use of his arm, but after two eventual surgeries, it was doubtful he would ever have full function of the arm again.

John walked the panting dog to the car and eased him inside along with all the blood-spattered leashes and equipment. When they got home, it took two hours to clean and disinfect everything. John bathed Leon in baby shampoo two or three times to make sure he was clean and then returned to the station to write a supplement on the use of the dog. By then, the incident was all over the news.

That night, when John went to dinner with friends he got a call from the department's Public Relations Officer. She told him that the city phone was ringing off the hook with citizens asking about Leon's condition. In the video news reports, it appeared Leon was hurt when the heavy suspect landed on him in the car. The Public Relations Officer asked if John would do a briefing with the media that night. He told her he was out having dinner and said he didn't like interviews, but he assured her Leon was fine and was not hurt.

"Leon got an hour-long bath and had treats with dinner," he told the woman to placate her.

The following Monday, he got a call from her again practically begging him to do a media interview. Within an hour, John was meeting the press along with Leon who was nicely brushed for the occasion.

Leon spotted the only female reporter in the crowd and ran up to flirt with her.

"He sure is a friendly little guy isn't he?" she laughed.

Everyone in the room broke out into laughter as John pulled persistent Leon back.

"Dogs will be dogs," he said with a smile, "but I did not teach him that. That's the French in him coming out I guess."

John reached up and covered his own name tag bearing his French last name. The dog could not have been more French had he worn a beret.

In the following days, they were doing interviews constantly. Leon became a national celebrity. John's friends from Germany and Holland e-mailed him after they saw the story on CNN as Leon had climbed to international fame. John joked with everyone that he, himself, was just the dummy holding the leash, and if Leon could drive the car, the feisty little fellow would do the interviews himself.

In the shadows of the fanfare, John was very proud of Leon, who had performed far beyond the department's initial expectations. Leon was by far becoming the best K-9 the city ever had, and the skepticism years ago at the kennel proved groundless. The French Ring's loss was the Mesa Police Department's gain.

A few months after Leon's highway takedown, Court TV contacted the city and asked for permission to put Leon and John on one of their episodes. Sitting in front of cameras and bright lights and memorizing lines made John long to get back in his patrol car, but Leon deserved his moment in the spotlight. As the adulation died down, Leon and John returned to the streets.

The Mesa area had been experiencing a rash of ATM thefts for nearly two years. Two weeks after the hostage incident on the highway, an ATM was stolen from the M & I Bank. The usual procedure was followed. The suspects stole a forklift from a construction site and ploughed into the machine to knock the money machine off its foundation. They then loaded it onto a waiting truck and trailer that they had stolen to haul the heavy ATM. The only thing left at the bank was the stolen forklift.

A local officer soon spotted a truck hauling a trailer passing through a residential area at two in the morning. The weight of a stolen ATM made the trailer sag so distinctively in the back that it was quite obvious to the officer what was going on, even though the trailer was a distance away. Unaware they had been spotted, the thieves, this time using their own pick up truck, continued on their chosen route to hopefully slip quietly into the sparsely-populated Arizona desert. When the passing officer turned to intercept them, the nervous suspects abruptly stopped and bailed out of their truck.

A perimeter was set up to lock the suspects down, and shortly thereafter, John and Leon started to track them. After about a block, Leon put his nose to the ground indicating he had picked up a scent. Moving rapidly with complete focus, the meaty little dog pulled John past a few houses and north across the residential street to a block wall. Leon sniffed the wall and tried to jump up on it. Instead, the pair went around to the gate that led into the back yard, and again Leon started to pull. Once in the back yard, Leon pulled John to the east side of the house where the air conditioners sat. Suddenly, the animated dog started to bark and jump up and down. John called for the suspect to come out of his hiding place, but there was no response. He sent Leon down the side of the house and immediately heard a scream rise above the loud hum of air conditioning units.

"Aport!" John commanded Leon ordering him to pull the suspect out."

The shaken suspect having been dragged out stood up and began to fight with Leon. That made Leon fight even harder. More officers arrived completely overwhelming the man who was caught by the French-speaking dog. The suspect was taken to the hospital before beginning a trial and ten-year prison sentence. The bank had been robbed several times and after Leon and a fellow K-9, Lindsay, later captured more bank robbers, the personnel at the bank breathed easier safe from the risk of ATM theft.

About a year later, John and Leon were called out to once more assist the Tactical Team. They arrived at an apartment where a suspect hid inside. Numerous calls were made for the suspect to come out, but there was no response. A team member next fired a 37 mm tear gas gun into the apartment. The team waited for the clouds of gas to settle, and then they made entry into the apartment. John sent Leon in first to clear the front living room area. The team, dressed in black tactical uniforms and wearing gas masks, crept with great stealth through the dark apartment. A chorus of commands suddenly flew back and forth from man to man. Once Leon cleared the living room, one of the lead SWAT members gave Leon the French command, "Coucher!" at the kitchen and hallway entrance. Once Leon was in the down position complying with the command, the team moved in and up to Leon. The dog was then sent in to search the kitchen area. When Leon came back into the living room, he saw team member, Mike Beaton, kneeling down at the hallway entrance. His uniform did not look unlike the padded bite suit Leon knew from training. Leon emerged from the thick clouds of gas and smoke and in his confusion bit Mike on the upper forearm thinking he was the suspect.

Mike screamed in pain, and John thought Leon must have located the suspect hiding somewhere inside. John's sergeant yelled for him to come up and that is when he saw Leon biting Mike.

"Alt! Alt!" John yelled to immediately release Leon from the bite.

Then he pulled the dog aside. Another team member assisted Mike out of the room to a waiting ambulance. With the arrival of medical help for

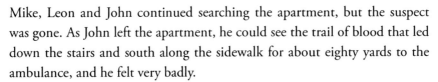

Mike, Leon and John continued searching the apartment, but the suspect was gone. As John left the apartment, he could see the trail of blood that led down the stairs and south along the sidewalk for about eighty yards to the ambulance, and he felt very badly.

It was not really anyone's fault though. The visibility in the apartment was zero, and all the men were dressed in black and wearing gas masks. John regretted not seeing the bite coming but was told not to worry about it, because there was no way to see everything inside the apartment. He drove to the hospital and met Mike in the emergency room. The bite to his arm was pretty serious, and it took thirty stitches on one side and twenty-five staples on the other to close it. Mike took it very well after John apologized for the incident, and Mike told John, as the others had, not to worry about it. Mike was down for a few weeks but made a full recovery and teased John later that he was determined to get a tattoo at the injury site that read "Leon was here!"

That incident changed the way the department deployed their dogs. It opened their eyes on training with tactical groups and taught them that when deploying the dogs, not to have them off leash near members that were kneeling down for lower coverage areas. They recognized that every dog was unique. While some could move through a group and never bite an officer, smoky haze or not, others saw things a bit differently.

A month later, in March, 2007, at 10:45 p.m., John drove to a location which was almost the center point in the city. A subject on a bicycle rode through the red light northbound, and John had to brake hard to avoid hitting him. He watched the subject ride east on the north side of the street, so he made a sharp U-turn to pursue him. The subject quickly turned in the opposite direction to avoid him, so John knew the man was suspicious. After he caught up with the fleeing bicyclist, John stopped him in a K-Mart parking lot located on the northeast corner. He demanded the subject's driver's license and radioed for a records check on him. John's suspicions were confirmed. The records check showed the man had numerous outstanding felony warrants for his arrest. The warrants were for probation violation on prior burglary charges, so John held the man where he was and waited for back-up. As time passed, the officer could tell the subject was getting nervous.

John had initially stood next to Leon's car door so he could open it if the subject tried to flee. For whatever reason, he moved to the opposite side of the subject as the man straddled his bike. Without warning, the panicked suspect abruptly pulled the bike up by the handle bars from between his legs and threw it at John, who reached out and grabbed him. Falling over the bike, John could hear Leon excitedly barking and scratching to get out of the car to help out "Dad," but he had no means to release the door. John lost his grip on the 19-year-old drug addict and fell to the ground. In what seemed like an instant, the suspect turned and ran south.

Equally fast, John stretched up from the ground and opened Leon's door, and the agitated dog jumped out. Leon hit the ground running, and John knew the fleeing suspect was going to be taken down. As John turned to follow, he did not realize just how fast the suspect was approaching the busy street. Leon was loping along with lengthy strides closing the distance quickly, and the suspect was fearfully looking back knowing that at any second he would be bitten by the dog.

It wasn't until John saw the suspect reach the road that he realized cars were approaching from the east. By the time he could react, the suspect with Leon close on his heels darted across the busy street. A car traveling west in the curb lane suddenly braked to avoid hitting the suspect. Leon followed after the suspect and ran in front of the stopped car.

Then everything went into slow motion for John. The inevitable was about to happen, and he could not alter it in any way. In excruciating detail, the scene played out in front of his disbelieving eyes. There was a second car he had not seen behind the first but about two car lengths back. The suspect leaped to the median just as Leon entered the middle lane. The driver of the second car did not slow down when he saw the other car braking in front of him but continued to drive past. As Leon entered the middle lane, the moving car struck him hard in the side. John watched in horror as Leon flew upward through the air and landed with a dull thud on the ground. The stunned dog momentarily tried to get up but could only struggle.

John raced to Leon and dropped down on his knees. He could see the dog was hurt very badly, and the distressed handler started to cry and yell at the same time. He called for paramedics to come, Code-3 with lights and sirens just as another officer arrived on scene. The younger, inexperienced officer was right out of the academy and could only stare in disbelief after seeing what had happened. John tried to pick up Leon to move him out of the street, but the injured dog was in so much pain that in his agony he bit John's left hand. John never felt it. He called Leon's name so the dog would know he was there, and he hoped the familiar voice would soothe his injured dog. At the sound of the voice he knew so well, Leon slowly released his hand and lay very still.

Leon's condition quickly deteriorated, and his breathing became labored. John knew he was not going to make it. As he knelt down to comfort Leon, the driver of the car that hit him drove around him and sped away without ever offering to help a police officer and his incapacitated dog. As best he could, John picked up Leon and ran to the car. There was no time to wait for the paramedics or think about a hit and run driver.

Placing Leon tenderly in the backseat, he told the fading dog to hold on. With lights flashing and siren screaming, John raced to the emergency veterinary hospital a few miles away.

"Hang on, Leon, hang on for your Dad," John begged for the entire trip.

John's vision blurred from the tears as he drove, and he apologized to Leon a hundred times for making such a poor decision. Both man and dog were well trained, but there were no guarantees in their line of work.

The emergency medical staff was waiting when the two finally arrived. John jumped out of the driver's seat and tore open the back door not knowing what he would find. It was too late. Once again, John had a last ride in the patrol car with one of his beloved dogs. Leon, his little French buddy, was gone.

The doctors pushed John out of the way and carried Leon into the hospital starting CPR on him as they moved swiftly inside. They took him into the trauma room and worked hard to resuscitate him, but they could not. The injuries were far too grave.

The doctor came out and told John, numbed by the pain of the loss, that they had placed Leon in a private room. John entered the room and saw the brave dog's lifeless body lying on the table. The grieving officer's emotions were a bitter mix of sorrow and anger. He second guessed his decision to send the dog, and at the same time he felt seething rage toward the young suspect.

John approached his friend and ran his hand over the soft little head as he had done a thousand times before. Leon had such a playful fun-loving personality and now he just lay quiet on the table. As John stood with Leon, one of the staff members entered the room and handed him a clay imprint of Leon's right front paw. He took it with his hand still bearing the marks of Leon's confused bite. John was grateful for the gift but would have preferred to bring his buddy home. They had had just over one year together. The department and public marveled at the dog's achievements in that short time. Now, like Ully, Leon was gone forever. John would return to a completely empty home.

John's lieutenant and other K-9 handlers arrived at the hospital to see how their colleague was doing. Handlers from the surrounding area responded also. No one was going to let the fleeing suspect on the bike get away.

The suspect was located by under cover units less then an hour later, and John would need to go make the identification. At such a time it would be hard to maintain one's professionalism and to keep emotions in check. John was driven over to the scene to identify the suspect by Tactical Team member, Mike Beaton, who still bore the scar from Leon's erroneous bite. Mike wanted to be with John and knew how much he grieved for his lost dog.

The defiant suspect repeatedly denied being at the stop with John despite the fact his driver's license was lying on the ground next to his bike in the parking lot. He was promptly taken away to face charges. The charge in Arizona for injuring a police dog was only cruelty to animals. The court did not charge the suspect with the death of Leon but pleaded everything down to just aggravated assault on a police officer and probation violation charges for which he was sentenced to just one year in prison. The court argued it was not the suspect's fault that Leon got hit by the car, as he was not physically touching the dog. No restitution for replacement of the dog and the handler's time to re-train a new dog was granted.

After Leon's death, the M & I Bank that had previously been robbed of its ATMs, donated $17,000 to the K-9 unit. The bank employees were deeply saddened by their friend, Leon's, death. As a final tribute, the bank posted a photo of Leon and John on the Megatron in New York's Time Square.

New York's Time Square pays tribute to K-9 Leon.
Courtesy of John La Fontaine

People from all over the country were touched by Leon's story. John received one hundred letters from citizens and schools all over the United States expressing sadness over Leon's untimely death. Whole classes of children wrote letters saying that they were "sad about Leon." Other citizens donated thousands of dollars to the K-9 unit in Leon's name. Some chose to send John photos and paintings of Leon. The loss was felt deeply by the entire public.

Coming from a construction work background, John had always utilized his skills to enhance the department's training facilities. Using his own money and charming willing donors, he started on a memorial project. Over a period of time, John built obstacles for the unit. Every nail he drove and every board he cut, he did for Leon. The K-9 unit had not had anywhere to train, so there were no training obstacles for the dogs to practice with. Soon, John supplied them with barrel climbs, A-frames, cat walks, tunnel crawls and fence jumps. Later, when an acre of land near the police shooting range was acquired, the unit built one of the finest K-9 training facilities in the area offering it to other agencies for use when they could not afford their own. It was called, "Leon's Field."

Officer John La Fontaine trains a new recruit at Leon's Field.

Courtesy of John La Fontaine

A fitting tribute to a brave dog

Courtesy of John La Fontaine

John's two strong hands that had softly petted his two cherished dogs built an additional memorial to Leon after the dog's tragic death. Off a curved concrete walkway that leads from the kennels at the training facility sits a place of solitude. A circle of benches surrounds a strong and mighty tree there. A stone pillar supports a plaque the department gave to John to remember Leon's heroism. The face of a familiar smiling canine adorns the plaque and looks out over Leon's Field, where other brave Arizona canines train. Within the circle of benches, a Chinese Pistachio tree, donated by a local nursery spreads its lush full branches to become a canopy of cooling shade for anyone who stops there on a warm Arizona day to pause and remember.

John need only look out over the facility or sit beneath the spreading Pistachio tree to remember the two dogs he served with and loved. The tree is growing well, and after training given in all Dutch commands, John's two new canines, Kino and Spike, often rest in its shade. The Dutch command of "Los," has replaced "Aus" and "Alt," keeping John far more than bilingual. The foreign dogs are the bearers of a torch passed from their forerunners. They are the guardians of the master and the night, never replacements, but always watchful sentinels who continue the tradition and serve with honor.

John with the two Dutchmen
Courtesy of John La Fontaine

John's new Dutch dogs, K-9s Spike and Kino, anticipate a cool dip in the pool.

Courtesy of John La Fontaine

*Cooling off on a hot Arizona day, K-9 Kino takes a
running leap to retrieve his ball from the pool.*

Courtesy of John La Fontaine

The Arizona Police K-9 Memorial that was proposed and overseen by Gordy Leitz, handler of K-9 Lindsay, stands in Phoenix and holds the names of all the fallen police K-9s that served heroically in Arizona. At the top stands a bronze sculpture of a stately Arizona K-9. Warmed each day by the bright sun, the gleaming bronze figure of German K-9 Ully, whose likeness was used by the creating artist, stands in a pose of eternal alertness. Beneath the imposing figure of Ully is engraved the name of his former Belgian housemate, K-9 Leon. The memorial preserves the memory of two international and formerly ownerless dogs that found a loving home in Arizona. With Officer John La Fontaine, they served with distinction and will rest forever far from their native countries, but in their adoptive homeland where, serving with him, they experienced much joy.

K-9 Memorial in Phoenix, Arizona

Courtesy of Jim Frost

K-9s Zeke, Bullet and Snap

"Tracker's Trilogy"

Joe "Tracker" Mastrangelo finished a distinguished K-9 career working for New Jersey's Mt. Laurel Township Police Department. During his twenty-four years of service, he was paired with three magnificent dogs, Zeke, Bullet and Snap, each dog unique in personality and well-skilled in the field of crime fighting. Their battleground was a town of twenty-three square miles occupied by forty-eight thousand residents. By noon, on any work day, the experts knew that about two-hundred-fifty-thousand people passed into the town, so there was always a sea of unfamiliar faces. In his years of service, Joe noted that for that reason there was never a shortage of new criminals being processed through the system. They came in all ages, sizes, shapes and colors perpetrating a wide variety of crimes. By the time he retired, Joe figured he had pretty much seen it all.

In 1983, Joe and one-hundred-ten pound German shepherd dog, Zeke, his first partner, were both rookies on the force. Neither of them knew a whole lot about police work when they started, but by trial and error they learned together. The mammoth dog knew what Joe was thinking and performed perfectly, sometimes before Joe could even give him a command. Soon the dog was well-versed in the technique of the "habious grabis," that he gladly demonstrated on any suspect running from him. Often, the neighborhood children came to Joe's door to ask if the gentle giant could come out and play.

Zeke's sheer size made him particularly intimidating,
but he remained a gentle and friendly dog.

Courtesy of Joe Mastrangelo

Under Joe's watchful eye, Zeke demonstrates the "habious grabis."
Courtesy of Joe Mastrangelo

"Zeke was a big old boy with a heart of gold," Joe remembered, "Every kid in the neighborhood knew him."

Early in his career, Joe got a call regarding a burglary in an industrial business area. He and Zeke responded to the call enthusiastically. The bad guy had broken into an office and had stolen the petty cash, which was fully understandable, but what was not was the fact that the long lanky burglar felt the need to pick up the keys to the sizable tractor trailer parked there and take the vehicle with him.

"Evidently," said Joe, "being inconspicuous was not one of his major concerns as he made his get away in the easy-to-spot rolling vehicle."

The search was on and about an hour later the truck was identified driving down a long country road. Much to his dismay the driver realized he had been spotted.

"Being the rocket scientist that he is," Joe said, "the guy bails out of the truck and runs into a corn field that has to be at least three-hundred acres."

The vast field of stalks would prove challenging to the searchers. It was hard to know where to begin the difficult track. Splattered with an occasional turn-of-the-century farm house, the road where the truck was abandoned was edged by oceans of identical corn fields. Patches of dense forest separated the scattered farms that popped up from time to time like mushrooms along the road and presented yet another venue for the suspect to hide.

Neither Joe nor Zeke were particularly feeling the call for a nature walk through a corn field on a hot afternoon late in July, but regardless, they started the track.

"The corn field was mature, seven-foot high or better, and the frond-like leaves and shafts were sharp and saw toothed. You needed only to brush by them to get cut. It had rained hard the night before, like a cow peeing on a flat rock. The bases of the corn rows were high, and the furrows were deep so the soil was like chocolate pudding."

The torrent of rain that soaked the thirsty corn only complicated matters as Joe tried to navigate the ruts between the now-quenched corn rows. The yellowing stalks held a post-rain jungle-like steam within their crackling leaves, and the stifling mist rose like a steam bath into the muggy morning air. The tall crops provided a haven for crawling insects and humming mosquitoes lying in wait for some fresh blood.

As the two mucked along though the squishy quagmire, the long slender husks slapped against them and rustled with each touch. Stalk after stalk, Joe pushed the brown tassels away from his face. Cotton-like fibers stuck to the sweat on his face and neck, creating a torturous itch reminiscent of encounters with fiberglass insulation. Joe's feet grew heavy, laden with caked mud, and as Zeke plodded along through the mire, soft mud pushed up between all of his toes.

The pair tracked intensely, but not for long when they came across a scarecrow. The tall figure had its arms stretched out horizontally and stood quite still. It was wearing an old black t-shirt, soiled, oversized droopy work pants and a filthy gray hooded sweatshirt—all fitting scarecrow attire.

Joe squinted through a panorama of cracked corn still clinging to the drying stalks. He pushed his way through swishing leaves, dried and stiffened by the hot sun and stepped forward to view the stationary figure.

Then it moved.

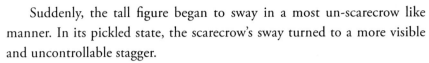

Suddenly, the tall figure began to sway in a most un-scarecrow like manner. In its pickled state, the scarecrow's sway turned to a more visible and uncontrollable stagger.

"O.K., O.K., O.K., you got me." it slurred.

When the scruffy fellow eyed Zeke's persuading teeth, warning him to stay put, he snapped upright and stiffened again standing as straight as the aging stalks. He eyed the excited sharp-toothed dog warily.

The sorry staggering scarecrow was handcuffed behind his back with Zeke's 15-foot tracking lead hooked to the chain between the cuffs. Joe held the other end in his right hand and held Zeke on a very short traffic lead in his left hand, the idea being that he could order the man in the direction he wanted him to go from a controllable distance behind. The scarecrow's eyes remained transfixed on Zeke's persuasive smile.

From past experience, Joe knew that trying to march a handcuffed prisoner out of rough terrain caused the suspect to unceremoniously fall down multiple times. For a man who had stood mute surrounded by whispering stalks, the scarecrow became more verbal as he plodded through the rows of corn. His two wayward feet would not fit next to each other in the furrow at the same time and given his state of intoxication, he was having trouble controlling them at all. With each stumble and fall that reintroduced him to the muddy morass, the profane scarecrow uttered his favorite chosen words often punctuated by invoking the name of his sweet Jesus. Joe pulled him back up as best he could with a sucking sound that could only be compared to a cow pulling its stuck hoof out of the mud.

"By the time we finally got out of the cornfield, the drunken suspect was a mud-covered, scratched up, bleeding man who looked like he got into a fight with a landscaper's electric grass whip! I looked pretty good because he had thoughtfully knocked down a nice wide path for me and Zeke to walk on."

The game had ended with a score of Zeke, one, scarecrow, zero. Joe found out later that the man had been out of jail for just twenty-four hours after serving a two-year sentence. At the next trial, the judge was not particularly sympathetic, so the scarecrow got four years for his trouble and two more for parole violation.

Six years passed, and Joe moved on to a bigger police department. Zeke had retired, and Joe needed a new dog.

"The average K-9 Patrol Dog class in Atlantic City in those days would have anywhere between twelve to twenty-five dogs and handlers. Months before the class started, the trainers and handlers scoured the tri-state area shelters and made appointments with pet owners (donators) so that we could test as many dogs as possible before the class started."

Out of one hundred dogs tested, only a few showed promise. Coming up short of enough dogs, Joe was pleased one day when he received a lead on some dogs living at a Brooklyn, New York, junkyard. He and a few other handlers drove all the way to Brooklyn to test the dogs.

"The junk yard was in a dilapidated neighborhood and was several acres in size. It looked bad even for a junk yard. The owner, a short fat man in dingy clothes and in need of soap, water and a wire brush greeted us at the gate of an eight-foot chain link fence. He was accompanied by two large shepherds."

The handlers followed the owner deep into the yard to an area with mountains of crushed rusting cars stacked like pancakes. In the claustrophobic surroundings, the handlers tested both dogs and found that one might have potential for patrol work. While stowing the testing equipment, a handler pointed to what looked to be a mangy underfed black mutt scrambling out of the trunk of an old burned-out car. The ragamuffin dog ran right over obviously wanting to be greeted. As bad as he looked, he appeared happy and ready to play. The yard owner explained that the dog was about eight-months-old, an unwanted product of his shepherds and was going to the dog pound along with the other shepherd right after the handlers left.

"Well, police dog handlers are softies at heart, and we couldn't leave that puppy there. We figured we'd find him a home somewhere. We loaded him and the tested dog into the van and drove back to Atlantic City."

When they returned to the Atlantic City Police K-9 kennels, the pup was placed in a run along with the other candidates. Over the course of the next few months, the puppy was name Bullet and was cared for by most of the men in the class. At first, Joe thought the pitiful animal had a jet-black coat until a first bath proved otherwise. The more Joe scrubbed, the more clearly he could see the classic markings of a true German shepherd dog. What emerged from the suds was a soggy dog that showed all the signs of police potential.

*Scrubbed clean, the junk yard dog showed all the
beauty of a classic German shepherd dog.*

Courtesy of Joe Mastrangelo

Released from the filth of a junkyard, K-9 Bullet starts a new life with Joe.

Courtesy of Joe Mastrangelo

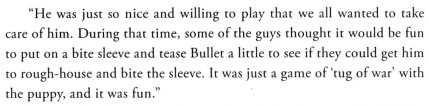

"He was just so nice and willing to play that we all wanted to take care of him. During that time, some of the guys thought it would be fun to put on a bite sleeve and tease Bullet a little to see if they could get him to rough-house and bite the sleeve. It was just a game of 'tug of war' with the puppy, and it was fun."

Joe was already two months into the training class watching his dog partners wash out left and right. A friend who had spent much time around Bullet suggested Joe give him a try. Joe had only two months of class left to cover eight weeks of training time and that was hard enough to do even with a mature dog. He spent a lot of time just getting the "happy-go-lucky" pup to take the training seriously.

"As he grew, Bullet didn't have a serious bone in his body. He wouldn't listen for squat," Joe observed, "I thought I'd never get him squared away. But Bullet turned out to be a pretty hard biter for a dog that was just having fun. Somehow, by the end of two months and with the extra help of all those guys in the class, Bullet turned out to be one of the best police dogs I have ever seen. And he proved it throughout his long career. He remained a puppy his entire life and had a place in his heart for all of the 'human puppies' he would entertain."

The 85-pound dog soon eased into the job with the comfort of an old shoe and picked up right where Zeke had left off. But he became an escape artist of sorts having learned to turn door knobs, lift latches and jump fences. Once loose, Bullet wandered twenty-minutes away from home to the local canine grooming parlor to socialize with any dogs that happened to be there being cleaned that day.

In the police car, he became proficient at pressing his body against his cage and butting his head into the door to pop the latch while Joe was out of the car. Once free, Bullet jumped to the front seat of the car and manipulated the pull handle on the passenger's door and let himself out. More than once, he pressed his paw on the button on the siren box near the console as he exited the car, thus signaling his own escape to Joe who came running to round him up.

Just after Bullet turned eleven-months-old, the new partners did a track of a burglary suspect. Bullet tracked the bad guy and found him hiding under a tool shed. The suspect didn't want to be arrested, but Bullet changed his mind after some perfectly-timed "porcelain persuasion." That's when Joe knew he had something special. Track after track followed, and Bullet gained a reputation for having an excellent nose.

A few years later, Joe and Bullet went back to school to learn narcotics detection. The dog had a natural talent, and he breezed through the class. Because of his previous positive exposure to the public, the next step was public relations. Bullet was called out to perform in demonstrations for the public, and with each demo the happy-go-lucky puppy that had emerged from the shadows of a car trunk never lost his enthusiasm. Soon, Bullet was known by thousands of adults and children. Out on the streets he was recognized as a star.

"Hey, Bullet," admirers called when they saw the team working, "Who's that guy that works for you?"

Bullet was an excellent competitor in the United States Police Canine Association's Regional Competitions and earned several trophies including first place in obedience and second place mastering the obstacle course.

"He was one of the first dogs in the New Jersey area to receive national certification in patrol, tracking and narcotics search," said Joe proudly. "Not bad for a junkyard pup."

Riding around on patrol one day, Joe heard the crackle of Dispatch relaying information regarding a small business garage being burglarized. Lights flashing and sirens screaming, Joe wheeled his car around and headed for that location. Officers on the scene told Joe that the "perp" had been seen leaving on foot just minutes before the police arrived. The suspect stole the petty cash and keys to one of the trucks, but he got scared off before he could take the truck for his get away. The track was on.

"So Bullet starts making like a vacuum cleaner on the ground, sucking up the bad guy's scent and moving fast through the woods."

Continuing at a fast clip, Bullet stopped at the edge of a creek that was narrow enough to step across. There, he found a work boot stuck right in the middle of the trickling water helplessly sucked into the mud. Someone less knowledgeable about mud than Bullet would be missing that boot on the rough terrain.

The two continued to track but strangely, Bullet started to track in random directions as if the suspect was purposely turning and changing direction to throw him off. Bullet tracked in circles in one direction, and then he abruptly started off in another as if some crazed person with no plan in mind at all went for a confused stroll in the woods. Further on, at the edge of the woods, they eventually came to a residential area where they crossed through a few back yards and followed the track right up to the back door of a house.

"Bullet has it in his head now that he wants inside."

After calling for back-up, Joe knocked sharply at the door, and a woman dressed in a flowered Hawaiian muumuu, kitchen apron and house slippers shuffled over to open it.

"I live alone," the woman stated firmly but not in an unfriendly manner, "except for my son who just got out of jail today."

She invited Joe inside. Upon entering the home, Bullet and Joe saw a long lanky man passed out drunk on the couch, and they could not help but notice he was wearing just one work boot. There, for better or worse, lay the scarecrow from years ago! Once more their paths had crossed.

"O.K., O.K., O.K., you got me," he slurred in his old familiar tone.

History repeated itself as the man was tried and sentenced to four more years for the burglary and an additional two more for another parole violation. He just couldn't seem to stay away from other people's cash and trucks.

There was a new score to post for Tracker's team. Bullet, one, scarecrow, zero.

Several years later, Bullet and Joe worked the midnight shift, and as the shift was nearly over at 5 a.m., the day was already growing warm. It was one of those lazy early June days when things were unusually quiet. Before finishing up the shift and heading home for a peaceful long sleep, Joe decided to check out the businesses along the hotel strip. The sun was not yet up and as he pulled through the intersection on a highway that came out of a residential area, he saw a late model car with two men in the front seat. They sat nervously at a red light waiting to cross over the highway when Joe made eye contact with the driver. Instantaneously, the car accelerated onto the highway almost side swiping Joe as it shot out in front of him and sped away.

Joe had been around long enough to recognize all of the earmarks of a stolen car, and the chase was on.

"It wasn't a long chase, but it did get a little crazy."

Joe followed the two onto a jug handle that went onto the interstate northbound. But the thieves wanted to go southbound and immediately crossed over five lanes of traffic, seventy-feet of grass median and another four lanes of southbound traffic before they turned south onto the interstate. Joe was driving a full-sized Bronco and had no problem negotiating the erratic course so he pursued them in the southbound lanes. Fortunately, the traffic was not heavy, but there were enough vehicles on the highway to cause Joe some concern.

It was becoming apparent that the thieves were not skilled drivers by the way that they handled the vehicle, and Joe thought they figured that out about the same time he did, because they slowed down as they and Joe went under the overpass. As both cars came out the other side, the driver and passenger both bailed out of the passenger's side door, rolled onto the soft grass shoulder, got up and started running. The stolen car was still moving southbound at about 20 mph, and with no one behind the wheel, it headed back across the interstate towards the northbound traffic. Thinking quickly, Joe got out and opened the truck door, and Bullet jumped out into the darkness.

"Get 'em boy!" he called, and four feet hit the ground running. Bullet headed straight for the bad guys while Joe pursued the driverless car.

But the men were quick, and Joe watched helplessly from his Bronco as the bad guys ran up a hill and climbed over a six-foot fence with Bullet following not too far behind them. Fortunately, the stolen car rolled into a ditch in the center median and stopped. Upon seeing that, Joe screeched to a stop and got out running, simultaneously calling on the radio for back-up and watching Bullet jump the fence.

The area on the other side of the highway fence was residential, and as Joe reached the top of the hill, he could see Bullet clearing a fence about three or four yards away. Joe didn't know it at the time, but when he yelled his initial command to Bullet back at the overpass, it was the last thing Bullet would hear him say that morning and for a long time to come.

"When God made Bullet, He said, 'This one will be a police dog,'" Joe said.

Any time Joe put Bullet on the track the eager dog took it seriously.

"But there are some things that a dog cannot easily accomplish. If you take two young men in good shape and several fences just high enough and just close enough, the guys can sometimes stay ahead of the dog. Bullet was no spring chicken when we started this adventure, and he was suffering from arthritis in his left ankle, which he had seriously broken several months before this incident. If you knew Bullet, he didn't care. He was working at what he loved best!"

Joe continued the pursuit, jumping fences and trying desperately to catch up to Bullet. There was no moon so Joe couldn't see well ahead of him, but he could hear Bullet barking and then someone yelling. Joe changed course and headed in that direction. When he got to the area where he thought the noise had come from, they were gone.

Soon, he came up to an eight-foot chain link fence that surrounded an apartment complex. On his side of the fence he found a bare human foot print. Then he found a left sneaker and a bloody torn sock, but, unfortunately, no one was in it. On the other side of the fence Joe could see the large indentation of a right sneaker, a left bare foot print and two palm prints in the soil. But he didn't see Bullet's foot prints on the other side.

By then the rest of the troops had set up a perimeter to contain the bad guys, but the thieves had covered so much ground in such a short period of time that there were not enough police to surround the area even with the help of two other police departments who got involved when the thieves ventured into their jurisdiction.

Joe paused for a moment to process all of the information he had collected on the ground. He knew that Bullet caught up to at least one of them, but what happened? The best he could reason was that Bullet caught the no doubt terrified suspect as he was climbing the eight-foot fence.

"He must have forfeited his left sneaker, sock and a little flesh to get away from Bullet and then fell hard enough from the fence on the other side to hit the ground on all fours and leave the impressions in the soil."

Joe couldn't track any farther as the track went out onto the blacktop and concrete, and he lacked Bullet's sensitive nose to accomplish anything.

"Now I'm thinking, the heck with the bad guys. I just want to find my partner and make sure he's o.k."

Joe spent the next hour looking for Bullet and yelling out his name. But the dog was nowhere to be found. It was as if he vanished into thin air, but Joe surmised that he was still on the trail of the bad guys.

The problem was that Bullet could not get over some of the fences that the bad guys scaled so easily. So the dog attempted to go around the obstacles to head the men off. The other problem was that Bullet continued to get farther and farther away until he could no longer keep up with them. And he was probably more tired and unable to jump fences that he had already cleared. With a sinking feeling, Joe realized that Bullet could not get back to him at all.

"I knew from experience what was inside my dog's head. Ask any seasoned handler, and they will tell you the same thing."

Joe also considered the possibility that Bullet confronted both of the men at the fence and may have been injured by one of them. He didn't care for that option, but it was in the back of his mind. Either way, he needed to find his dog.

By 9 a.m., Joe hadn't seen Bullet for almost four hours. A command post was set up on the other side of the residential area behind a small shopping center. Joe had gone over the track area several times and still couldn't find Bullet. He really starting to sweat thinking that Bullet was hurt or trapped, and he was frustrated that he couldn't help his partner.

The sun edged up over the Jersey skyline starting a new day and after a few hours, it beat down relentlessly. As the day grew hotter, officers from surrounding departments, firemen, township employees, family members, truck drivers on CB radios and civilians offering their assistance all populated the area. Even after a reward was offered, Bullet remained missing.

"So, I do the only thing that I could do. Bullet has friends. They have noses just like him and partners just like me. If there is one thing true about K-9 handlers, it's that we have the tightest brotherhood of all police organizations."

Joe made a phone call, and within one hour thirty more K-9 teams arrived to join the search. Many of the handlers and dogs Joe knew, but there were just as many that he didn't. Joe was a fellow K-9 handler in need and that was all they needed to know. Many came from as far as one-hundred-miles away to assist their fellow officer.

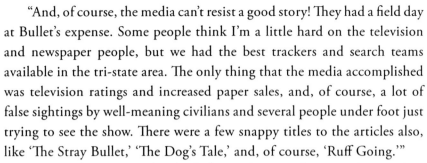

"And, of course, the media can't resist a good story! They had a field day at Bullet's expense. Some people think I'm a little hard on the television and newspaper people, but we had the best trackers and search teams available in the tri-state area. The only thing that the media accomplished was television ratings and increased paper sales, and, of course, a lot of false sightings by well-meaning civilians and several people under foot just trying to see the show. There were a few snappy titles to the articles also, like 'The Stray Bullet,' 'The Dog's Tale,' and, of course, 'Ruff Going.'"

The search went on relentlessly for twelve more hours without a clue. And then at 9 p.m. that night, the searchers received a phone call from a television station stating that they had conducted an interview with the people who found Bullet.

"Naturally, they called the television station first. These two 'heroes' had found my partner. With the assistance of fellow officers, Bullet was safe at home with me shortly thereafter."

The story went that the two "heroes" were entertained by Bullet from about 10 a.m. that morning until the time that they called the television station at 9 p.m. claiming to have just heard the broadcast about Bullet and had just realized who he was. They didn't think he was a police dog, because he didn't attack anyone they said. Bullet was in good shape, and Joe was grateful to have his buddy back safely, but as the story later enfolded, the "heroes" seemed a bit less heroic.

Joe lived about five miles from the original spot where Bullet started to chase the bad guys, but it was a "you can't get there from here" situation. The two "heroes" actually lived three blocks down the street from Joe's house. It seemed that Bullet at some point decided that he could no longer catch the bad guys and changed his priority to that of finding his way home. He had crossed two major highways after finding his way out of the backyards of that area when he met the two "heroes."

Bullet was exhausted and extremely thirsty from the heat. As he passed the men's residence, they offered him water and coaxed him into the house thinking he was a stray dog. And by some odd quirk of nature, they said they did not notice the shiny metal police badge hanging from his neck. Bullet, being the well-mannered, well-trained police dog that he was, knew that they were not the two bad guys that Joe had given him permission to bite and did not take offense at their kindness.

It was later discovered that shortly after Bullet was taken in, several of the men's neighbors became suspicious of the "new pet" and told the two "heroes" that it was probably the police dog that everyone was looking for. Finally, one neighbor threatened to call the police and report them. The "heroes" offered to split the reward if he would wait awhile longer, but he declined their offer.

"He was the real hero. When I finally got all the facts, I was hot and looking to put the "habious grabis" on two particular individuals, but the media had made such heroes out of these two guys that it was more prudent to let sleeping dogs lie. So they skated!"

Once Bullet was safely back with him, Joe tried to look for positives.

"Even though we didn't arrest the car thieves, at least one of them wasn't going dancing that night, and we got the car back. Aside from being tired, Bullet was in good shape and at home. A well-trained police dog was ordered to bite two suspects, was exposed to the public without the handler for an extended period of time and was non-aggressive towards people other than the suspects. If Bullet had not been distracted by the "heroes," he would have miraculously found his way home on a route that he had never walked before. He was only three blocks down the street from his home. I realized how much the community cared about their police officers and their hairy partners. I knew that I could always count on my fellow officers and K-9 handlers in times of need, and lastly, Bullet was the most famous police dog in four states and had the fan mail to prove it!"

By 1996, old Bullet had retired and spent his days sprawled out on Joe's couch watching reruns of Star Trek and Hill Street Blues. Like most K-9 handlers who never think they will be able to work with another partner, Joe found a dog who would not take no for an answer. Snap, a Belgian Malinois, was that dog.

"That guy was a 'one of a kind!'" He only weighed about fifty-seven pounds soaking wet with rocks in his pockets. But, forty pounds of it was brass, and the rest was love for me."

Handler, Joe Mastrangelo, with his partner, Snap

Courtesy of Joe Mastrangelo

Snap demonstrates his agility on the A-frame.

Courtesy of Joe Mastrangelo

Snap didn't have an ounce of fat on his body, and he ate twice as much as Bullet did. He was a high energy, "search and destroy" kind of dog who could never sit still. He was a dog that always had to be doing something, and the police department gave him plenty to do.

"Snap was a little guy who would never give up. He could run like a jaguar and jump like a kangaroo!" Joe remembered.

In no time at all, Snap was patrolling the streets and racking up little "bad guy" stickers on the side of the K-9 truck just as fast as the jobs kept happening. At the first call of the night, the two were off. A report had come in of a utility pole getting hit out in "cow-tipping country." Mt. Laurel was a farm community that was slowly but surely being devoured by real estate developers. There were great wooded gaps between developments, so the suspect had great opportunities to hide.

Then the radio transmitted another curt message. A man, now irate, had stopped to get a cup of coffee and left his truck running outside a Wa Wa convenience store. When he came back outside, the truck was gone. Dispatch asked the caller for a description of the truck.

"It's a tractor with a flat bed trailer loaded with steel," came the surprising reply.

This was not your typical stolen vehicle.

Another voice cut in. An officer stated he was going out to the "hit pole" call when he spotted a tractor trailer going the other way leaving a tell-tale trail of steel off the back of the truck bed as distinctive as the trail of bread crumbs sprinkled through the forest by Hansel and Gretel. After swinging his car into a quick U-turn, the officer headed out after the truck swerving from side-to-side avoiding the steel bread crumbs heaped on the blacktop and maneuvering his car as skillfully as a slalom racer down a ski slope. When he finally caught up with the tractor trailer and got it to stop, the driver darted from the cab and headed for some back yards on foot leaving behind not much more than an empty liquor bottle of Mad Dog.

Joe and Snap arrived at the scene to start the track. Snap was on a mission! He wasn't letting this one get away! The woods were thick and overgrown, and Joe could not see a foot ahead of him in the pitch black, but Snap continued to track hard. Sticks cracking underfoot at each step, Joe followed the dog's rhythmic pants in the darkness and tried to navigate the difficult terrain that he had come to know well.

"See, when God made South Jersey, He said, 'You know, sea level isn't low enough. Let's make a big swampy hole in the middle of this woods right here, and I think I'll create a new plant to cover it all over. We'll call it 'beggar patch' and wrap it in another plant that we'll call 'wait-a-minute vines.' 'Beggar patch' is that bush with the little round sticker balls that no matter what, you can't get through it or around it. And if you get near it, these little sticker balls grab you and tangle you up. 'Wait-a-minute vines' are those thorny vines with no leaves. They are easy to identify because as soon as you get into them, the first thing that comes out of your mouth is 'Yow! Wait a minute!' And, of course, the township buys their cops polyester uniforms so that when you come out of the woods, you look like a giant blue fuzzy!"

The thickets became more dense, and Joe fell to the ground to crawl on his hands and knees through the entangling undergrowth of "beggar patch" for the next mile with Snap on his leash leading the way. In the blackness of the forest, Joe tried in vain to avoid the calculated and demonic attack of the "wait-a-minute vines."

Just up ahead, Joe finally saw light from a condo complex. Bruised and battered by nature, he emerged from God's playground. The light was shining from around the side of one building and into an alcove shared by four apartments. Suddenly, the hair ridge down the middle of Snap's back stood straight up. In quick pursuit, the dog edged closer to the light and then dashed into the alcove. From behind, Joe could hear a disturbance there. But it was not a violent disturbance. Joe listened to what seemed like a resident with arms filled with groceries, perhaps, leaning and sliding against the apartment door while fumbling about trying to blindly and unsuccessfully fit a key into the doorknob beneath the packages. Then a voice rang out.

"O.K.., O.K.., O.K.., you got me," a male voice suddenly and unexpectedly yelled.

Joe pointed the dancing yellow beam of his flashlight towards the surrendering voice. The profile of the face was strangely recognizable—the drunken sway of the body familiar.

"S.O.B! It's the scarecrow! Pickled as usual."

Recognizing Joe, the familiar figure fell to his knees and cried.

"This ain't right. It just ain't right!" the inebriated man wailed.

Twelve years after their last social engagement, Joe assured the scarecrow that once again sweet victory and truck ownership would not be his. The man's favorite Jersey cop was there one more time to sign his dance card.

Immediately, Joe began to laugh. What started as a subdued giggle evolved into a full-out belly laugh that echoed through the dark woods. Within minutes, all the back-up officers arrived to find the source of Joe's merriment. And the more that showed up, the louder the collective laughter became. With each additional chorus, the scarecrow repeated his disbelief and dismay and philosophical thoughts on the "rightness" of things. He had been out of jail only six hours, just long enough to go to the liquor store, get drunk, spot the lovely truck of his desire and steal the steel.

"You know," said Joe, as he led the deflated man away, "you are single-handedly responsible for assisting me in training all three of my patrol dogs."

It was a recognition the scarecrow did not want. All he wanted was a truck. Now it was back to jail until the next opportunity arose, probably another six years in the future. The scarecrow, the dog and the handler would be older and slower by then. But with any luck at all, Joe would be working a new dog most likely the last patrol dog of his career. By then Snap would hopefully be retired and home on the couch watching reruns of Deep Space 9 and NYPD Blue as the scarecrow, with no forethought or intent, would again expertly train the new dog. And to paraphrase the scarecrow, in Joe's estimation, that would be "right---just right." Snap, one, scarecrow, zero.

"So it's late September, the leaves are starting to fall, but it's still hot enough for mosquitoes and green head flies to be out at night. Me and the Snap, we're working night watch humping calls in the 4th district when we get a call to assist in a car chase for two burglary suspects going on in the town next door. So we fire up the woody wagon and start over that way. While I'm driving, I'm listening to their channel so I can get the scoop before I get there."

From what Joe gathered on the radio, a patrol unit was shaking hands with doorknobs of the businesses along the highway when the officer saw "a couple of city boys" out in front of a supermarket after closing. They saw the officer, jumped into a running car and sped away. As the officer passed the front of the store, he saw that the window was smashed out so the chase was on. The suspects were part of a black market cigarette ring working out of the city, and it was about the seventh store they hit that night. The car was loaded with cartons of stolen cigarettes from all over three counties.

"You have to appreciate the area we work in. This area used to be South Jersey farm land outside of the city, and now overnight it's been developed. So there are a lot of wooded and swampy areas in between shopping centers and developments. So the cop starts chasing these guys up and down the highway and, of course, around a few of our famous 'South Jersey Highway Circles.' As I'm getting into the area, I hear one of the good guys say that the car is slowing down in front of a pretty good section of woods. Now I hear, 'one just bailed out and is running into the woods.' The car keeps going for about another quarter mile, and the driver bails out, and he runs into the woods. Okay, I'm awake now and getting excited, because this is my kind of turf!"

The section the suspects were hiding in was about one-mile-long and a half-mile-deep. Evidently, they were not on a first name basis with "beggar patch" and "wait-a-minute vines," or they would have found a better place to hide. The unwelcoming area was surrounded on one side by highway, two sides by shopping centers and the back side by an intimidating twenty-foot-high cliff face.

The good guys set up a perimeter around the general area thinking that the suspects were still inside the woods, but they were not really sure because there was always a lot of confusion is such situations. For all they knew, the bad guys could have doubled back behind them and crossed over the highway with their stolen smokes while the police were trying to stop the patrol car, keep one eye on traffic and the other eye on the suspects. It made it even harder knowing the suspects had bailed out a-half-mile-apart.

"Five minutes later, me and the little buddy are at the spot where the first suspect bailed out. The plan at this point is to track them one at a time. I'm putting the tracking harness on Snapper, and he's already moaning 'cause he wants to get started! I hook Snap up to an 18-foot tracking lead, turn my baseball cap backwards on my head, make a fist around the end of the lead with both hands and hold it up to my forehead. Now you might ask, 'what's that tracking lead and forehead stuff about?' Well, I've been tracking in God's sense of humor for seventeen years now. Snap is smart enough to know that the only way to deal with 'beggar patch' is to go under it. And I got tired of getting my hat knocked off and landing on my butt. Use your imagination."

The suspects' cigarette habit would keep Joe and Snap busy for many more hours.

"Okay, I give Snapper the high sign, and we take off into the woods. Snap's sucking up the scent of the bad guy, but the swamp is tough. It's like trying to walk on top of that familiar chocolate pudding that's three-feet deep, and, of course, let's not forget the 'beggar patch!' Then we would hit dry spots, but they were only two-feet square, and a tree was growing out of them.

Well, about two hours later, we finally track out to a section of bull rushes and swamp cedars. The grass is so tall and thick that I can't see Snap at the end of the tracking lead. The next thing I hear is what I can only describe as the mating call of the Jersey Devil! It's one of those 'gotta be there' kind of things. Needless to say, the lead went tight, and Snap put the 'habious grabious' on the bad guy. And that guy was screaming like an Irish tenor. So, I call the pup off and start handcuffing the bad guy while Snap's guarding him."

With one down and one to go, Joe and Snap continue on.

"The next thing you know, Snap takes off, and I'm yelling for him to come back. I don't have a clue what he's up to, but I'm worried. We're in deep, and Snap is the only one who knows the way out. He gets about ten-yards-away, dives into the bull rushes and disappears. Two seconds later, Snap reappears, but he's got a foot in his mouth with a leg and a man attached to it. And this guy must have been the female Jersey Devil, because he's answering that mating call I heard earlier. Somehow, these two knuckle heads managed to find each other in the swamp, and Snap decided he wasn't leaving without both of them! And I agreed with him. Besides, I told Snap that I knew what he was doing the whole time. I think he believed me. Well, Snap cleared about seven burglaries that night. And you wouldn't believe how many other burglaries these two confessed to Snap on that long walk out."

Called often, Joe and Snap worked both night and day shifts. It was the kind of beautiful fall morning in mid-October before the frost of winter made its first showing—crisp but not cold, as Joe and Snap were finishing up the night shift. The leaves on the trees were showing off the early colors of autumn under the first rays of sunrise, and Joe had just finished a quiet night shift. As he was putting Snap in his "canine condo" at home, the phone rang. Joe's wife, Joan, reported that it was Police Dispatch calling to find out if Joe had fed Snap yet.

"I know what that means, because I've heard it many times before, and Dispatch knows that I won't work Snap for at least four hours after I've fed him. I don't want him to flip his stomach (gastric torsion). I've seen dogs and horses die from that."

Dispatch wanted the team to go way up to the north end of the county to assist one of the towns there. A residential burglary had occurred while the owners were home, and the bad guys had tied them up. The husband and wife victims were elderly and not in good health. Their description of the bad guys was poor at best, because the burglars were wearing masks when they broke in. Joe met up with the detective on duty in the town. The situation was a bad one, because there was no way to identify the bad guys.

"The police want us to do a track with no loss of continuity. That means that Snap can't lose the scent anywhere along the track. Even if we catch the bad guys, if there is any loss of continuity, they walk, because I can't testify that the track was unbroken. In most states, the courts are in agreement. A police K-9 track is as good as an 'eyewitness,' as long as it starts at the crime scene and ends with the bad guy without any interruptions. This put a lot of pressure on Snap and me, because tracks are seldom perfect, and the whole conviction now rests on our shoulders."

Not only would the track be difficult, it would be dangerous.

"To make matters worse, the two 'perps' managed to get away with the homeowner's loaded revolver along with some jewelry and the mattress money. This area of the county was mostly farms and woods that abutted a big military base. The only thing around to break up the woods is an occasional highway. The town did have a small 'Stop & Rob' (7-Eleven gas station) and a bus stop. But that is a good five miles away, as the crow flies."

It was beginning to look like it might be a long time before Snap got his next meal.

"I decide to have a short conversation with Snap about this whole situation before we started the track, and he assures me that it's a piece of cake. Right— the lying little SOB!"

The track started out fairly well. As soon as Joe brought Snap out of the truck, he went right to the house's back door, put his nose on the ground and started dragging Joe across the yard with the well-dressed detective following right behind.

"Now one might expect that the track would go up or down the highway a few hundred feet and stop, because that's where the getaway car would be. Not this time. We head right into the woods. The detective, of course, is wearing a suit and penny loafers. He's determined, but he's not prepared for what is about to happen."

But Joe felt the kindest thing to do was allow the spiffy detective to learn for himself that dapper dress suits and "beggar patch" were seldom a good GQ combination.

"The woods were some of the worst I had ever encountered in South Jersey. We were on our hands and knees for a long time crawling through the 'beggar patch' and the 'wait-a-minute vines' that I love so much. And, when we finally did hit a clearing, it's covered with a bed of poison ivy. See, if you want to get ivy poison, you have to find some late in the season, like October, when the leaves are mature and shiny from the resin."

While they were crawling along in the dense woods, it occurred to Joe that the whole thing didn't seem right. Normally, there would be a car waiting somewhere. Burglars didn't often go into the woods unless they were chased. Even then, they usually hunkered down a little ways in, because they were afraid of getting lost. But Snap had the scent and said, "They went 'that-a-way,'" so that's the way Joe went. He understood that the dog knew more than he did so Snap was in charge when they were tracking.

"I was just along to carry his water and talk on the radio!"

After about four miles, the three searchers spilled out of the woods.

"The detective," said Joe, "looked like he was 'road hard and put away wet.'"

The disheveled man had lost one of his penny loafers somewhere back in the woods, and as he stumbled out to the clearing, he was extremely unhappy. The trio found themselves at the top of a ridge and down below was a road that accessed the military base. As the exasperated detective grumbled, Snap took everyone down the hill to the side of the road that turned away from the base and headed in the other direction. Joe and the once nattily-dressed detective followed Snap along the side of the road for another mile where Joe saw a signpost that said, "Army Base." It had an arrow that pointed in the direction they had just come from. Snap headed right for the sign and started sniffing the ground right under it.

"Naturally, the detective that's with us already has an attitude, because he thinks we're on a wild goose chase. He's minus one shoe and dry cleaning won't fix his suit, so he's gonna seize the opportunity to suggest that Snap took us the long way just to pee on that sign."

Just as the detective gave his last derisive comment about Snap, the briar-covered dog started digging the ground up under the sign. Dirt flew upward just missing the surly detective, and moments later Snap had a revolver in his mouth. It was the same one that was taken from the house. The dirty-socked weary gumshoe, who had been quickly transformed in Snap's world from GQ model to unkempt hobo, hopped on one foot, and Joe left him there with the gun and told him to keep digging and call it in. Lacking Snap's toenails and not having so much as a small sharp nail file to dig with, the detective would have to improvise.

Snap, wearing his same basic all-purpose beige fur suit, became very charged up after his find and started dragging Joe down the road. After another three miles, they came to the center of a small town. First, they crossed the highway and went up to the pay phone outside the 7-Eleven. Then, they turned back across the highway still heading away from the base. Suddenly, there were people around, and Joe was worried that they would become too much of a distraction for Snap, but the dog was truly driven, and he kept going like the people weren't even there.

Joe had watched a bus go by as they crossed the highway near the 7-Eleven, where the vehicle had evidently dropped off the people. Snap finally stopped tracking at the enclosed bus stop, where many people still stood. Circling the little structure, he refused to leave it.

"So now my brain starts smoking, and I get this idea. I call the local Police Dispatch and have them put out a 'stop and hold' on the bus that just left the area. Well, we get lucky. One of the local cops stops the bus about four miles further down the road before any other passengers exit the bus. I guess the cops up this end of the county don't worry much about public relations, because he orders everyone to stay on the bus and then escorts the bus back to the bus stop where I'm waiting."

When the bus full of grumbling detoured passengers returned, it was all Joe could do to hang onto Snap as the happy dog dragged him up the steps and into the bus. Puzzled and wide-eyed, passengers watched as Snap pulled Joe straight down the aisle to the back of the bus where the dog started growling at two men who were bleeding from scratches all over their heads and hands.

"And these darn little prickly things are stuck all over their clothing. You can well imagine the look on their faces when I tell them they're under arrest. And Snap is a little upset when they don't resist."

The men were paraded off the bus, and their fellow passengers were relieved to get back on the road after such an unexpected bit of excitement. Once more, despite the fact that he and the Snapper were tired from the long and difficult track, Joe took away the positives.

"The mattress money was found in the 'perps' pockets. The bus driver confirmed that he had just picked up the two guys who we arrested. The detective that we left behind to dig found the stolen jewelry in the same hole where the gun was located. During their interview, the 'perps' said that they had been partying all night with a buddy who was stationed at the Army base. They ran out of money, had no car and decided to rob the old people so they could get back to New York. They didn't realize that they were so far from civilization and got lost in the woods. When they finally came out of the woods to the base entrance, they were afraid they would be caught and decided to bury the gun and jewelry under the sign so they could give their buddy a landmark to dig it up later. Last but not least--that detective? He told all the boys that he never had a doubt about Snap. As a matter of fact, he knew what Snap was up to the whole time, and I never said otherwise."

Joe retired in 2004 taking a host of memories with him. His dogs had been his life, and next to his family, there was no one he was closer to. Joe was an expert witness in police K-9 tracking, training and narcotics recognized by two different New Jersey Superior Court Judges. He conducted annual tracking seminars along with another K-9 handler and has been a guest speaker/lecturer at the Burlington County College/New Jersey Institute of Technology on the subject of animal behavior, in particular the reading of animal body language. His artistic ability allowed him to create popular cartoons featuring his beloved Snap.

"Snaptoon," drawn by Joe, featuring courageous and able K-9 Snap
Courtesy of Joe Mastrangelo

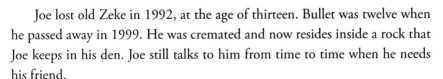

Joe lost old Zeke in 1992, at the age of thirteen. Bullet was twelve when he passed away in 1999. He was cremated and now resides inside a rock that Joe keeps in his den. Joe still talks to him from time to time when he needs his friend.

After partnering with Joe for thirteen years, Snap suffered a stroke after retirement and became partially paralyzed. On the sad day that Joe had to have him put down, the Snapper went out with the same high energy and spunk that he had lived. After receiving a sedation shot from the veterinarian, he still had the strength and desire to lift his head, lick Joe's cheek and turn to the bite the hand of the vet before the sleepy dog drew his final breath. He was cremated and also resides with Joe in the place that all the dogs called home.

Joe "Tracker" Mastrangelo attributes his successful tracking techniques to three dogs who dragged him through the best "beggar patch," "wait-a-minute vines," mud and swamps that South Jersey had to offer. And he still has the scars to prove it.

K-9 Vago

"On This Earth to Be a Police Dog"

He was a born New Yorker, strong, brash and independent with a bravado normally seen in a dog far beyond his tender age. The son of K-9 Lago, a strong Schutzund III dog that was bred to produce fight drive, the little pup was bought sight unseen by Lt. Chris Bracco of the Binghamton Police Department, who trained dogs with the non-profit Southern Tier Police Canine Association in New York.

The officer went to the kennel to visit when the little dog was just six-weeks-old. From all appearances, the puppy was clearly the alpha of the litter, and it was comical to see the other pups scatter when he asserted his dominance after he'd had enough of their horseplay. The dark brown searching eyes watched Chris intently from inside the pen following his every move as the new owner spoke with the caretaker of the pups. The dog seemed to be a likely candidate for police work, but Chris needed to test him.

Always on a mission, the pup was all business. He passed all Chris's puppy police tests with flying colors sinking his razor-sharp teeth into a burlap tug with much determination and pulling it with all the strength he could muster with his clamped baby jaws. He was fully-committed to hold on and keep his grip bracing his tiny paws hard against the ground and struggling with all his might to edge his small rotund torso backwards. As Chris tried to wrestle the tug away from him, jerking and swinging it with increasing intensity, the puppy gripped it in his mouth with not the slightest thought of releasing it. Chris recognized the behavior as a good indication of fight drive, courage and spirit.

Yet, for his age, the little dog was calm, steady and focused, simultaneously exhibiting incredible hunt and chase drive. Chris plunked down $800 of his own money and scooped up the one-pound bundle to take him home. He couldn't wait to introduce the new family addition to Dana, Chris's one-year-old Doberman pinscher. Dana had always been a bit of a diva, and Chris believed she knew she was gorgeous, and he wondered how the two would get along. Dana, or "Lulu" as she was affectionately known, needed a buddy for the long hours she was alone when Chris worked the night shift. This would, indeed, be a canine version of the Odd Couple.

Chris set the squirming little dog down on the living room floor for their first introduction. Immediately, the pup's first reaction was to boldly step in front of his new officer and bark at the startled Doberman. At first, Dana appeared shocked, but in her aloof way she decided to ignore him as one would briefly wave off an irritating insect. Then Chris lay down in the living room with Dana at his side to watch television. Having made his initial statement and impression, the self-assured pup confidently wandered into Chris's bedroom to go to sleep on floor. Bemused, Chris thought it was strange behavior for one so young but later came to understand that independence and confidence were characteristics of good police dogs and those genetic traits would serve the dog and officer well throughout their future endeavors.

After owning the pup for a full week, Chris was embarrassed to tell his fellow officers that he still had not named the animal. He gave the task some serious thought. Vago rhymed with Lago, the pup's strong father, and it sounded like a solid respectable name to match the new dog's personality, so Vago it was he proudly announced.

K-9 Vago and Chris
Courtesy of Debrah H. Muska – Animal Images
animalimages.com

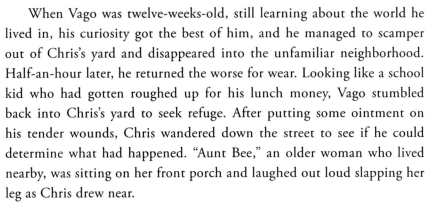

When Vago was twelve-weeks-old, still learning about the world he lived in, his curiosity got the best of him, and he managed to scamper out of Chris's yard and disappeared into the unfamiliar neighborhood. Half-an-hour later, he returned the worse for wear. Looking like a school kid who had gotten roughed up for his lunch money, Vago stumbled back into Chris's yard to seek refuge. After putting some ointment on his tender wounds, Chris wandered down the street to see if he could determine what had happened. "Aunt Bee," an older woman who lived nearby, was sitting on her front porch and laughed out loud slapping her leg as Chris drew near.

"That little puppy of yours just got a whuppin' from a group of alley cats that hang near here," she said with a broad smile and hearty laugh.

She explained that Vago had approached one of the cats to check it out and was mauled by not only that cat but all of its buddies before tearing out of her driveway, tail between his legs to skitter back towards home. After the street-cat incident, Vago never ran off again, and brave as he was, he never warmed up to any cat.

As the weeks passed, Chris started to bring Vago to the police K-9 training facility. It soon became obvious to the others there that Chris had a special and talented potential police dog. The first thing they noticed was that Vago was a dog that loved to bite. Since biting gave him such great joy, it was slowly integrated as a reward into all of his training, and the initial training progressed very smoothly. Vago eased through agility training, drug detection and tracking. As long as he got his bite, he could be taught anything.

But some of the experienced officers grew alarmed when they were getting bitten in Vago's enthusiasm when he decided to forego the thick bite sleeve to favor an actual warm bare arm or whatever appendage he could grab. Some felt that the training was moving too fast and putting too much pressure on the pup, for Vago was only sixteen-weeks-old and participating in training sessions with older and more-experienced police dogs. But it all felt so natural to Chris, and he was having so much fun that he ignored the critics. He and Vago continued to develop and succeed as a team with no problems. Despite Vago's young age, Chris felt his dog had made sufficient progress and was ready to deploy.

But, there were already three canine teams working for the department and, unfortunately, there were no current openings. Knowing what he wanted and feeling young, confident and as aggressive as his new pup, Chris enrolled in the New York State Bureau for Municipal Police Basic K-9 assuming the risk that a spot might not open up in the department. He knew he would have to attend the training with Vago on his own time.

So sure was he of his dog's potential that Chris worked the nighttime streets for five months and during the day attended the K-9 Academy. In the summer of 1997, he graduated from the Academy and awaited a coveted spot for himself and Vago. In the meantime, he took Vago to K-9 demonstrations and functions with established department handlers hoping to catch someone's eye. Upon one occasion, he attended a "Night Out Against Crime" demonstration at an inner city park where the mayor was in attendance. Afterwards, the mayor approached Chris and commented that he didn't know Chris was in K-9. Chris told him he wasn't and at that, the mayor assured him that he would be.

While Vago waited for an assignment, he contented himself with his favorite passion—a tennis ball. He greeted visitors in Chris's home with the ball in his mouth daring them to try and take it. Sidling up to uninitiated visitors, he casually and innocently dropped the ball on the floor, but when the visitor started to pick it up, quick as a flash, Vago grabbed it with his mouth just seconds before it could be claimed. For that reason, Chris could never play fetch with him as a regular dog would play. Vago called the shots. In order to have any interaction with Vago and the tennis ball at all, Chris had to devise a new game. Gathering together thirty tennis balls and a bat, he hit the balls one-by-one out into the yard for Vago. Each time a new ball was hit, Vago changed course from chasing the first ball to chasing the new moving ball. Eventually, at game's end, Vago trotted into the house with the bat in his mouth before returning to the yard to retrieve just one carefully-selected ball, which he brought into the house. Once inside, he lay atop the bat, ball in mouth until Chris agreed to play the game again. The modified game of catch seemed to satisfy both dog and handler.

...just waitin' for a ball game
Courtesy of Chris Bracco

Between games, Vago dropped his beloved ball everywhere. He dropped it in his water bowl, behind the couch, on the coffee table, on the dinner table and once with a great splash into the toilet bowl causing a gigantic overflow that flooded Chris's home.

Idle game time was curtailed when in January, 1998, Chris and Vago joined the K-9 Unit and officially hit the street.

"This was probably the greatest feeling in the world. I was in a marked police K-9 vehicle with a young stud, K-9 Vago, just waiting to put him into action."

That action came quickly. The Endicott Police Department, a neighboring police agency, did not have a K-9 Unit at that time, so Chris and Vago were dispatched to provide mutual aid. The neighboring department had seized a large amount of cash recovered during a drug raid, but at that time there were legal technicalities in claiming it. If a narcotics dog indicated on the money alerting to the odor of the narcotics, it made it far easier to legally seize the money. A small agency like Endicott didn't have a large drug-seizure fund, which would allow it to purchase much-needed equipment, so they were really counting on getting a positive indication "by dog" so they could keep the cash. So the department devised a test to prove that the dog could identify the correct bag.

The investigators placed several bags inside one of their interview rooms and told Chris that one of the bags held the drug money, and the other bags were controls with cash that was uninvolved with the case. He was asked to have Vago sniff all of the bags. Chris was extremely nervous, haunted by the persistent thought that he and Vago had never trained for such a specialized task. A lot was riding on Vago's successful performance. Despite his apprehensive state, Chris proceeded with Vago by first showing him his tennis ball. With a swift arc of his arm, Chris pretended to throw the ball into the room. Bright and alert, Vago entered the room to look for his ball and circled the room's interior passing by and ignoring several bags. Momentarily forgetting about his ball, he suddenly pounced on a paper bag sitting on a desk. Chris watched anxiously as Vago attacked the bag wildly clawing and ripping at its contents. He worked like an old pro, and the officers watching behind him diligently trying to contain their excitement immediately became both ecstatic and relieved. They confirmed that the dog had chosen the correct bag, and Chris rewarded Vago by giving him his tennis ball. Chris had not been nearly as sure of himself as Vago had been, and his doubts were obviously ill-founded.

"I walked out of there with a high that is difficult to describe. I had nailed my first call."

Chris's trainers had told him early on that Vago was way ahead of him in terms of grasping K-9 usage. They joked that if the dog could drive, he wouldn't need Chris at all. Chris had seen the phenomenon before when new handlers were given great dogs whereby the dogs' confidence and ability initially carried their not-so-confident handlers. It took time for the handlers to "catch up." Now he was in that same position.

That first year flew by and with the passage of time, Chris and Vago gained valuable experience responding to K-9 calls.

"To this day, I firmly believe that the best training for a police dog is a street call. There is no way to duplicate the rush of adrenaline and excitement in the air and most importantly, the human elation that is passed on to the dog when he succeeds."

The time working together fine-tuned a psychological component that allowed Vago and Chris to think as one, each one feeding off the other's energy, mood and assessment of the situations they found themselves in.

"The adrenaline in the air starts with a scent a dog picks up coming from the handler. They know when we're driving on a hot call versus a routine call. It's also my mannerisms. I'm nervous, moving faster, talking faster and my voice changes. An animal picks up on this. There is also the scent of fear from me, which is good fear. Then there is the suspect's odors, most importantly fear, which I believe Vago thrived on."

Even off the job, Vago read Chris's feelings.

"Vago could also sense when I was happy for the same reasons. My voice when I praised him changed, and there are probably scents I kicked off when I was relieved and secure after being stressed. If you don't have these emotions that kick off scents, the dog won't kick in. That's why they say that the dogs are often spitting images of their handlers. Lax, apathetic handlers equal dogs that are nothing special. So it is the scents that the dogs smell, coupled with the physical characteristics of the handler, that change as situations change."

On days when Chris was upset about something, merely thinking about that issue while Vago was in the car caused Vago's demeanor to change. One look could tell Chris that Vago was concerned or wondering if Chris was mad at him. His ears fell back slightly, and he appeared submissive. Chris was his leader, and he depended on Chris for everything.

"He was always studying me and reading me to see what was up," Chris remembered, once more visualizing the familiar canine image.

In March of 1999, a lot was up. Chris was assigned to the day shift and was out patrolling his post at 1:00 p.m. when he got a call that would lead to, hands down, his greatest and most intense moment as a handler. He was routinely driving south on a two-lane street that connected a seedy section of downtown to a south-side residential area. Chris cruised slowly past apartment complexes and multiple-family dwellings punctuated by scattered single-family dwellings. He had been accustomed to seeing street people wandering downtown, but on this occasion he looked up to see that strangely enough, a vagrant was walking from the nicer residential area back towards downtown. Chris had seen the male earlier in the day exiting an alley in a questionable part of downtown, and now it appeared the man had traveled a good distance. Incongruent too, was the fact that the man carried with him three nice leather bags that looked exceedingly out of place. Taking a closer look, Chris could see the top of a VCR sticking out of one of the pieces of luggage, and the bags all appeared to be full of electronics.

From Chris's side view mirror, he noticed the man picking up his pace abruptly turning and quickly walking in the opposite direction. Chris swung his car around in a U-turn in traffic, but by the time he was headed back north the man was gone. Figuring that he must have stepped onto the grounds of an apartment complex just off the street Chris continued to pursue him.

Growing even more suspicious, Chris exited his vehicle and walked into the apartment complex where he had last seen the individual. There, Chris asked a maintenance worker if he had seen the suspect, and the man pointed towards the rear of the complex.

"He went that way," the man said.

Chris ran to the rear of the building and there in the grass sat the luggage, but there was still no trace of the man. Chris opened the three bags and saw electronics, video games, money and seemingly all the fruits of a recent burglary. With that discovery, he ran back to his car to deploy Vago.

Still a relatively new handler, Chris held Vago's tracking lead in his hand and let the dog run free as they made their way around the building to the luggage. In retrospect, it was one of those incidents where the dog was still in charge instead of the other way around, the kind of memory that rookie cops and all handlers remember well.

Moving quickly and freely, Vago sped past the luggage and without warning ran over to and down a steep embankment. The grassy hill that ran from the rear of the apartment complex was fifteen-feet up and then another fifteen-feet down as it sloped towards the riverbank. Another seventy-five yards of river bank ran between the hill and the deep river. Vago continued to run east along the river bank before Chris could recall him. Fearless, the dog raced straight for the river. Seeing Vago disappear, Chris realized that he had no control of the dog, and he regretted that he had not initially hooked Vago's tracking lead onto his excited partner's collar.

Minutes passed like an eternity, and Vago was nowhere to be seen. Growing more nervous and bewildered, Chris ran several hundred yards down towards the river. His concern was so great that he hadn't even taken the time to use his police radio. Instead, he spent every second trying to locate Vago. At a loss as to what he should do next, he stood quietly on the hill for a moment and stared at the brownish river that rhythmically lapped at the bank's edge. The muddy Susquehanna River, two-hundred-yards wide, ran through the city intersecting with the Chenango River downtown which ran south along the length of city. The current was steadily flowing, and apprehensive Chris found no comfort listening to the steady rush of the moving water.

His mind raced imagining what could have taken place out of his sight. He could visualize Vago jumping into the treacherous river after the fleeing suspect. He had never taken Vago swimming at all. He was not even sure the dog could swim. The current of the river looked intimidating, and it would have been extremely difficult for a dog to survive its power. The river ran east for miles and miles, and there was no telling how far a struggling dog caught in its wrath would travel.

Chris had never known such panic. He took off running along the murky river.

"Vago, come!" he screamed over and over.

There was no response—only the constant flow of the river echoed back to him.

Chris strained his eyes to look further down the embankment through sparse leafless trees and along the damp ground anchoring clumps of dead grass and the remnants of the end of a cold winter. He focused on the river's fifteen-foot expanse to locate the man or dog helplessly bobbing in the swift-moving current, but he could no longer see either.

"What if the guy drown Vago or he, himself, drown in the river's depths, and now Vago was floundering in the current going down river trying to stay afloat?" Chris thought, as he tried to erase the image from his mind as quickly as it formed there.

As he ran faster and faster, seemingly breathing heavier with each stride, a nearly paralyzing fear overtook him. But Chris continued to make his way east along the river bank driven to find his dog. With some relief, he began to see fresh footprints and to his even greater relief, he soon spotted little paw prints that followed them in the squishy mud.

"Good boy, Vago," he thought.

Somewhat comforted at the sign, his mood changed from one of abject fear to measured relief and optimism. Only then, did Chris grab his police radio to call for assistance indicating that his K-9 partner was chasing a burglary suspect along the riverbank and to request a perimeter. He added the admonition to the responding units that they should use caution, as there was a police dog running loose.

After making the call, Chris traveled another quarter-mile, and every so often he saw a human footprint with paw print impressions in the mud following closely behind. Through his radio came the call that someone reported a dog chasing a male in the area.

"To this day, I'm not sure who called in that report of what they saw and where they saw the chase, but I remember thinking at the time, 'I sure hope Vago is chasing the suspect!'"

As he drew near a brushy wooded area, Chris could see the silhouette of someone running through the thickets. Just behind the moving figure, he saw his partner bouncing up and down bounding through the brush like a spring lamb. Then he saw both the suspect and Vago emerge from a patch of prickly brush and head across a creek. Vago was in hot pursuit and sensing the close proximity of the dog to him, the suspect abruptly jumped into the nearby cold creek and paddled across to other side. Without a moment's hesitation, Vago followed, jumping in with a loud splash and quickly swimming across behind his prey. Chris watched helplessly from the embankment.

"Get 'im!" he yelled from where he stood giving the dog's bite command.

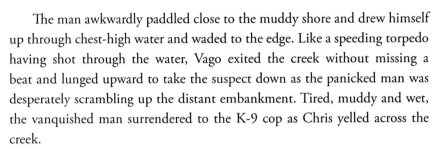

The man awkwardly paddled close to the muddy shore and drew himself up through chest-high water and waded to the edge. Like a speeding torpedo having shot through the water, Vago exited the creek without missing a beat and lunged upward to take the suspect down as the panicked man was desperately scrambling up the distant embankment. Tired, muddy and wet, the vanquished man surrendered to the K-9 cop as Chris yelled across the creek.

"Don't move!" he called to the weary man, who obeyed him immediately.

The man instinctively knew that any motion or noise would trigger Vago to bite, so he remained completely still lying on the cold ground. Then Chris cupped his hands to his mouth and commanded Vago.

"Down!" Chris yelled to him from across the creek

Vago looked across the creek assuredly at him and then looked at the suspect. Vago knew the down position well that he used to guard and did not need to be told twice. He responded immediately and lowered himself to the cold muddy ground where he was content, yet serious and still all business.

Arriving officers on Chris's side of the creek wore heavy bulletproof vests and gun belts, and they carried walkie talkies. After a brief discussion, they decided that there was no way any of them was going to cross the deep creek. It was freezing, the water was chest high and their cumbersome equipment would make it impossible to cross. They did not dare take off their gun belts not knowing if the suspect was armed. It was up to the dog to hold him.

The most expeditious thing to do was to radio for other units to approach the creek from the opposite side. Minutes seemed like hours as they held their collective breath and waited for the units to arrive. All they could do was stare across the watery expanse and trust the dog's training. Five minutes later, back-up arrived on the other side of creek. The suspect lay motionless and for the full time before the units arrived Vago never moved. Fear of the K-9 kept the man in his place. Chris had not been able to see what transpired during Vago's pursuit, but from what he could judge as the man was taken away, the dog had not bitten the suspect. He saw no discernable evidence of bite wounds on the man's winter clothing.

"I was totally surprised to see Vago go into that creek after the suspect. I was new at K-9, and every day was like my first day at work."

When he was finally arrested, the man would not admit to anything other than to say he had been smoking crack alongside the creek when the dog approached. The dog prints had been sporadic rather than following a straight line behind the footprints. Chris would never know just how Vago pursued the man, and Vago wasn't talking.

After the man was taken away, Chris called for Vago, who eagerly leapt into the creek and paddled back across. Dripping wet, he stood creek-side and with a hard shake, he splattered water from his wet coat. As Vago bounded into the police car, Chris thought how thankful he was to have his dog back. Chris slid behind the wheel and cranked up the heat in the car to warm Vago on that cold March day as they headed back to the luggage that was left behind the apartment complex. Thankfully, it was still there. Chris secured the luggage and its contents in his car trunk and began looking for the scene of the burglary.

Several blocks away, he found a home that had been entered by someone breaking its rear window. The police were able to contact the resident who responded and identified the luggage and items as his personal property. The captured wet suspect was charged with burglary in the second degree and was eventually sentenced to a lengthy prison term.

The creek incident proved that Vago really was something special. He showed initiative and a drive that could not be taught. That intangible quality that eludes many dogs was always palpable for Vago.

"You can't instill in training the qualities he demonstrated on that call. Nor could I possibly have prepared myself for that type of situation. As the years went by, every call had its own twists and variables. I just remember thinking after those calls, 'thank God for Vago.' Just as Vago arrived at my home as a puppy and independently went into another room to sleep, he confidently left my side to track down a violent criminal. Vago was put on this earth to be a police dog."

Several months later, the team was involved in another memorable K-9 call that started with highly-charged street theatre and ended with a dramatic apprehension. On a warm June day, Chris and members of his unit were participating in cadaver training alongside a small lake in the adjoining town of Vestal, New York, where the dogs were trained to find drown individuals or crime victims. A call came in that the drug unit had been involved in a vehicle pursuit in which two of the operators threw a large amount of cocaine out the moving car's window. It was later found in a residential front yard. After discarding the illegal drugs, they crashed their car and fled. Steve Ward, handling his striking red and black German shepherd dog, Brando, participated in the cadaver training with Chris and Vago, and now both teams were called to respond. Brando and Vago were both alpha males who had to be kept apart, but duty called, and two K-9 squad cars roared up to the Practical Bible College after information developed that one of the suspects was last seen running into a dormitory.

As the cars arrived, Chris felt as though they had just pulled into the filming of a movie. Media outlets that had scanners monitored the police chase that resulted in the suspect fleeing and entering the college. Reporters and cameramen mingling with police chiefs anxiously paced outside the college waiting for the dog units to arrive.

Just before noon, with sirens wailing and police lights blazing, the dogs arrived, and all cameras turned to film them. With great drama, the handlers unloaded the dogs from their cars. Photographers, as aggressive as Hollywood paparazzi, followed the dogs at close range as the two handlers tried valiantly to keep their alpha dogs a safe distance apart. The officers spoke with an array of police chiefs standing there holding court discussing what should be done. The chiefs requested that both dogs conduct a search inside.

"It's not normal to allow two dogs to be unleashed into same building. We did it because we were new, and the chiefs requested this."

The plan was unconventional at best and a recipe for disaster at worst, since both dogs were alpha males that didn't get along. And now they would roam together in the same building while their handlers waited outside. What was appearing to be a dramatic and impressive police operation could in a heartbeat quickly disintegrate into a fiasco reminiscent of an episode of the Keystone Cops.

Both apprehensive that the two dogs might erupt into a fight before the rolling cameras and appear as a noteworthy segment on the nightly news, Steve and Chris reluctantly and warily took their dogs to the front door. The chiefs' decision was firm. The dorm was large enough they reasoned that both dogs could be utilized, so a plan was in place. Steve and Chris hoped for the best, and the handlers felt somewhat more at ease deploying their dogs on different floors. Chris went up to third floor and called out his announcement.

"Binghamton Police K-9. You are under arrest. Surrender yourself now or I will release the dog!"

Procedure dictated waiting thirty seconds.

"This is your final warning! Binghamton Police K-9. You are under arrest. Surrender yourself now or I will release the dog!"

With no reply, he gave the next command to Vago.

"Go get 'im!"

Chris cut Vago loose from the third floor stairwell, and Steve released Brando on the first floor. So far, so good. Vago ran down the tiled hallway, and about midway he stopped abruptly and stood up on his hind legs sniffing the walls between two rooms.

"He's got 'im," Chris confidently told the investigators behind him.

They obviously didn't believe Chris and asked that he and Vago go down to the second floor and begin a search, feeling that a room-by-room search would be more thorough. But although Chris acceded to their wishes, he thought, "Why? We know where he is."

Following their orders, Chris and Vago descended to the second floor where a lot of the dorm rooms were open. As Chris stood further down the hallway and watched, he saw Vago trot out of a room he had just explored. And much to his surprise, Chris watched as Vago's old nemesis, Brando, happily trotted right out behind him. Then they went into the next room and just like two old buddies, they came out again without incident.

"You just can't make this up. No aggression, no problems--both were all business."

After more fruitless searching, Chris grabbed Vago as Brando wandered off elsewhere in the building. Eventually, the dogs bumped into each other again without incident on the second floor. The investigators and Chris then devised a plan and decided to make a K-9 announcement in the doorway of each room and release Vago if they got no response. Vago entered dozens and dozens of rooms, each time running in and about-facing and then running right back out realizing there was nothing there for him. On the side of caution, Chris checked inside the first couple of rooms after Vago exited, not completely trusting the dog's judgment, but he caught himself, recovered his complete trust in Vago and stayed out in the hall watching the dog work.

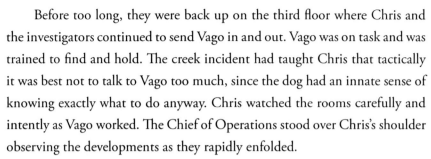

Before too long, they were back up on the third floor where Chris and the investigators continued to send Vago in and out. Vago was on task and was trained to find and hold. The creek incident had taught Chris that tactically it was best not to talk to Vago too much, since the dog had an innate sense of knowing exactly what to do anyway. Chris watched the rooms carefully and intently as Vago worked. The Chief of Operations stood over Chris's shoulder observing the developments as they rapidly enfolded.

At a room in the middle of the hallway, Vago ran in almost routinely and turned around quickly as he had done so many times in other rooms and then ran back towards the door. But this time something was different. This time, he paused and stopped completely. Then he circled back into the room. Chris watched as Vago threw his furry head back and began to air scent. With his nose still high in the air, he jumped at a wooden cabinet with his front legs pushing it towards the rear wall. The cabinet moved, but it didn't fall back against the wall as one would expect. Chris looked back over his shoulder and caught the awed expression on the face of his Chief of Operations.

"I think he's got im!" Chris said excitedly.

Vago stuck his head around the cabinet where he uncovered the man he had always known was there. The dog bolted forward and grabbed hold of the suspect's arm as the hiding man lay curled up on the floor. Chris could hear Steve yelling enthusiastically in the hallway knowing Vago had his man.

"Then the cavalry came into the room and pulled the cabinet back and piled on the bad guy like they do in football when someone fumbles."

The atmosphere was electric. Instantaneously, men scrambled, and bodies flew everywhere in the thrill of the moment. The subject was arrested and after a trial was sentenced to approximately fifteen years in prison. The search and capture that had begun with so much Hollywood drama had ended without incident, and the alpha dogs proved they were up to the task when necessity demanded it. Later encounters might find them at odds again, but for the moment, two happy handlers took their well-behaved dogs home after a stunning success.

Patrolmen Chris Bracco and Steve Ward pose at the Binghamton City Hall with their "cooperative" dogs, K-9s Vago and Brando.

Courtesy of the Binghamton Police Department K-9 Unit

Vago was at the pinnacle of his success. Bright, determined, agile and mature, he fulfilled all of Chris's expectation of a "good dog." And with each success another case came their way to further test his abilities.

But a call on July 12, 2001, tragically changed the quality of Vago's life, and afterward he would never walk or run with the speed and joy he had always known. It was a warm summer evening, and Chris was accompanied by Officer John Ryan as they rode on routine patrol. Just before midnight, they stopped for coffee and then drove along a quiet residential street. Off to the side, Chris observed a male nonchalantly walking along with a female down the sidewalk. At that time, the department had active warrants out for a dangerous criminal being sought for attempted murder and robbery. Chris knew the criminal's face and ever watchful and cautious, he focused on the male on the street more closely. As the man saw Chris slow up in the patrol car, he quickly turned his face away. Feeling some assurance that the man could be the one he sought, Chris commented to John that the walker looked like the criminal who was wanted. John agreed so they pulled over to the curb where John exited the passenger side closest to the sidewalk to make a positive identification.

Like a shot, the subject took off running up the street with John following closely behind. Chris bolted from the car, called Vago out and went around the car to the sidewalk. Vago was eager to join the chase and galloped up the street passing John as both turned right and ran onto the sidewalk of a bridge. Chris looked ahead watching the chase under the white glow of the bridge's long line of illuminating streetlights. The dog and suspect ran about thirty yards on the sidewalk of the bridge when the man reached for the top of a five-foot barrier wall that ran the length of the bridge. To Chris's amazement, he leapt over it disappearing into the night with the dog following right behind him.

"Vago leapt over the wall after him, and I think my heart stopped. All I could see was the flow of the black Chenango River below."

The fall was about thirty feet. In quick pursuit, Vago had pushed off the top of wall and both he and the suspect landed with a thud below on a hard dirt surface covered with small rocks and weeds. The glittering light from the streetlamps reflected off the dark moving water as the reality of what had just happened hit the dog and the suspect. Now on the river bank, precariously close to the water, they were just fifteen yards from the river, and the current was swiftly flowing south.

Frozen with fear and dread, Chris quickly gathered his wits about him and ran back towards the street from which they had come and stumbled down a steep hill to the river bank. As he drew closer, he could hear not only the ominous sound of the dark moving river but the distinct cry of his beloved dog. In the shadows of the bridge, Chris saw Vago circling the suspect who was lying on his stomach motionless at the river's edge.

Pathetically, Vago held his front right leg up, and Chris could see his paw dangling loose, obviously dislodged from its joint. Having landed with such force on his right paw, Chris could tell that Vago sustained a bad break, yet the vigilant dog hopped on three legs around the motionless suspect on the ground, a strong sense of duty overcoming severe pain. Other officers arrived and stood by as an ambulance was called for the escaping suspect. It turned out that he was fine and was tended to by the ambulance medics and treated for minor wounds. Vago did not fare as well.

*After racing in pursuit across the East Clinton Street Bridge, Vago leapt
down from the back, southwest corner sustaining a leg injury.*

Courtesy of Binghamton Police Identification Unit

Whining pitifully, helpless Vago knew he was hurt and continuously cried
out, badly needing Chris's help. He let Chris approach him, and his officer
scooped him up tenderly and carried him up the forty-foot hill to the car.

"Okay," Chris whispered to him gently as he labored under the dog's
weight, "Goooooood boy," he repeated soothingly trying to calm his dog and
ease the pain.

Staggering up the hill in the dark with the heavy dog proved very difficult,
but Chris was determined to carry him as slowly as possible to prevent further
trauma and pain.

"I have never felt so helpless. I tried to get him into his kennel, but he
needed both front legs to stabilize his body due to the angle needed for him
to climb in. I'll never forget the scream he let out."

It was past midnight, and Headquarters was able to find a vet who agreed
to meet them at her office in fifteen minutes. Vago's leg was broken in two
places. The doctor put a make-shift splint on it and made an appointment with

a bone specialist in Ithaca, New York. Then she gave Vago pain medication and sent him home that night.

After several days, Chris drove an hour to Ithaca to consult the veterinarian there. It was the first of many trips he would make there over the years for treatment and follow-up surgery.

Vago underwent surgery on the injured leg that week, and the surgeon placed screws and a metal plate inside the shattered leg. The dog had half of his body shaved, and his injured leg was cast so that it could not reach the ground.

"I felt guilty," said Chris sadly. "No one could assure me that Vago could run or work again."

The days and months crept by slowly, and Vago gradually learned to move around quite well on three legs. Three months later, he went back to the specialist, and the cast was finally removed. Vago's scrawny pale leg was in the shape of hook. His paw turned inward toward his body, and the misshapen paw never would straighten out fully again. The paw remained stiff from metal and screws, and due to the bones being fused together, Vago lost the range of motion where the paw would normally bend. Although the specialist told Chris that the leg should loosen up a bit, it was really never the same. Vago was good about letting Chris massage the deformed leg as he was instructed, but the dog was reluctant to put pressure on it.

The out-of-commission police dog learns to walk on his bad leg.

Nurse Dana watches over her patient.

K-9 Vago poses with the gifts and cards he received after his injury.

Chris and Vago accept an award from Binghamton City Council just before K-9 Vago retuned to work.

All pictures courtesy of Chris Bracco

The vets told Chris he'd have to get Vago moving in order to speed up the recovery, so Chris decided to bring him back to training. The dog that had been top-notch and agile on so many prior visits to the familiar training facility entered more cautiously, nowhere close to his former image. But in no time, memories of his training kicked in, and Vago seemed to forget about his leg and started putting his paw down during exercises. It was a joyful sight to see. Within weeks, he was moving pretty well but would never walk or run without a noticeable limp. But even with his disability, Vago was still faster than a human, and Chris got the green light to take him back to work.

The city gave Vago a warm welcome back that included a press conference and lots of recognition. Chris received a framed certified Resolution of City Council honoring Vago and himself for Outstanding Performance. It acknowledged and formally commended them both for bravery and valor in apprehending a dangerous criminal. The Council also wished Vago a full and speedy recovery. Best of all for Vago, he received a gift package including a monstrous bone that he loved dearly.

During his first call back, Vago dug out a drug stash from the siding of a home, and all Chris's worries about him being able to function started to subside. Unfortunately, throughout the remainder of his career Vago had problems with his leg. During certain weather conditions and on some other days, he carried his bad leg up off the ground and operated on only three legs. But during a call, probably because of the rush of adrenaline, he put the leg down as much as possible. His desire to work overcame the impediment.

Nearly a year later, Chris responded to a call in a downtown residential area of a male attacking a female in the street with a knife. As he arrived on the scene with rookie officer, Anthony Wood, he could see that the male wielded a knife in one hand and a sinister-looking elephant hook, its sharp pointed end and catching curved side hook at the ready, in the other. He could see the man slicing at the female with the razor-sharp knives, so Chris instinctively grabbed for Vago as he exited the vehicle. Just as Chris released Vago towards the male, the maniacal man swung back with the hook towards Chris and Anthony. In a blinding fury, Vago lunged upward attaching himself to the subject's back, and he held on tightly. Wood maced the man, temporarily rendering him sightless, and in that instant, Vago swung him hard to the ground. The knives and the elephant hook, as dangerous as they were, were no match for the gripping teeth that Vago sunk into the man's back. The man quickly realized he was defeated, and he surrendered, was handcuffed and led away.

"I really don't know how this call would have ended without Vago, and we will never know.

Chris and the dog with the permanently-injured leg received a commendation for that call. More were soon to follow.

In July of 2002, almost a year to the day from Vago's injury, the team was dispatched to a south side home for a possible burglary in progress. Upon arrival, the shift's acting captain told Chris that the first officer responding was met by two males exiting the residence pointing handguns at him. The captain also stated that the males fled in a vehicle, and the female who called 911 was believed to still be inside. No one knew what had happened prior to their arrival, but the officers assumed it was something bad and deciding to err on the side of caution, the captain wanted the dog to enter the home alone first.

Chris made several announcements warning that a K-9 was going to be released. No one answered from inside the nicely-kept single-family home. Chris gave Vago a pat on his side and sent the slightly limping dog into the home and waited in the doorway. After about thirty seconds, Vago appeared on the landing of a stairwell between the first and second floors. He looked at Chris momentarily and then made his way back up to the second floor out of view. Vago was completely silent, which was extremely strange. It did not fit his normal predictable pattern of behavior. Normally, he would either bark or there would be some commotion indicating he found someone. It was hard to know what to make of it, but Chris ventured a guess.

"I believe he has found someone," Chris told the captain, judging from the dog's reaction, odd as it was.

Together, Chris and the captain went up to the second floor proceeding cautiously. Vago met them, leading the way gingerly yet softly. He entered a bedroom and approached a blanket on the floor. Softly, he sniffed at the blanket careful not to disturb its contents. When Chris entered the room, he saw Vago looking down at the blanket. Then he began to circle it. To everyone's surprise, inside was an infant, alive and well. Vago appeared to be just letting the officers know it was there and was most anxious to continue his search. An officer scooped up the infant and took it back downstairs and outside.

Vago's compassion seemed most human-like following an inner sense he had of the fragility and the circumstance of the small child. He was trained to go into a building, locate human scent and engage, and that he had done but in a way that was seldom seen by K-9 units.

The officers cleared the rest of the second floor and then the first floor and finally arrived at a door in the kitchen leading to the basement. Chris creaked open the door and made several more K-9 announcements, but again no one responded. All was eerily quiet. He released Vago, and the dog eagerly ran downstairs to search, steady on his three good legs.

A short time elapsed, but the dog did not return. The officers carefully eased down the stairs into the basement and continued into a dimly-lit finished lower-level living room. Vago stood quietly over a dead female lying on the bloody carpet. Next to the woman was a dead adolescent child no older than thirteen. Both had gunshot wounds and appeared to have been executed. Vago was up on his back legs air scenting above the deceased victims indicating that he had human scent, but he was looking for someone else to apprehend. It was as though he got to their scent and something wasn't right so he didn't engage them. He was circling around them nose in air trying to figure out what just happened and where there was a live body to apprehend.

217

A mother and her child were murdered inside of their residence by intruders, and a sensitive dog had found them. He had not alerted in his normal animated way. He failed to bark as he normally would have done, and he sought no reward.

Two suspects were eventually caught and sent to prison for the brutal slayings, and the images of that night would forever be indelibly imprinted in the memories of those who responded.

"I will never forget that night, specifically the manner in which Vago treated the infant and the deceased was, again, almost human-like."

It was more validation of the superior quality of an animal named Vago. He was a dog that had different layers. He could match whatever situation he and Chris were involved in with the appropriate response. He was super aggressive when he needed to be, but he was also super smart. Time and time again during foot pursuits Vago ran past officers to catch a fleeing criminal, always one step ahead of the humans. And when he needed to, he could exhibit exquisitely sensitive emotion that would not be expected of a dog.

As a handler in an urban area, Chris had frequently seen the presence of other animals, both domestic and wild on K-9 calls he made and knew what a distraction the animals could be. Vago was disinterested in other animals and able to stay on task in those situations and his apathy regarding other animals was a benefit. But not all animals could be so easily ignored.

Detecting narcotics meant that Vago and Chris spent a good deal of time in less-than-desirable city locations. Much of the team's time was spent frequenting perpetually dismal neighborhoods, decrepit and depressing, with shabby buildings symbolizing all the gray hopelessness of the downtrodden areas. The crime-ridden streets teeming with all the vices that reflected the bleak surroundings kept the police returning repeatedly. Dog fighting, the blight of so many similar areas was no stranger to the urban area. In such areas, vicious pit bulls were bred to fight and inflict fatal wounds upon each other, all for their owners' financial gain. The ferocity and viciousness of the pit bulls was well known, and a chance encounter with one could cause an intruder serious harm or death.

Several blocks from the city's ghetto and notorious drug area sat a worn residential area where Chris and Vago met up with federal agents at a rundown apartment suspected of being a drug house where the agents were executing a search warrant.

Upon Chris's arrival, the agents warned him at the door that a number of pit bulls were running loose inside the apartment, and although the men had fared alright, they questioned bringing Vago in. Knowing that Vago pretty much ignored other animals Chris was not overly concerned, but he cautiously peeked inside to have a look to assess the attitude of the pit bulls. A slow smile eclipsed into a broad grin as he saw six pit bull puppies romping and hiding, oblivious of their shabby surroundings and just being puppies. Feeling less anxious about the situation, Chris deployed Vago who characteristically ignored all of them.

But the puppies wanted to be part of the action. Organized as well as a group of playful puppies could be they lined up behind Vago and went on the drug search. Trailing along behind the serious drug detector, the yipping puppies marched along on their tiny legs double time trying to keep up with Vago's longer strides. New tiny recruits and soldiers in the war against drugs, they pranced along with great zeal. Like ducklings imprinted on their first image, the pups fell in naturally behind the big dog. They knew better than to nip at him, even playfully, but they took great delight in jumping at him and annoying him.

From room to room, the yapping high-pitched canine parade led by Vago made its rounds. Finally, the dog and his tumbling entourage entered a bedroom where agents were standing. Vago began to scratch around the area of the bed and then stuck his nose between the mattresses on the bed. He caught the edge of a large freezer bag of marijuana and pulled at it frantically. He had found what he was looking for. Chris handed it to the agents who were most happy to receive it. When Vago was rewarded with his ball, the puppies jumped up on him with glee and continued to follow him everywhere as co-victors on the hunt. Vago kept moving away from them, but mission accomplished, he seemed to finally relax and enjoy the attention. The dog returned to his squad car, and the puppies were left behind with other residents after executing their very first drug search.

During a later call, Vago acquired his nickname, "the furry missile," given to him by members of the night shift. He may not have been able to run as well as he used to, but he could fly. He responded with Chris to a hotel for a report of an armed robbery of a front desk clerk. While canvassing the area, Chris was waived down by a man working hotel security who followed the suspect out of the hotel to a residential street.

It was late at night, well past midnight, when Chris quickly got his K-9 out of the car and sent him into the yard. As night shift officers watched, Vago chased the male out of the yard and across a street. They both disappeared out of view once again going down towards the dreaded river bank. Vago closed a gap of thirty yards between himself and the suspect firing like a missile locking on accurately to the target. It was as though he had been launched from a cannon, and those who saw it would not forget it.

As Chris ran towards the area, he could hear the suspect shouting. Unlike most suspects who usually surrender or submit, this subject decided to fight Vago. He continually punched Vago in his side and screamed at him. Yelling, kicking, rolling and grunting, the man wrestled wildly with the thrashing dog his guttural tones intimidating to no one, especially not to Vago. The dog had seen and heard much better when he was trained as police officers posing as decoys accustomed him to the intimidating shouts and mannerisms of a suspect.

"Vago dug into the moment, and I could tell he was having a good time. Vago had such intense fight drive that I think he'd been waiting for this guy for years."

It was a cause the man was unlikely to win. The suspect finally was taken to the ground by Vago and had no fight left in him. All he got for his trouble was an arrest for robbery and trip to the state prison.

On cold nights or often when Chris was tired, he drove over to the Binghamton Mets stadium parking lot at night to play Vago's favorite game. After letting Vago out of car, he threw the dog's tennis ball deep into the lot. Chris then got back into the driver's seat and closed the door leaving the window rolled down. In the darkness, he watched Vago limp back with his found ball. The happy dog jumped up on driver's door resting his front paws on the opened window's slot. He held the tennis ball tightly in his mouth refusing to let go. Gradually, once again on Vago's terms, he dropped the wet slimy ball onto Chris's lap to initiate the next toss. So many nights, Chris sat face-to-face in the black of night with the dog that held the cherished ball and calculated the time of the drop. The bright searching eyes shone in the darkness so close to his own. The soft pant and the focus of purpose were so distinct there in the quiet twilight hours.

"I remember thinking that someday this would be a memory and that my invincible partner would be no more."

He would enjoy every day and night with Vago for as long as they would have left together.

For all his ferocity, Vago was also a comedian in his own right. He was supposed to stay in his kennel while Chris exited the police car, but Chris always left the cage open with the car's front window open just in case he urgently needed his dog. One night, Chris was inside a convenience store when someone walked in and asked if his dog could drive. The man told Chris that the dog was behind the steering wheel. Curious, Chris walked outside to check, but Vago was in his cage, and Chris paid it no mind.

On several later occasions, people at the scene approached Chris when he was out of the car to tell him that the dog was in the driver's seat. Each time, Chris went to check on him, and every time, he was in his cage.

One night, Chris decided to set him up. He walked into a convenience store that night and positioned himself at a side window at the rear of the store to spy on Vago. Peeking behind a rack of food snacks near the window, Chris observed the dog. Not seeing his handler, Vago slyly left his cage and jumped up into the driver's seat. He was thoroughly enjoying a little freedom, the comfort of a soft warm seat and the luxury to hang out and look into the store when Chris returned to the cash register at the store's counter. Once there, Chris quickly whirled around toward the car, and quick as lightning, he saw Vago jump back into his cage.

"He had been watching me all these times pulling the wool over my eyes."

Vago had been found out, but the game had a good long run before it finally came to an end. The dog was a bit of a trickster and magician all rolled into one, operating in the shadows of his master for a bit of fun, but at the same time keeping careful watch of the man in his life that meant the most to him.

Over time, Vago endured additional surgery on his deformed leg. As the years passed, the selfless dog whose dedication to Chris and the Binghamton Police Department could not be curtailed, even by the limited use of one leg, carried on until he could no longer serve.

When Vago was nine-and-a-half, Chris had to face the uncomfortable thought of retiring his friend. It had always loomed in the distance, but the reality was soon immediate. Chris had pushed out the thought of Vago's retirement that occasionally surfaced in the Mets' parking lot during ball tosses, but Chris's fellow officers envisioned Vago's retirement more clearly with objective eyes. Vago was more often picking up his injured front paw as well as his rear leg during training. The old gentleman in some ways was no longer at the top of his game. Chris could no longer put off the inevitable.

Chris married in 2005, and his new wife, Heather, brought to the marriage of all things, a cat. Memory of Vago's puppy encounter with alley cats never faded, so he maintained a respectful distance from "Brownie" just to be on the safe side.

On Chris's honeymoon, he received a call indicating that a dog was being sold by the Royal Canadian Mounted Police. K-9 Storm was too much dog for his present unit. Chris said he would have to think about it. He spoke with Heather about the talent of Storm and how acceptance of the dog could be a blessing in disguise. With great guilt and still some apprehension, he called back and made arrangements to take the available dog upon his return home.

"I remember feeling, 'how is it possible that something positive feels so negative?'"

Once more, he put the thought out of his mind.

Post-injury, K-9 Vago and friend, Dana, pose with the happy bride and groom.
Courtesy of Chris Bracco

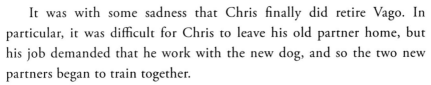

It was with some sadness that Chris finally did retire Vago. In particular, it was difficult for Chris to leave his old partner home, but his job demanded that he work with the new dog, and so the two new partners began to train together.

"Storm was perfect, drive oozing out of everywhere, young, sharp, like a thoroughbred. I remember throwing his ball, and as he raced after it, I cringed with memories of how Vago would pull up lame at times during ball tosses."

On the day when Storm went to work in place of Vago for the first time, Chris brought Storm to the side of his police car in the driveway and opened the rear door. The strong and nimble dog jumped into the back, and as Chris closed the door, he saw Vago on the other side of the fence separating the driveway from the backyard. Vago sat motionless, confused and as sad as a dog could look. As Chris backed out of the driveway and headed down the street, he looked back and could see Vago's eyes following the car.

"All the joy and excitement Vago brought me just nosedived into ultimate sadness. But I knew when I signed up for this work that there was a business side to it."

But Storm proved weak in narcotic detection. All of his accolades and talents were connected to his tracking and apprehension of suspects. With Chris's new role working alongside the Narcotics Task Force, that had to change. Chris worked diligently with Storm trying to bring him up to speed and to Vago's distinguished level, but Storm wasn't ready for the rigors of live narcotics searches in an urban environment.

Chris made a command decision. He kept Storm in a cage in the middle of his Jeep Grand Cherokee and after emptying out the back end of the vehicle of cargo and equipment, he found a perfect place for his old friend, Vago. Trusty Vago would ride with them and handle actual drug searches, while Chris continued to train Storm.

One night, Chris responded to a residential side street in a downtown neighborhood known for drug activity after being called to assist members of the street crime unit. Officers had just apprehended a male after a foot chase on the street after observing the male in possession of a bag with suspected narcotics.

Upon searching the suspect, no drugs were found and the feeling was that he must have tossed the baggie during the chase. Chris walked towards his Jeep to get his K-9 to deploy. Two dogs awaited him. He reached for Storm but hesitated. It was no time for training, and the job needed to go to the dog that could get it done. He popped open the rear hatch and helped lift, and then place, aged but professional Vago onto the street. Chris grabbed a tennis ball, and the old partners walked towards the driveways where the chase began.

Vago went into several driveways and backyards searching and within minutes he was scratching at an empty plastic baggie lying in the grass. Vago then indicated on a chain link fence next to the baggie which separated two driveways. When the suspect threw the plastic bag, the drug pieces fell out and flew farther into the air into an adjacent driveway. Chris looked over the fence, and there on the other side were five small plastic knotted wraps of suspected cocaine. Chris threw Vago his tennis ball.

"Nice work, Vago," he thought.

"The street crime guys were happy and this strengthened their case. I walked Vago back to Jeep, opened the hatch and carefully lifted him into vehicle. That was Vago's final call for service, and he showed Storm "what was what" and how to be a police dog for the Binghamton Police Department and for his handler, whom he had served for years with great honor and loyalty."

Storm was soon up to speed and riding with Chris alone during their shifts. Vago watched them every day load into the car and head down the street. That aspect never got any easier for Chris.

The two dogs were kept separate at home. Chris felt that if left alone together, Storm could hurt Vago, but Vago kept close tabs on Storm who was kept in a kennel in the backyard. Vago, the senior, had the run of the fenced yard, and he often barked at Storm but then curled up next to the cage where both dogs slept peacefully side-by-side.

"I truly believe Vago loved Storm and understood what had happened in his own life."

Storm was quite the magician, and one night going down to laundry room which had a doggie door used by Vago, Chris was surprised to find Storm there. He had found a way out of his kennel and was in the laundry room with Vago getting along famously. Chris's dogs were full of surprises.

Vago had a tender and gentle side, and it was sometimes shown when others least expected it. After the dog finally retired, Heather revealed a secret about Vago. When Chris got up and walked to the bathroom during the night, she confessed that Vago entered their bedroom on the sly, jumped up on the bed and gave her his canine kisses. As soon as Chris came out of bathroom, the dog would hear him, and as silently as a ghost slipping though a wall, Vago disappeared from sight with Chris never the wiser that he had visited. Never once in all the times he played the game did Chris catch him.

"He was a gentleman for a dog and truly respected in the law enforcement community. I'm proud to say that Vago set the standard very high for police dogs."

Vago's love of his job was transferred to his love for Heather and daughter, Emma. He followed their every move and to Vago, Heather became his new handler. Heather was extremely special in her care for aging Vago. She took him on daily walks in the neighborhood ending in the park that he loved. She brushed him, played with him and kept him company while Chris was away at work for hours on end, which gave tremendous relief to Chris knowing is old friend was in such good and loving hands. In return, Vago taught their new dog, Timmy, a Chihuahua mix, how to walk on a lead still demonstrating a high standard until the very end.

From day one, when as an independent feisty pup, he pulled fiercely on the burlap tug, Vago had been on a mission. Eventually, the elder statesmen of dogs began to fade. He had been "all business" and the very image of uncompromising and unconditional trust. He had served the public well. Finally, his mission was fully accomplished and done so with distinguishable honor. Vago was laid to rest on October 26, 2008.

A portrait one of Binghamton's finest, K-9 Vago...a life well lived.

Courtesy of Debrah H. Muska – Animal Images

"I miss him so much," Chris freely admits. "I feel proud though. Vago was put on earth to be police dog, and he did his job well."

K-9 Gina Marie

"Treasure of the Tidewater"

She is a four-year-old Akita that proudly wears a complimentary Virginia State Trooper plastic badge, yet she has never made an apprehension or participated in a traffic stop. Her handler is a card-carrying member of the Virginia Police Working Dog Association, yet the dog has never walked a beat out on patrol. But K-9 Gina Marie's reputation is such that she is recognized by agencies that normally have a closed and exclusive membership, and all are delighted to make an exception for her.

When Tom Luna, Gina's handler, and his wife, Suzanne, decided to find another dog to join their Labrador mix, Lexis, they wanted a dog who could work in search and rescue. So on a crisp February morning in 2005, Tom drove from his home in Norfolk, Virginia, to a more pastoral setting of small farms surrounded by acres of unplowed fields to reach the home of Akita breeders who lived in the peaceful Virginia countryside. The setting was a perfect locale for any happy dog.

Tom and Gina Marie

Courtesy of Charles Hartman, Cathy L. Benton Photography

cathybenton.com

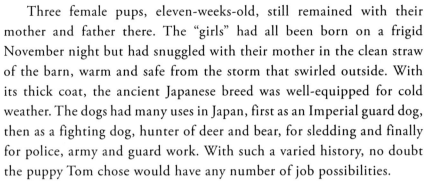

Three female pups, eleven-weeks-old, still remained with their mother and father there. The "girls" had all been born on a frigid November night but had snuggled with their mother in the clean straw of the barn, warm and safe from the storm that swirled outside. With its thick coat, the ancient Japanese breed was well-equipped for cold weather. The dogs had many uses in Japan, first as an Imperial guard dog, then as a fighting dog, hunter of deer and bear, for sledding and finally for police, army and guard work. With such a varied history, no doubt the puppy Tom chose would have any number of job possibilities.

Tom sensed something good was about to happen as he eagerly waited by a big red barn while the breeder went inside and brought out the mother Akita who was then followed by a parade of plump tumbling pups. The mother's kindly face was not unlike a bear, and her thick fur framed it beautifully. As Tom played with the puppies, the mother stood calmly observing. She remained docile and friendly and completely relaxed around the stranger who showed interest in her babies. Unlike many mother animals, she trusted him implicitly with her brood.

Tom knew he had a tough decision to make. How could he ever choose between the little canine bears and take just one home? He asked to see the father of the pups, and soon a large dignified wolf-like dog strode forward with an almost royal aura, revealing a very confident stance and expression. The sheer size of the parents could have made them ferocious or intimidating, but almost as quiet and deferring as the gentle Geishas of their land of heritage, they signaled nothing but serenity.

In the bright sun, surrounded by budding trees, Tom sat watching the pups play in order to garner a bit more knowledge about each dog's personality. He knew the pup he chose would be his for life, and he wanted to choose wisely. As the playful pups leaped and stumbled towards him, he found himself fixated on one with a black mask. Tom then hugged all three pups but then reached for the black-masked puppy. After completing the necessary paperwork, Tom carried his new masked friend to the car, opening the back door and placing the pup on a soft worn sweatshirt on the seat.

"I drove down the gravel driveway with a song in my heart," Tom remembered.

Once on the interstate heading towards Norfolk, Gina Marie quietly stood up on her tiny hind legs on the back seat behind the driver's seat and stretched upward, gently planting a puppy kiss on Tom's neck. She then returned to the soft sweatshirt to curl up and sleep. For the first time, she communicated directly with him, and her tenderness seemed to imply that she was most grateful for being chosen by him.

Suzanne greeted Tom and the pup upon their arrival. She remembered that when she was a young teenager, she worked for a wealthy family in California who had an exquisite German shepherd dog named Gina. The soft baby dog she now held in her hands seemed very worthy of such an honorable name. She felt the dog needed a middle name and decided Marie was a good fit. Gina Marie had an uneventful first night, and for the first two months he owned her, Tom slept beside her in the guest room cementing a strong bond.

Every free moment afterward was spent socializing Gina Marie. Tom knew the City of Norfolk and its brilliant waterfront views well, and he took Gina everywhere. Walking along the downtown waterfront, where he had for so long seen the tugboats and visiting cruise ships glide along effortlessly among rows of sailboats bobbing in the water, his new friend trotted by his side. Merchant ships vied for position in the busy harbor that for so long moored a variety of ships during Norfolk's three-hundred years of naval heritage and maritime history. Cool morning salty breezes, signaling the turn of the tide along the shimmering coastline of the Tidewater State, played with the snapping sails of the sailboats that floated not far from the U.S.S. Wisconsin battleship, which for years graced the sparkling harbor. Tom shared it all with Gina. In the shadow of the hulking Wisconsin they could see the booming guns now silenced, where once they had pounded Japanese positions and installations during the raging battles of WWII. Gina sat tall breathing in the salty air and listening to the plaintive cry of the sea birds that swooped low and dove with great precision into the harbor's water. Living at the site of the world's largest Navy base provided the opportunity to ponder United States power and might first hand.

The USS Wisconsin in the Norfolk harbor
Courtesy of Tom Luna

But power and might did not always necessarily mean large displays of force or an aggressive, intimidating demeanor. It did not always come packaged like the mighty threatening warship in the harbor. Might could tread softly on large but silent paws and quietly move mountains. Tom's new dog was proof of that. He knew that regarding canines, the right mix of genetics and DNA could produce an exceptional dog. As he got to know his new dog, he found that gentle Gina Marie was that exceptional dog, one with solid strength of not only body but spirit. She needed to find her niche, and Tom would lead the way.

Four months later, Tom enrolled Gina in classes with a personal trainer. After successful completion of her "lessons," Tom practiced obedience with her every day and noticed she chose to comply with his commands willingly and not for the reward of a toy or edible treat. Her nature was to please.

Eight months later, they were invited by a Virginia Search and Rescue Organization to a state park where search and rescue dogs practiced, and the candidates were evaluated. When it came time for Gina to be tested, the tester told Tom put her in the sit position and then hand him her leash. Then Tom was directed to turn and act excited with Gina as she sat by the handler's side.

Tom did so and then ran into the woods and hid behind a pine tree. A few moments passed and Gina was sent to find him. She did that willingly, but when Gina was given the same test with a stranger, she showed little interest in the game of hide and seek. After a few futile attempts to rouse her interest, and after encouraging her to locate the strangers, the handler noted that she was not responsive and would need to do a lot of practice during the week if there was any hope for her in search and rescue. Other breeds were ready to run and search when released indicating their intensity was extremely high. But Gina's intensity was markedly less, and her future looked dim in search and rescue. Having eliminated that possibility, her future needed to be reconsidered to fully utilize her skills to their highest potential.

Tom next took Gina to a Schutzhund Club in Virginia one drizzly Sunday morning to see if she was skilled for agility and apprehension work. Gina Marie was the only Akita there, but she was one of the largest dogs that had arrived. Dobermans, German shepherd dogs and Belgian Malinois barked with excitement and thrived on the activities awaiting them. Gina remained more passive surveying the scene with quiet interest. A well-known Virginia police officer, who had many successful dogs in national competitions, approached and assessed Gina's chances for success. He told Tom that Akitas generally showed little interest in bark and hold or sleeve-biting exercises, but he would test her anyway.

When the officer tested Gina Marie with a leather bite sleeve, Tom saw that what the man had said was true. Gina remained indifferent and showed no interest in wildly biting the sleeve as the other dogs had done. She was a reserved dog and simply not motivated to attack or hold anything. Her thoughts were clearly elsewhere. Tom tried to be optimistic and continued with some agility and obedience work with the club, but one day the K-9 handler pulled him aside.

"Gina Marie is an awesome dog, "he said, "but my dogs are bred to apprehend criminals and detect drugs and bombs."

Tom and Gina would leave the other breeds to enthusiastically pursue work in law enforcement without her. She would never successfully fulfill the needs of the police K-9 handlers. That was not Gina's gift. Tom opened the car door for the placid dog and took the big Akita with the teddy bear face and soft eyes back home.

After passing the AKC Canine Good Citizenship Test with a perfect score, Tom considered using his dog as a therapy dog. He contacted Therapy Dogs International and scheduled her for testing. Gina was one of fifteen dogs applying for just eight open slots at the local hospital, so competition would be stiff.

Nicely brushed and groomed, Gina arrived at Children's Hospital, where she was the first dog tested. The hospital had hired two animal behaviorists, and the testing room was a hospital room where a young girl of ten simulated the role of patient. As Gina and Tom entered the room, he noticed the testers had a Labrador retriever sitting between them. Gina casually glanced the dog's way, but her interest was not on the dog at all but on the young "patient." Her focus and devotion to the girl was complete. She was curious but gentle, and to her there was no one else in the room but the young girl.

"I remember the day we took the Therapy Dogs International Test for therapy dog certification and registration," Tom said. A regional evaluator, after testing Gina, quietly said to me, 'Sir, you have an exceptional dog.'"

Feeling cautiously optimistic, Tom waited a few weeks for the testing results. Happily, he soon learned that Gina was selected. He gazed into her soft face and shared the news with her in many of the "conversations" they always had. He realized that her gift was not in the high-powered police world, speeding along in wailing police cars waiting to pounce and apprehend "bad guys." Nor would it be in the intense world of search and rescue. Her sweet nature would not find her racing through woods or climbing over rocks and fording streams to find the lost or injured. She was a cerebral dog, according to her vet, and her intensity was not physically overt, but it manifested itself in the way her mind worked. Gina Marie would help the lost and injured in another way. Her world would be more serene but not without its emotional hurdles. The gift she had to give would be in the tender care she would provide and in the simple love of a child. She had ranked first out of the fifteen dogs that applied, and not long afterward, Gina started her hospital work.

Gina Marie's Buddy Brigade trading card
Courtesy of Tom Luna

Gina Marie resting at the Butterfly Garden at Children's Hospital
Courtesy of Charles Hartman, Cathy L. Benton Photography

The expressive and kindly face of Gina Marie
Courtesy of Charles Hartman, Cathy L. Benton Photography

Gina was an eighty-five pound furry Florence Nightingale padding along the slick hospital corridors bedecked in her bright blue hospital coat. Her large frame, as intimidating as the U.S.S. Wisconsin itself, made many skeptical that she could make a good therapy dog, but one look at her caring face and casual observation of her gentle ways changed many minds quickly. Gina Marie became the newest member of the "Buddy Brigade" at Norfolk, Virginia's, Children's Hospital of the King's Daughters, and her teddy bear face and sensitive eyes would comfort hundreds of sick children who eagerly anticipated her visits.

Gina's alertness was so obviously stable and her demeanor so calm that she fell naturally into the work of therapy dogs. She quietly observed everything around her and quickly assessed situations with exquisite accuracy allowing her to give the appropriate responses necessary to each of her patients. Even outside the parameters of the hospital, her instincts were phenomenal.

One day when Gina and Tom were shopping for pet supplies in a huge store, the dog slowly ambled down the wide aisles. As they walked along and visited with employees, Gina's leash suddenly became taut.

Tom made "eye contact" and softly said to her, "Show me." At a quick pace and seeming to be on a special mission, Gina trotted to the front of the store. Tom knew she was searching for somebody. Before reaching the check-out counters, Gina made a quick right and then abruptly stopped. About twenty feet away stood a mother and her teen-age daughter. Gina focused on the young girl intensely and then made the approach quietly and directly. The mother looked on with some apprehension.

"When my daughter was a very young child," the mother explained, "she was bitten several times by an Akita. She has been petrified of large dogs ever since."

But the girl maintained a peaceful expression and faced Gina squarely. Gina patiently continued to sit and await the girl's response. Soon the patience was rewarded as the girl slowly offered her hand for a kiss.

The mother looked astonished as the daughter stood there having accepted Gina's kiss. Gina had gently made friends in her own loving way. She found a need to address and did it with her own proven technique.

"Today, your dog has brought healing to my daughter," said the woman. Thank you."

It is hard to say how Gina had sensed that the young daughter was in the store and to understand what motivated her to deliberately find the formerly-frightened girl. Before Tom could obtain the mother and daughter's names, both were gone. Without a word, Gina had erased years of fear from the young girl's heart, and Tom never figured out how the dog knew it was even there.

Gina's gift bordered on extrasensory perception, and at times seemed almost magical. She demonstrated it time after time. One afternoon, as Gina and Tom were making "rounds" on the seventh floor of the hospital they walked by the nurse's station. One of the nurses noticed Gina and called out to the other nurse.

"Look, there's the dog!"

Tom stopped and inquired what she meant.

"A few weeks ago, Gina Marie was visiting a young seven-year-old boy from Chicago," the nurse said. He was in his bed, and his parents were with him. When you and Gina entered the room, and the boy began to pet Gina, he seemed happy to have the visit from her. When you and Gina left the room, something wonderful happened to the boy. His parents excitedly related to the medical staff that their son who had speech difficulties, and who was very reluctant to speak, suddenly began speaking normally. The parents believed Gina was instrumental in bringing about their son's recovered speech."

Tom was gratified to hear such news, but he was not wholly surprised.

"All the children who have been touched by Gina Marie's visit have received a 'blessing,'" Tom explained. Her presence, the feel of her soft double-coat, the expression in her eyes and her gentle kissing of the child results in an almost supernatural touch. Countless parents from many parts of the United States have taken photos of her with their child."

Gina Marie's entrance into the hospital room of a sick child can immediately fill that room with warmth and calm. Officially adorned in her Buddy Brigade vest, she makes her entrance after first receiving an invitation. Upon her vest the children see her American Kennel Club Canine Good Citizen patch, her "Buddy Brigade" patch and a Red Cross patch, along with her Therapy Dog International Registration number for the current year. She is a dog that is hard to mistake.

The worried parents keeping vigil over a sick child at the hospital hover near the bedside and welcome the chance to stand alongside or sit by Gina Marie. She could easily jump up and snuggle with a child on the bed, but Gina has learned that children like to play with her on the floor so she patiently awaits their climb down from a bed to join her for some fun. Tom offers the young patients a chance to walk down the hall holding Gina's leash, and the many takers forget their pain and circumstances to proudly walk along with the big dog. In a hallway filled with bustling nurses, doctors, visitors, parents, I.V.s swinging from long poles and children in colorful hospital gowns, Gina can often be found plodding along hooked to the wheelchair of a giggling child riding along in a vehicle suddenly transformed into a grand magic coach being pulled by a prized pony. There is no shortage of smiles as Gina and her charge navigate the hospital corridors.

Bayley takes Gina Marie on her leash for a walk down the hospital corridor.

Bayley plays with Gina Marie on the floor of her hospital room.

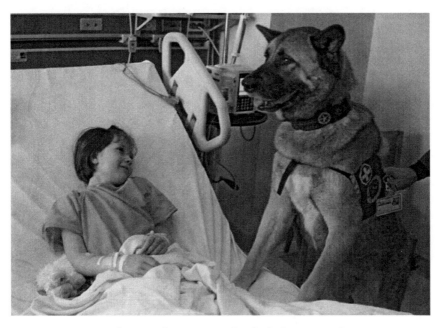

*Gentle Gina demonstrates her bedside manner for
patient, Anika, just recovering from surgery.*

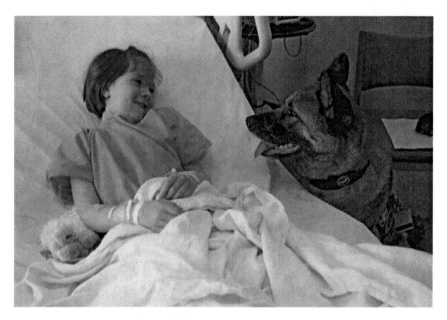

Anika and Gina Marie exchange smiles.

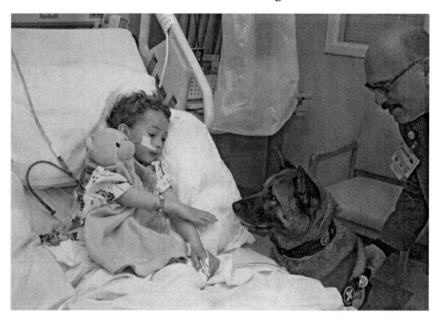

Post-surgery, Hunter reaches for the soft fur of Gina Marie.

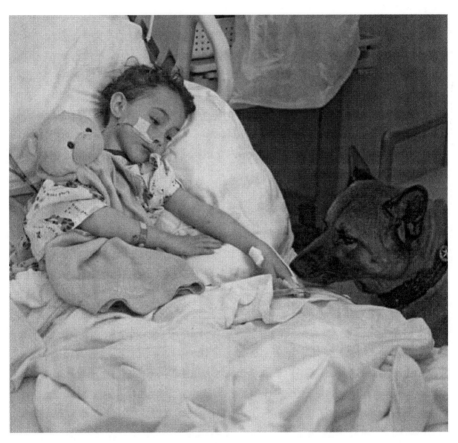

Gina rewards Hunter with a soft kiss.

All pictures courtesy of Charles Hartman, Cathy L. Benton Photography

A young girl of twelve lay severely burned from her head to her feet. The nurses were constantly at her bedside when Gina and Tom paused at the door and asked permission to enter. As they were invited in, the severely burned girl tolerating excruciating pain made eye contact with Gina, and with much effort managed a smile for the visiting dog. As painful as it was for the stoic girl, she could not resist Gina's charms. Tom left Gina's trading card with the young patient with the hopes of keeping the smile upon her tender face. For those few moments with Gina, the girl's thoughts were turned away from her pain, and Gina's visit provided a brief respite from the misery proving, once again, that Gina's was a noble calling.

As she made her rounds, Gina came to know all the medical staff at the hospital. One doctor met Tom outside a patient's room and commented on Tom's "unique" ministry. The doctor asked if he could go in and observe Gina with the patient.

"This is great work your dog is doing for these children," the doctor later commented.

Such words reinforced the thought that Tom had that he had chosen the perfect path for Gina Marie. It was reinforced further when their visits took them to the Transitional Care Unit where infants born with congenital physical defects were cared for.

One special eighteen-month-old boy, Jake, quickly became one of Gina Marie's favorites. Since his birth, he had never gone home. The sterile hospital became his only home, and the staff there became his family. Jake could not speak, and with Gina Marie's help, he was just learning to walk. Just seeing her made the little boy literally dance towards and around her. His severe head deformity and manifestations of his other physical differences were difficult for some to look at, yet Gina Marie found him beautiful. A bond began to grow and often it was hard to separate the two, as Jake's sobs rang out when it was time for Gina to leave.

Gina Marie's capacity to pull many miracles from her Buddy vest to give to those who needed them the most is no surprise to the medical community. The hospital filmed the interaction between the two friends recording a lasting history of the joy such a dog could bring to a broken life and spirit.

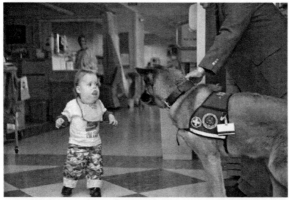

Gina Marie interacts with her beautiful friend, Jake.

All pictures courtesy of Charles Hartman, Cathy L. Benton Photography

In the early spring of 2007, the likelihood of any smiles in Virginia seemed remote. In just nine minutes, a disturbed student went on a rampage and killed thirty-two fellow students at Virginia Tech University. The sheer number was staggering.

As soon as he heard the news, Tom knew that he and Gina needed to be there to help heal the pain that had swept the campus like a tidal wave and lingered as the families there were swallowed up by it coming to terms with their grief.

So many times in the past, the healing task had involved work on an individual basis. Now the magnitude of the work ahead was so overwhelming and the numbers of the grieving so large that Tom wondered how such pain could ever be assuaged. So on an uncharacteristically cold and windy day for that area, a day that seemed to reflect the mood and tenor of the times, Tom and Gina left before dawn to drive to Roanoke. It would take five hours, leaving much time to contemplate what lie ahead. The university had made arrangements for Tom and Gina at the elegant Inn at Virginia Tech. The inn had housed all the major news network employees who arrived to cover the horrific events, and now after their departure the hotel still housed the State Troopers and their K-9s. Gina settled down that night in the beautiful and comfortable room, taking her spot facing the door to keep watch and to listen as the K-9s returned from their duties late each night. The task ahead of Tom and Gina in the morning would be great.

For two days, Tom and Gina walked the 2600-acre campus for eight hours each day greeting students and family who dealt with their grief there. Tom led Gina along paths of plants just emerging into the new spring. Past shrubs, across awakening lawns long brown and dry from winter's dormancy and past the campus goldfish pond, they walked to finally rest on cedar benches and to sit at the tables there to relate to anyone needing a friend. Students approached Gina and asked to pet her. They ran their hands through her soft coat and looked upon her understanding face. Smiles slowly emerged where there had been none, and the students wearing their new smiles parted company with her as she continued on her way. One student who was watering plants asked if Gina would care for a drink, and the thirsty dog took a long cool drink from the garden hose. Refreshed, she moved on. There were so many more to see there.

With some trepidation, Tom and Gina approached the Drill Field in the center of campus where the temporary Student Memorial was located. There was a mood of deep respectful silence there broken by the occasional hushed tone of a voice sorrowfully remembering a familiar name. Later on, the sun warmed the day, and hundreds of students walked in all directions. Tom straightened Gina's beautiful multi-colored amber bandana that was tied neatly around her broad neck and made a mental note of how elegant she looked.

Virginia Tech campus police ringed the memorial and bent over to greet Gina as she passed. People milled about in silence with no one wishing to disturb the dignity of the memorial space. Students, faculty and the public stopped to linger at each slain person's area. As Tom did the same, Gina, who remained by his side, sat down next to each name. The smell of flowers left there in tribute sweetened the breeze and added a splash of color to the somber surroundings. Small American flags marked each name, and Gina stepped softly past cuddly stuffed animals, written notes, candles, balloons, toys and a simple written statement, "The world has no words to describe our sadness." All the time Gina knew.

Student Memorial at Virginia Tech
Courtesy of Tom Luna

Past the memorial, Gina and Tom walked toward a nearby area where counselors offered students ice water, fruit, crackers, Bibles and pamphlets about tragedy and disasters that sought to answer the eternal question, "Why God?"

After a night's restless sleep at the hotel, the pair headed back to campus. At the Drill Field, a professor grasping a briefcase lingered and stood alone wiping away many tears. Two grandmothers prayed there and turned to greet Gina as she neared them taking a moment from their grief to take a picture of the attentive dog. She readily accepted their hugs and for a brief moment each of the women retreated to her own private thoughts while burying a sad face in soft welcoming fur. A group of Virginia State Troopers stood quietly. Some took pictures of the memorial while others stood too dazed to express any emotion. Indeed, there were just no words.

In early evening, Gina and Tom strolled over to Norris Hall where the killings had taken place. They saw a six-foot chain-link fence ominously covered with a green canvas. State Troopers patrolled the area. When Gina caught the eye of one of them, the man called her and Tom over. He expressed his thanks for having a gentle canine like Gina on campus. As a show of his thanks, the Trooper gave Gina a plastic State Trooper badge. It would become a sacred treasure of remembrance for Tom, and Gina would wear it proudly.

A light drizzle began to fall, and the sun was slipping down to the horizon. With her plastic badge affixed to her collar, worth more than gold to Tom, they paused for one last look at the memorial site. Gina had brought some smiles to weary faces during her visit, and with time the sun would shine brightly once more for the Hokie community. In the cool mist, Tom led Gina from the campus. It was time, once more, to go home.

A few months later, Gina and Tom received a letter from the President of the University thanking them for their efforts on the college's behalf. He said that a framed photograph of Gina would be in the archives of the University Library marking her service during the days after the horrific incident. The largest newspaper in Hampton Roads, Virginia, wrote an article praising Gina's intervention, and it was accompanied by a picture of her and Tom at the Virginia Tech memorial site.

Gina's impact during the tragedy at Virginia Tech proved the effectiveness of canines in time of disaster. She is currently completing training to allow her to respond to disasters such as hurricanes and terrorist attacks.

Just a mile from the Elizabeth River, Tom and Gina find great peace in the dark wooded area there as they walk among the pine trees at 5:30 each morning. In total silence and with her expert sense of scent, hearing and alertness, Gina moves skillfully through the underbrush observing everything around her and listening for the sound of "critters." Tom and Gina have developed a natural and intense communication and trust, and eye contact with each other speaks volumes. Their moments together early each morning prepare them in both mind and spirit for the day ahead.

Gina Marie in her favorite woods hunting for critters
Courtesy of Tom Luna

Although Gina did not end up working for the police department, Tom maintains a strong relationship with the Norfolk Metro Police. He wrote a proposal to the Chief of Police offering Gina Marie as a special "therapy" to dedicated, hard-working officers going on or off duty. That winter, she and Tom were invited to the Police Department's 2007 Christmas Social at the Police Academy. In a festive crowd of over two hundred attendees, they met the police chief, his staff of officers and many other department personnel. Gina Marie made a solid impression, her physical appearance seeming to impress the police.

"She looks like a German shepherd dog and seems physically larger that some of our K-9s," one commented. She reminds me of one of the top K-9s in our unit."

Gina's imposing presence now serves double duty at the hospital. As her popularity continued to rise, hospital Safety and Security took notice of her and soon Gina was asked to make her presence known on the hospital grounds and around the medical school. For one hour, twice a day, she greets doctors, nurses, students, professors and employees as they walk from parking garages to the hospital and medical buildings. Always uplifting everyone's spirits, she now serves as an escort and protector after being issued a police security badge to wear on her collar.

The fire department in Norfolk also found solace in her presence. Ladder #14 fire fighters having just returned from battling a raging a fire found Gina waiting for them when they returned. Weary and soot-covered fire fighters climbed down from their truck to remove the heavy equipment, and then one-by-one, they came to Gina Marie, knelt down and patted her. Some buried their faces in her strong warm neck and enjoyed the minutes of relief and total respite they found in the comfort of the dog.

Gina Marie has the best of both worlds. Tom personally joined the Virginia Police Work Dog Association as an Associate Member because he believed in supporting the local and State K-9 teams. His involvement with them keeps him and his special dog in close association with a very important police presence in Norfolk.

Ladder 14 – Norfolk, Virginia
Courtesy of Tom Luna

The gracious Akita is a fine representative of her breed. It was a totally blind and deaf woman in the 1930s who brought the first Akita to the United States. When she was asked to do a speaking tour of Japan, Helen Keller, heard the story of a brave dog in the Prefecture of Akita there. She was impressed by its courage, and she said she would like to have such a dog. As a measure of the respect in which she was held, a policeman in that prefecture presented her with an Akita puppy called Kamikaze-Go. The dog assisted handicapped Keller just as Gina assists her tiny patients today. In Japan, small statues of the Akita are often sent to ill people to express a wish for their speedy recovery and to parents of newborn children to symbolize good health. The patients at Children's Hospital are fortunate that they have not statues, but the "real thing."

As a member of the Therapy Dogs International, Organization, Gina Marie's work brings her in touch with so many who admire her gentle nature and intuitive gift for healing. She never cared to hold a bite sleeve or hold a suspect, but she, herself is held in the hearts of all she comes in contact with. Furry paw touching frail tiny hand, Gina has her own special "hold" to bridge the gap between canine and human with often astonishing results. In the naval town of Norfolk, she is the port in many storms.

In the evenings when Tom takes Gina on their nightly walks, he speaks to her of many things.

Tom praises his exceptional dog, Gina Marie. The song in his heart is unending.
Courtesy of Charles Hartman, Cathy L. Benton Photography

"Gina will listen," Tom says confidently, "In my heart, I know Gina is thinking, 'We are a team, let us remain humble and obedient.'"

It is a humility and obedience that no one can teach, but which exudes from the gentle dog from Norfolk, Virginia, the ever-tender, Gina Marie.

Born to serve, the dog that everyone loves—Gina Marie
Courtesy of Tom Luna

K-9 Bear

"Thunder Down Under"

A remote land of rugged beauty, and the world's smallest continent—dry and flat, encompassing coastal wilderness and aboriginal culture, Australia's wild and windswept ocean beaches stand in contrast to the scorched red desert of the sunburned "outback." A land of shipwrecks, stunning floral displays, indigenous kangaroos, wombats and koalas and some of the most venomous snakes in the world, the land down under is a diverse geographic mosaic of lush rainforests, rich farmlands, timbered woodlands, broad grasslands and mysterious mangrove swamps. The land of December summers and July winters duplicates the United States in size, but only twenty-one million people live in its vast and sometimes unexplored interior.

Adjacent to the desolate outback, lies massive river redgum country, an area of mountains and lush farmland where the giant eucalyptus tree offers welcome shade, and beyond the outback lies the "gibber plains," the inhospitable barren land so named by the aborigines, covered with closely-packed angular rocks making it difficult for man or beast to transverse. Like any other place, perhaps many less exotic, the varied landscapes of Australia can also be a place of crime.

Senior Constable Bryan Whitehorn, a born and bred Australian, had spent seventeen years policing in regional South Australia but was also familiar with the less-welcoming underbelly of Australia's big city life. He had been posted to the South Australian Police Dog Operations Unit in 2000, and most of his work was based around the metropolitan capital of South Australia, Adelaide, Australia's fifth largest city. With a population of just over a million residents, the city stretched between the ocean of Saint Vincent's Gulf and the Adelaide hills sprawling twenty-miles-wide from coast to mountains and pushing seventy miles into Australia's interior at the edge of the agricultural farmlands and beyond that, Australia's rugged outback. Bryan spent many hours racing north to south and east to west covering the large city and chasing down its crooks. What he needed was a companion to extend his law enforcement capabilities, a good and faithful working dog.

Since the fall of the year, participating in his initial police dog training course, he was having great difficulty training a good dog. For six months he worked with a variety of donated dogs that were all unsuitable.

"They just didn't have a high retrieve drive, which is paramount in teaching a dog how to track. One of the dogs could track well, but his criminal work (bite work) was not up to standard. Some were lazy and others just simply didn't have the high drive and outgoing temperament that we needed."

Because the department did not have a breeding program, the force was reliant on donated German shepherd dogs, and after many of them failed to meet Bryan's expectations, he was offered yet another one.

In 2001, a man had experienced a broken marriage and his huge dog, Kane, who had become accustomed to living in a house with a decent back yard, suddenly found himself moved to a very small unit with the man's mother. The dog had only a very tiny yard to play in, and so cramped was his area, that one day the bored dog escaped the yard several times by climbing a tree that had fallen down across a back fence. There were no children in the family to play with, and he was quickly becoming a very unhappy animal.

Because he was such a full-on, high-drive dog, the owner thought he could be well utilized by the police K-9 section. On the off-chance that finally a donated dog would work out, the police arrived to take a look. What they found was a gigantic unusual-looking animal with a long-flowing coat. There had been very few long-haired German shepherd dogs with K-9 units before, and the size of the dog was startling. Kane was removed from the confining surroundings and taken away. Time would determine if the dog was beauty or beast.

After a few days of testing, the dog showed some possibilities, and it was decided that the unit would take him as a potential police dog. The unit already had a dog named Kane, who worked with the other nine general purpose police dogs, and although it would not be likely by appearance that the two dogs would be confused, the new dog needed his own distinctive name. The training officer who had originally picked him up decided that the name Bear suited him well, and the police would see if Kane took on a new persona to match his new name.

Bryan was assigned to find out. He had been trying unsuccessfully to train a Rottweiler and the effort was becoming obviously futile. He was less than optimistic when he was allocated Bear to train, but they immediately hit it off. What had been a difficult six months because of the unsuitability of the former dogs suddenly became easy because Bear was so trainable. The dog was sociable and very friendly and after a few weeks working with him, Bryan began to feel that he had found a dog that could not only be easily trained but could become a valuable member of the force.

Bryan Whitehorn and K-9 Bear
Courtesy of Bryan Whitehorn

They finished what was supposed to be a fourteen-week basic dog training course in about ten weeks, and they were soon out on the road. It took Bear awhile to settle into his new life as a police dog, but he was so very grateful to be out of that cramped backyard. Bear went to quite a few "taskings" before he managed to catch his first crook, but in retrospect, Bryan felt the slow start probably had more to do with him being a new handler and getting the hang of things than any deficiencies on Bear's part.

That first apprehension was much anticipated by Bryan, and he could not wait to celebrate it. The satisfaction of proving his dog could do well had thus far been elusive, but he knew when that day came it would be a joyous day for both himself and Bear. Each time they were called out would provide another opportunity for the forever-remembered first "win."

Very late one evening, Bear and Bryan were called to a city street where an adult male offender had assaulted two people outside a nearby restaurant and fled into a large construction site. Bear was deployed in an "on lead" search, and there was no question he knew just what he was doing. All his training kicked in, and he remained focused and determined. Eventually, he located the hunted man hiding in a townhouse construction complex. With the hope of remaining hidden and unreachable, the man climbed onto the roof of the yet-to-be-completed building and refused to come down. A one-hour standoff between him, Bear, Bryan and numerous police began. When suggestions and demands that he come down were fruitless, a negotiator was called in, and the man was finally convinced to come down off the roof. He was promptly arrested, and Bryan was enormously proud of his dog.

Bryan was ecstatic, accepting the congratulations of his colleagues on the scene. He and Bear had caught their first crook! He praised the dog lavishly, and Bear appeared just as pleased with his own performance. There were smiles all around, and the tedious evening would end on a high note. Officer and dog were beginning to click as a team during that night of their first triumph.

Several minutes later, the State Duty Inspector, who was at the scene of the stand off, received a telephone call. Her previous smile faded, and her face grew ashen as she intently listened to the message. Then she relayed what she had heard to Bryan and his colleagues. The date was Tuesday, September 11th, 2001, and she had just been advised that terrorists had just flown planes into the World Trade Center in New York. The police team on the ground in Australia stood in disbelief and shock as did the rest of the world, and the celebratory atmosphere of the moment was shattered. An enormous dark blanket of sorrow suddenly hung like a pall over the celebration of Bear's first "win," and the mood turned somber as the men so far away from the tragedy considered the full magnitude of what had happened.

Australia's criminal element took no such pause at the horrific event, and shortly after hearing the stunning announcement and still reeling from the shock, Bryan was deployed on the other side of the city to search for a car thief who had run from police. The man had dumped the car, but Bear located him hiding in the backyard of a suburban house. Now Bear had two wins on the same night, but the luster of the night had been forever tarnished by the tragic news from New York.

Bear and Bryan followed the arresting patrols to the nearby watch-house, one of the major cell complexes for the Adelaide Police, where the man would be locked up and where his details would be recorded. While there, Bryan watched live on television as the World Trade Centers crashed to the ground in a moment of unbelievable tragedy. It was a bittersweet night for Bryan, and the unforgettable date would always give him cause to reflect back on the night of Bear's first win. Suddenly, the win did not seem nearly as significant.

Bear and Bryan formed a strong bond and worked across South Australia, and as the years progressed, Bear's win ratio quickly began to escalate as did his reputation among the members of the South Australian Police. The long-haired police dog was instantly recognizable to police officers, and he soon became a favorite among his fellow police officers. During his working life, Bear remained a big dog. With long-flowing hair, he was one-hundred pounds of muscle and ran on paws as big as a grown man's hand. With a head the size of a bucket, he was unmistakable. He could be a ferocious beast or magnificent beauty depending upon whom he encountered.

A year later, the beast side of Bear was called upon to hunt down an armed hold-up offender. It was 2:00 a.m. on a clear cool morning when the people of Adelaide were fast asleep. On a major road in a residential area, Bear and Bryan were called to search for two offenders who had robbed a man at knife point. When the officer and dog arrived on the scene, police were already chasing a twenty-year-old man along the street. Bryan watched helplessly as the nimble suspect quickly climbed over the roof of a house and disappeared into the rear yard. Bryan grabbed Bear, and the two raced to the side fence to gain access to the yard but found the fence was heavily-fortified and their path was blocked. Minutes of delay meant that the robber would cover a great distance before the team could catch up with him. And a protective backyard dog would most likely have a go at Bear. Bryan pounded on the door of the home hastily awakening the homeowners to get them to unlock the gate. With their entranceway now open, Bear pulled at his lead to get into the backyard. Thankfully, no pet dog appeared there.

Once there, Bear quickly indicated against the rear fence. Without any thought for his own safety, he leapt up and over the five-foot-high galvanized iron fence. Bryan scrambled after him further away from the illumination of street lamps. They found themselves in a pitch black environment along the steep banks of a creek. Bryan could hear the shallow waters gurgling below. There was a drop off of twenty-six feet, and Bryan followed along behind Bear as carefully as he could in the dark hoping not to lose his footing. He was sorely tempted to use his torch (flashlight), but doing so would have given away his position to the man and tactically would have ruined his night vision. So he put one foot in front of the other in the darkness, his only security being Bear and the lead.

Bryan could hear Bear's pants in the blackness as the dog pulled hard along the embankment. Moving along at a quick pace, he dragged Bryan along about half a mile until just up ahead, Bear showed great interest in a tree. Standing against that tree was the offender. With the dog's excellent night vision and riveting sense of smell, he had spotted him easily. Only then, did Bryan switch on his torch to light up the hiding man. The man was blinded by the bright light and tried to shield his eyes from the direct beam.

"Police with a police dog!" Bryan screamed, "Get down on the ground… stay still!"

That was not the man's intent. In a flash, he jumped from his hiding place and dropped down into the shallow creek with a soft splash and scrambled to climb up the other side. Disappointed his prey had gotten away, Bear had only one thing on his mind and began to immediately pull hard down the steep embankment, which was slippery with slick wet stones and a layer of thick mud at the bottom. Bear pulled so fast and hard through the mire that in an instant Bryan half-tumbled, half-slid down the embankment to the rippling water's edge. The water was flowing, but it only covered the bottom of the creek, and Bryan was relieved that it was not raining heavily then or the creek may have been flowing fast and full.

Bear pursued his prey non-stop. The racing dog's muddy feet followed up the other embankment, where Bryan saw the silhouette of an array of houses. Through front and back yards Bear ran climbing up and over numerous fences. He knew his prey was near, and he was relentless. Just ahead, was an area of tall grass. Bear was excited by the prospect of reaching it. With a gigantic leap, he came down upon the back of the man who had tried so hard to escape him. The man had been trying desperately to conceal himself there and now found himself buried under the dog's long-flowing hair. Bear and the man thrashed about in the grass and when Bryan heard a loud scream, he knew his dog had made a direct hit. The defeated man offered no resistance, and Bryan made the arrest.

It was a great win for Bear because of the difficult terrain and the many fences he and Bryan had to climb. Out of breath, Bryan was relieved the chase was over. He stood in the street with Bear afterward speaking with the patrol sergeant, when he started to feel pain in his knee. He learned later that the fall down the embankment had torn the medial ligament in his knee, but he had the satisfaction of knowing that despite the injury the babbling creek, the thick mud and the break-neck speed of the chase, he had gotten his man. Bear's long coat was a matted mess and filled with broken twigs and debris he had picked up along the way, but like Bryan, if he'd been asked, it was all worth it.

"Because of the nature of our work," Bryan emphasized, "police dog handlers are often subjected to difficult terrain, slippery creeks and rivers, armed offenders and the curse of most dog handlers, hanging flower baskets and clothes lines at head height!"

Due to Bryan's injury, the team was out of commission for several weeks. During that time, Bear paced anxiously and hated being off work and was chomping at the bit to get back to into the thick of things. Playing in the yard and taking VERY slow walks with Bryan were difficult for a dog with such drive, and no one was happier to get back to work than the long-haired dog. Soon he was off with Bryan to Mt. Schank, an extinct volcano located in Australia's rich farming area where cattle and sheep peacefully grazed. Similar extinct volcanoes were scattered about the training venue and provided a remote and enjoyable place for a dog and his handler to train.

Training among sheep, cattle and extinct volcanoes
Courtesy of Bryan Whitehorn

Bear continued to be a high-performance police dog and was called upon to participate in STAR Operations (Special Tasks and Rescue) high-risk incidents when necessary. His win ratio had become the best in the Unit, and he produced year after year of high-level arrests as he trod along catching his crooks through the extreme temperature differentials of Australia. His long coat served him well in the snowless June and July winter times when temperatures dipped to -17F. When the temperatures soared to 113F during the long hot summers in January and February, the blistering Australian heat was a real test for Bear. To help him cope, Bryan constantly drenched him in water at jobs and at home to keep the large dog cool.

Using high-risk tactical equipment, Bryan and Bear train to ready themselves to work with STAR Operations on high-risk incidents.

Courtesy of Bryan Whitehorn

In June of 2005, Bryan sped to a street in the western suburbs of Adelaide where a carload of men had dumped a car in a driveway after having committed violent robberies in the eastern suburbs. A police patrol had spotted their abandoned vehicle a few hours after their rampage. The men had been robbing pizza bars and takeaway stores and threatening and assaulting the owners with pipes and bars. After they dumped the car, they began jumping fences to get away.

Bryan released Bear to search a massive cordoned residential area for about an hour with no success. When someone "rung up" to say they thought they saw someone jump the fence into the airport grounds, Bryan and Bear moved their search area outside of where the police had established the cordon. Towards the back of the Adelaide airport, they started their area search.

While walking down a street well outside the cordon area, where Bryan really felt it was unlikely the men had fled, Bear immediately pulled hard up the driveway of a house and trotted swiftly down the side of the house. In the distance, was a pile of broken branches that attracted Bear like a magnet. Edging closer, Bryan could sense the dog's instincts were correct. Beneath the branches, Bear found two of the robbery suspects who had jumped over a fence and had pulled the broken branches over themselves to hide. The two robbers were nearly a mile outside the cordon area, and it was because of Bear's keen nose and hunting skills that the two violent criminals were arrested. Like so many, they had underestimated the power of Bear's canine nose and his intelligence in putting it to work.

Bryan found that robbers never seemed to learn their lessons. In September, 2006, he was called to yet another robbery incident, where a bus driver had been "bashed" and robbed by three violent youths on the suburban streets of Adelaide. Three against one, they had beaten him with their fists and then stole his belongings. By 1:00 a.m., Bryan and Bear were on the job. The distraught driver could only give a description of the thieves, and in his rattled state he pointed where he had last seen the three men fleeing.

Bryan fastened Bear's tracking harness and cast him around the area where the bus driver had pointed. Bear immediately picked up a track of the men. By that time, the incident was almost three-quarters-of-an-hour old, which greatly diminished Bear's chances for success. Being night time, there was no pedestrian movement and that gave Bear a huge advantage. He began tracking down the street, across a corner and down another street for about ten minutes until he came to the driveway of a house that sat in total darkness. Bear tracked left up the driveway to the front door of the house and stopped. It was a normal brick house, neat and tidy in the leafy eastern suburbs of Adelaide and situated in an area considered to be a normal middle class neighborhood. It was not the kind of place that would give Bryan the slightest suspicion that the criminal element lived there. Bryan brought Bear back out into the street and cast him past the house and across the street, but stubborn Bear was determined and kept returning to the one house.

"At first, I wasn't sure, but you always want to believe them," Bryan remembered, "but after I cast him past and in the street, and he gave me nothing, I was pretty confident this was where they had gone."

So sure was he of Bear's indication that Bryan called the uniformed police and detectives in and told them that he thought the trio had gone into that house.

It was a busy night in Adelaide and before Bryan could learn the outcome, he and Bear were summoned to another job leaving the search of the house in the hands of the detectives.

Half-an-hour later, the detectives rang Bryan to tell him that they had searched the house and located the three men inside still wearing the same clothes that the bus driver had described, and they were in possession of the bus driver's property. The robbers could not imagine how the police had picked the house to search, but they should have known that Bear was always on the job. Without Bear's tracking skills, the three young criminals would never have been caught. The driver's jacket and wallet were returned to him compliments of the giant dog with the long fur coat, and the violent offenders were then off the streets.

Bear was popular at schools and community visits because of his gentle nature and good demenor, and he didn't display any aggression when he was in the company of people who admired him and just wanted to be his friend. But when in the company of those who chose to break society's laws, Bear changed dramatically and became a hard, aggressive and terrorizing foe in the fight against crime.

The Many Faces of Bear

Courtesy of Bryan Whitehorn

As Bear faced the twilight of his career, he was involved in probably two of his highest-profile and most-satisfying police dog wins. He was seven-and-a-half-years-old but still keeping pace with his contemporaries when in November, 2006, a prisoner had escaped from the low-security Cadell Prison in the Riverland area of South Australia, nearly one-hundred-sixty miles northwest of Adelaide. The vastness of Australia meant it would take two-to-three days to drive from one side of South Australia to the other, and any work that Bear and Bryan did in the outback usually required a plane or helicopter.

The escapee had run through a field and had been on the run for over twenty-four hours. The police at one point spotted him on the riverbanks of the Murray River, but he eluded the police causing them to put up a large cordon around the area. The scrubland area of about one-and-one-half miles long by a mile wide was ringed by police. From the ground, it was difficult to say what the interior of the area looked like so Bryan took Bear to the airport where a helicopter waited.

Bear had flown in fixed-winged aircraft before to jobs in the rugged outback and had previously gone on flights in the helicopter for other jobs in nearby country areas. He took flying in his stride and sat calmly looking out the window. The helicopter was the smaller one used by South Australia Police, and Bryan and another police officer climbed into the tiny compartment and tried to squeeze giant Bear in between them. Wedged in tightly, Bear took off traveling the most expeditious way he could to the forbidding outback on the forty-five minute flight.

The scrubland below wasn't entirely desolate, although it was quite harsh country. The River Murray, used for irrigation, nourished the scrublands which were often very thick with the vegetation feeding off the river, but the further one moved away from the river the land became quite dry. Far below the whirr of the chopper blades, koalas slumbered in the leafy treetops of the towering eucalyptus trees where brilliant native birds soared through the blue skies. The gray galahs with accenting brilliant pink plumage, one of the most beautiful of cockatoos, screeched their high-pitched "chill-chill" calling to their mates, but Bear paid them no mind. It was the man who had taken flight that Bear was interested in. The serenity of the locale was broken by the intrusion of the escapee, and the men and dog were determined to find him.

As the helicopter circled, Bryan looked below to get an idea of the type of country that he and Bear faced.

"Doesn't look too bad," he observed.

But once on the ground, he had a different opinion. Bryan and Bear faced thick dense scrub with massive river gums and thick thorny bushes nearly ten-feet high. The sharp thorns tore at Bryan's clothes and skin and pulled at Bear's long coat as they pushed their way through the bushes that were a most difficult impediment. It was slow going through the tangles and thorns, and Bear's coat would drag much of the growth from the scrub home with him. In the past, he had experienced many deep ingrown prickles, and the clinging seeds from the grassy country had clung tenaciously to his silky coat. The scrub would adorn him with yet more prickles and thorns that would need to be combed out when he returned home, but it was a hazard of his job and did not stop him from proceeding forward.

It became impossible for Bear to search while still on lead so Bryan had no choice but to release him. Before he did, he issued his loud challenge.

"Police with a police dog, come out now or the dog will be released! This is your last chance!"

There was no reply.

"Find him!" urged Bryan and with the words he waited to hear, Bear lunged ahead through the vegetation.

After Bear was cut loose, he did what he did best even under the difficult circumstances. Amazingly, after a very short time, the dog lifted his head indicating he could smell the hidden offender. Bear took off racing at full pace through the thick scrub out ahead of Bryan as the handler struggled to fight his way through the dense growth.

Bear continued his drive towards the hidden place where the offender lay low and then dove under the thick bushes there. After a brief skirmish with the dog and man thrashing about wildly in the foliage, Bear dragged the escapee out by his pants.

Bryan grabbed at Bear to pull him off his prey so that the man was not further injured.

"Lie face down and don't move!" ordered Bryan.

Then he called the other police in to make the arrest.

Bryan poured water from the large bottle of water he carried on the helicopter for Bear. The dog had earned a cooling drink and slurped water from his portable water dish before boarding the helicopter for a ride home.

The escaping man could never have been seen where he was hidden from the ground or from the air. Yet in just fourteen minutes, Bear was able to accomplish what the other police and a helicopter had been unable to accomplish in over twenty-four hours. He was a professional in every sense of the word.

Bear's second-to-last offender provided opportunity for his highest-profile win. He was eight-years-old and his step was a little slower, but his enthusiasm never waned.

Late one night, in March, 2007, towards the end of the hot Australian summer, the air was still warm. An alarm had sounded at a school, so at 2:00 a.m., Bear and Bryan reported there to search looking for a thief who had been involved in a large-scale serial crime spree breaking into schools to steal money and electrical goods.

The track started at one of the schools. Bear had tracked from where the man entered the building on through the school grounds and finally to the roadside curb where the track was lost. Bryan was convinced the man was using a car to move around between the various schools in the inner-southern suburbs. Bear was just finishing up the track when at that moment another intruder alarm screamed out at another school nearby.

Along with other patrol cars, Bryan and Bear made a quick dash in their car to the neighboring school, screeched to a quick stop, parking on the street and raced from the car. Two additional police cars with two officers each joined him at the school. Upon entering the school grounds, Bryan moved along with great stealth so as not to be spotted. Bear, as always, moved quietly along with him. Bryan looked toward one of the administration buildings, and through the window he could see the interior lights burning brightly. There stood a man in jeans and a dark t-shirt who was pulling drawers apart in his frantic search for money. Silently, and leashed to Bear, Bryan slipped along slowly and approached the door where the offender had broken in. When he was satisfied that the rest of the accompanying police had surrounded the building, he tore open the smashed door and yelled out his challenge, which echoed off the deserted hallway.

With no response, he released a pumped-up Bear into the building. Bear galloped down the hallway towards the very spot where the man had been seen. Caught by surprise, the startled man had entered the hallway only to see Bear thundering towards him.

The crook made a dash for a side door bursting out and through it and ran away as fast as he could into the cover of night. Bear continued to give chase across the school grounds ducking behind a large shed and then sprinting back into open ground across the grassy oval that comprised the school's play park. Bryan could hear the steady rhythmic beat of the dog's feet as he pounded across the park, and he could see the dog closing on the suspect. Halfway across the park, the offender turned and faced rapidly-closing Bear. Bryan was still ninety-feet behind the dog, and he tried desperately to catch up. Just then, the nearly-thirty-year-old male raised a treacherous tire iron across his shoulder and brandished it towards the attacking dog. Enraged, Bear lunged at him, growling and snarling with even greater intensity as the man struck Bear hard twice across the shoulders.

Anyone knowing anything about highly-trained police dogs could predict what would happen. The strike with the tire iron served only to make Bear angrier and more determined to get to his quarry. With increased ferocity, one-hundred pounds of growling fury lunged at the offender again seemingly oblivious to the deadly tire iron, and Bear grabbed the man across the side of his ribcage. The tire iron clattered to the ground, and with a final burst of energy, Bear knocked his assailant to the ground beside it. Bryan and the other police officers arrived within seconds as Bear ensured that the particularly nasty character was shown why it is not advisable to strike a police dog.

Bear had not been seriously injured, but he very well could have been or killed. A lesser dog probably would have been. The shaken offender was arrested and soon his car was located nearby. The investigating uniform police patrols who found the car located a map on the passenger's seat. The thief had marked the locations of a dozen more schools on the map and obviously had plans to hit them all in the next few nights. But Bear made sure the man's school days were over. Instead, he was charged with four serious breaking offenses leading to a long prison sentence.

Bear's heroics in chasing down the offender in the heat of battle immediately raised the interest of media outlets across Adelaide. Far from the thick outback or the busy city streets, Bear found himself in the midst of a media frenzy. The next night, Bear and Bryan were the subjects of numerous interviews about Bear's courage. School children later wrote the brave heroic dog letters and sent him lots of cards and small gifts. Bear shone in his fifteen minutes of fame. He was the darling of Adelaide's media, and his tale was told for some time until, as is the norm, another more important media event took his place.

Bear had one more win. He located a crook in a backyard for a simple property damage offense after searching just three yards and easily found him hiding underneath some branches of a tree.

"It was a bit liking shooting fish in a fishbowl," said Bryan.

Although his last win was anti-climactic, Bear was a dog that easily balanced the hard cases with the soft ones. For all Bear's brilliant tracking ability, his one flaw in that regard was possums.

"Despite everything we do as handlers to desensitize the dog from hunting animals, sometimes their natural instincts will still take over. For some reason, possums and cats were Bear's Achilles Heel."

He had fooled Bryan a time or two before.

"He's always been distracted by possums sometimes indicating into a tree. I've thought the crook might be hiding there," Bryan laughed, "and found it was just a possum."

A quick flick of Bear's "check chain" and sharp command of "off!" moved Bear past the distraction and got him back to work providing Australia's possum population some degree of safety.

On Friday, April13th, 2007, Bear jumped into the back of the police car for his last shift. The police communications operators were all aware that it was Bear's last night at work. The long-haired dog had become a real favorite of the police radio room operators. He and Bryan visited there regularly to put a face to the voice of those police officers that helped Bear hunt his crooks. On that last night, every radio operator wanted to be the one that got Bear his last win. Unfortunately, it was not to be, and Bear's last shift was a quiet one.

"Maybe it was karma, that the criminals in Adelaide all knew that Bear was leaving so it was not a good idea to be out doing bad things on the city's streets knowing that 'the big furry one' was looking for his last win. Maybe they were all too scared to face him one last time."

At 11:00 p.m., Bear signed off for the last time, and everyone who knew was sad. But at the same time, they were also happy for their friend for Adelaide's gentle giant would be given time to enjoy life as a normal dog at home in Bryan's back yard.

Bryan took Bear into the office that night, and the dog had his photo taken sitting in the boss's chair at the computer. Later, he also posed on the hood of the patrol car he had known so well. Bryan drove him home and gave him a warm pat.

A final pose on retirement day
Courtesy of Bryan Whitehorn

Contemplating computer work in retirement
Courtesy of Bryan Whitehorn

"Well that's it mate," he simply said as Bear gazed with questioning eyes into his handler's face.

For Bryan, it was a feeling of remorse, because Bear's career was over. His faithful companion had endured cut pads from glass, the odd scratch from sticks and fences, and he once hurt his back dragging a fleeing man off of a fence. He had grabbed the man across the backside, and as he dragged the struggling man down, Bear fell sideway twisting his back. He was rested for a couple of weeks and then was back at work. Bear was a dog that would give his all, and all of Adelaide loved him.

His career had been a full one. In the past, he had gone on training exercises in Australia's national parks where kangaroos grazed and, from time to time, he took off chasing them. Fortunately for him, the kangaroos like so many crooks he chased decided to flee, bouncing along the parkland on springy legs, hopping faster than a dog can run. The creatures were often a distraction to working dogs who trained there, and the handlers all knew that if their dog cornered a big one, the kangaroo would defensively lean back on its thick strong tail and use its back legs and feet to simply tear a dog open clean down its chest, killing it easily. Distance was always best at such times.

Bear's career was also a notable one. He had been called out for service 1153 times, had apprehended 160 criminals, and in his long career he recovered $15,127 in stolen property. He received much recognition.

Five months after retirement, Bear was honored for his services when the German Shepherd Council of Australia awarded him their "Outstanding Service Award." He was presented with the award at the National Breeders competition in Adelaide, and for Bryan it was a humbling occasion for his trusted partner to be recognized by the prestigious organization for services to the breed and the community. The award was only presented to two police dogs each year in Australia, and it was a significant and just tribute to Bear's distinguished career.

But Bryan's career needed to continue and in order for that to happen, he needed a new dog. A large new shadow was cast in Bryan's yard that caused Bear some consternation. A short-haired German shepherd dog, K-9 Shadow, arrived to leap into the backseat of Bryan's patrol car, much to Bear's chagrin. An interloper had entered the retired dog's premises, and Bear showed an incredibly jealous side he had never shown before. It was Bear's intention each day that he should be the dog to jump into the patrol car to go to work, but somehow the new fellow always beat him to it. Incensed by the new dog, Bear started to pick fights with Shadow and then Shadow reciprocated. Bryan soon had to keep the two dogs separate when he found that old Bear wanted to teach young Shadow a few "lessons." Life in Bryan's home became a constant dog-shuffling affair as the dogs exchanged places in the kennel to ensure they didn't end up in a "scrap."

Slowly, Bear became resigned to his fate, but he was never happy about it. And then one day, Bryan took the long-retired Bear into work on a weekend to give him a bath. It would take ten minutes for the bath and another twenty to dry him off with the blow dryer Bryan kept at work.

"He does tend to shed a fair bit of hair. Sometimes driving around in my police vehicle was like having my own personal snow storm going on inside the car."

Just getting to ride in the police car again was a thrill for the old gentleman. After Bear's long tangled coat was restored to its former beauty, Bryan took him to an abandoned nursing home in southern Adelaide where some other handlers were training. After doing some building search training, the other handlers asked Bryan what he thought Bear might be like after so long off the job. The dog had done no operational police work for eighteen months since his retirement. The group decided to test him.

Two of the handlers entered the massive sixty-plus room nursing home complex and hid in one of the bathrooms. A few minutes later, Bryan took Bear from the car, and the dog was suddenly transported back in time. He was back at work. A loud challenge at the front door of the building brought it all back to him and was all he needed to hear. Bear, with a new spring in his step, charged into the building. Within three minutes, he was standing outside the door of the bathroom where the two handlers were hiding barking and banging on the door just like old times. Bear had completed the exercise faster than any of the other current working dogs, just showing the young boys how a real pro does it. He had not lost it. He simply put the skills in a box until he needed them again. With that mission accomplished, Bear took one more ride home in the patrol car to finish out his retirement.

In his retirement, Bear is still popular. Bryan's adult children and his little granddaughter love the furry old man dearly, and he's a favorite of Bryan's girlfriend and her own children. The former police canine returns everyone's love in droves. Upon occasion he can still show a little resentment and make his wishes known when he digs a small hole not much bigger than his own feet just to remind Bryan that he hasn't taken him for a walk, but he is a mellow soul contented with his new place in life.

In his dotage, Bear still plays with the toys from the school children, and he doesn't mind an occasional dip in the cool blue ocean waves that crash upon Australia's golden sandy shores. On hot Australian days, he spends his leisure hours at home relaxing next to Bryan's swimming pool. On such days, it's not uncommon for Bryan to walk outside and see Bear standing on the top step of the pool with all four well-traveled feet cooling in the aqua water. He emerges after a good soaking with a massive shake as pool water from his long coat flies to spray everything around him.

Wet and bedraggled, the well-recognized police dog finds a sunny place in the sun to dream whatever police dogs dream. Four feet twitch and curved lips emit small high-pitched growls amid snores and low rumbles and once again, K-9 Bear is chasing the bad guys. He remains a reflection of his homeland—an heroic figure in the sun displaying the same classic and rugged beauty that is Australia.

Marilyn Jeffers Walton

Relaxing poolside in retirement
Courtesy of Bryan Whitehorn

K-9 Aron

"The Price of Valor"

In May of 1997, Terry Burnett realized a dream he had since he was seven-years-old. He was finally a police officer and was being transferred to K-9. Once with the unit, he was assigned a German shepherd dog named Charlie. Charlie was a donated dog, and the owners said he was just so aggressive they couldn't handle him.

"Let me tell you," said Terry, "Charlie wouldn't bite a hot dog. He was a laid-back, easy-going, loving-type dog."

As a result, Terry worked with him for five weeks trying to tease out or at least find a mere trace of that alleged aggression, but it just wasn't there, and the dog, with little regret on his own part, washed out. Terry was heartbroken. His dream job appeared gone. He was extremely attached to Charlie so the department let him and his wife, Jamie, adopt the laid-back washout. But that left Terry without a dog. The trainer told him that when he got a dog that really showed police dog potential, he would be amazed at the difference between Charlie and that dog that was truly meant for K-9.

About a week later, a dog crate was unloaded from a flight originating in the Czech Republic. K-9 Officer Allen Herald, Assistant

Trainer for the Metro Police, called Terry and told him to meet him at the airport. A dog had arrived. Terry went home and picked up Jamie, and they drove to the airport thrilled to meet his new partner.

At the airport, Allen told him a little about the dog named Aron. Then they approached the crate.

"This is your dog," smiled Allen, "You get him out of the crate. If he gets on you and bites you, hold on."

Allen advised Terry not to let the dog get loose in the area and that he would help get him off Terry, which made Terry more than a bit nervous. Holding the lead in his hesitant hand, Terry peered with some reserve into the unloaded crate. Two dark eyes stared back at him. There inside, he saw a long-legged sable-colored and very dirty German shepherd dog.

Terry called the dog's name, the massive head tilted and Aron emitted a low grumbling growl. With some caution, yet calling the dog's bluff, Terry slowly opened the door. Much to his surprise, Aron strutted out with curious interest in Terry and his new surroundings. Even after making the long flight and arriving in an unfamiliar place among strangers who spoke a different language, the dog showed an enormous amount of confidence. His ears and tail stood straight up, and everyone agreed he was a fine dog.

Terry hooked Aron up on lead, and from that moment on they began their K-9 career together. Allen went to his car and got a catch sleeve, put it on and walked back toward them.

"Let's see what he's got," Allen said.

Aron saw the sleeve and became very excited. From the way he immediately bit it, Terry could see his aggression level was high and that he loved apprehension work. Even Allen was impressed.

"Oh, my gosh," he said, "You've got a keeper there!"

Aron had new home. He never disappointed, and his training went so well that he quickly was put to work by Nashville, Tennessee's Metro Police. During the next months, Terry and Aron answered many calls for assistance, and the dream Terry had always had was finally realized.

Full-fledged partners

Courtesy of Terry Burnett

Terry Burnett and K-9 Aron train.
Courtesy of Terry Burnett

Early on the morning of May 14, 1998, just a year later, a twenty-five-year-old man prepared himself to go to the bank. He did not carry a checkbook or deposit slip. As he dressed, he covered a myriad of gang tattoos than stained his thin frame. He did not want to look too conspicuous. With unsteady hands, he carefully attached a fake beard and mustache to his face negating any previous thoughts he had regarding conspicuousness and then he slipped into a long-sleeved coat. He had a job to do. His drug debts were mounting, and his dealer was losing patience with him. He needed money to pay his debts, and he needed it fast.

After dressing, he found what he would need to assure him of success, two semi-automatic handguns. A 9 mm Glock in one hand and a .357 caliber Sig Sauer at his side would comprise the protection he needed. His heart pounded as he nervously loaded the guns and anticipated the trip to the Nashville's Regions Bank. His eyes darted nervously back and forth taking one last look to make sure he had everything, and he reviewed his plan in his mind. He had previously cut a hole in the fence leading to his escape route behind the bank to the near highway. Everything should work just fine. Although he was nervous, his criminal history emboldened him. He covered his dark hair with a hat and left for the bank.

Terry and Aron had been riding around for hours. Their shift started at 6:30 that morning. Already, it was getting unusually hot for that time of day. The muggy morning predicted the virtual steam bath that would follow later in the day when the sun had reached its zenith and the air became thick with moisture. For now, it was tolerable. The early spring heat had brought the trees and bushes to full bloom and even the weeds along the highways and in the fields were sprouting in full force, squeezing out any beauty that tried to grow there. Sleepy Nashville was just awakening, and soon traffic would pick up as the public headed to work. Terry's work day would be well underway by then, and he and Aron would be together for a long time patrolling the streets.

Terry was proud of the beautiful dog that shared his car and enjoyed working with his partner. He had loaded the big German shepherd dog in his cruiser that morning knowing he would have good company all day. They were both still fairly new to K-9 as Aron had only been out of training for about seven months. He was relatively untested during that time and certainly the day shift would do little to change that. Day shifts were often slow and lazy and afforded little opportunity for a young dog to demonstrate his finely-honed skills. Terry had great hopes for his dog as Aron had done well in training. He just needed that first test on the job to confirm Terry's faith in him. Would the dog perform as he did in training? Would he remember all that he had learned? Would he still remain focused in the haze of the adrenalin rush and excitement of an apprehension? That was what all new handlers pondered. Would the loyal bond that Terry had seen with other officers and their dogs be the same for such new un-tested partners? His attachment to Aron had been immediate, and already he felt great love for the big friendly dog.

At that time, the Metro Police did not have a permanent day-shift K-9, so officers from other shifts got assigned the day shift for a one-month period. They all yearned to be back on night shift where the action was, but the shift was a necessity and although they grumbled, they took turns patrolling by day.

"Day shift was not a very coveted shift, but when it was your time in the barrel, you just did it and made the best of it," said Terry.

So they would bide their time. The dog's time was coming. Terry knew that. Night shift was just around the corner.

Before traffic picked up, Terry drove to a local fast food restaurant to enjoy a little breakfast with his friend.

"Are you hungry, A-ron?" he asked the dog, in his soft southern style.

The question did not really have to be answered. Aron was a big dog tipping the scales at one-hundred pounds with not a bit of fat on him. Terry knew him as a real "chow hound," and the leisurely morning would allow Terry to get himself a cup of steaming coffee and some warm breakfast for them both to eat.

"When it came to food, he would wear me down by staring at me until I gave him part of my breakfast, which I really didn't mind doing it. I knew he loved sausage and cheese biscuits."

Terry pulled the cruiser through the drive-through and ordered. Aron's tail wagged happily as his strong front legs paced and his big paws tap danced in anticipation of the tasty treat coming his way. Besides being with Terry, the drive-through was a highlight of his day.

With a minimum of bites, Aron gobbled the breakfast biscuit snapping up the warm sausage and savoring every crumb. Breakfast over, the partners set out again to see what the morning would bring. Terry looked down and realized he had left his flashlight on its charger at home so he decided to run back by the house and pick it up and told Aron so.

When he got there, Jamie was up getting ready for work. It was still early so Terry took the opportunity to grab a second cup of coffee and sit down to talk for a few minutes. He expressed to Jamie how bored he was on day shift and how he couldn't wait to get back on night shift where all the excitement was. He and Aron were just coming to the end of their month-long day shift. Then it would be somebody else's responsibility.

"Just hold on," Jamie assured him, "in a few more days you'll be back on your regular shift."

She had enjoyed having Terry and Aron home at night so the day shift did have some advantages. Terry looked at his watch and saw it was only 7:30. He and Aron had many more hours to work so he led Aron to the cruiser and set off again for the city streets. Traffic began to flow by then, and nothing unusual had come up that needed to be attended to. So they cruised the streets for about another hour.

Then destiny intervened. Two paths crossed that muggy Tennessee morning, and a series of events was irrevocably set in motion.

A lone agitated man, holding two guns with his tattooed hands entered the Regions Bank. Brash and arrogant, he waved both guns yelling at bystanders and threatening to kill all of them. He pointed a gun at the teller and demanded money and then leapt up onto the counter to stuff a small bag he carried full of money. Bag in hand, he fled on foot barging out the bank's back door. In his haste to get away, he dropped the magazine from his pistol slowing his escape. He decided to leave the extra ammunition there as well as some of the money as he fled. It was more important to keep moving. At the same time, a teller sent a silent alarm to the police department to notify of the robbery.

Terry was slightly startled when at 9:00 a.m., Dispatch put out a Code 1000, bank robbery alarm, alerting him that he was needed at Regions Bank. It was so early in the morning and the banking day had only just begun. About the same time, a man working in the vicinity of the bank called Metro Police and advised that he had just seen a suspicious man go inside the bank, and the man's description was relayed to the responding units.

Terry turned on his lights and siren, and Aron probably just as surprised began to bark excitedly. In transit, further reports came in updating Terry on the situation. What he was hearing made him push the accelerator even harder to the floor. He was worried about the people at the bank and his fellow officers. Terry listened to each update intently. Just before he arrived, he noted that the suspect had just escaped out the back door as police arrived at the bank. At least one shot was fired by the suspect as he fled. Within minutes, Terry passed the fast-food restaurant next to the bank at a high rate of speed and swerved into the bank's parking lot. Before him, he saw the pulsating red and blue lights of many police cars and the flurry of activity as the police conferred and rushed to set up a perimeter.

After conferring with the officers on the scene, Terry was reminded about the magazine from the suspect's semi-auto pistol falling out and clattering to the ground in the bank's back parking lot. K-9 Officer Devery Moses, Terry's back-up, and his dog, Arco, met Terry and Aron and started their track at the spot where the magazine had fallen. Aron, at the end of a fifteen-foot leash, immediately picked up the suspect's scent and tracked across thirty yards of open ground to a wooded area behind the bank that abutted a six-foot fence. Aron threw his head up and started air scenting.

"Keep your eyes open," Terry told Devery, "the suspect's still close-by!"

Aron pulled hard to a place where the fence had been cut with a hole big enough for a person to climb through. Directly on the other side was a thick growth of trees, weeds and bushes. It would be hard to push through the barrier there. But Aron really wanted to go through the hole in the fence so Terry shortened up on the lead and squeezed through the hole in the fence with Aron leading the way. Given the quick indication by Aron, Terry felt sure that his dog would not require much time to locate the dangerous robber.

And he didn't.

The foliage looked more dense, and Terry could not see two feet in front of him. Through the thick leaves and branches that blocked him, he strained to peer through any opening he could find, but it was futile. All he could do was proceed with caution.

Five yards away hid the wild-eyed, drug-addicted bank robber, and he realized the handler and dog were closing in on him. The thick woods had slowed his progress as it had theirs. With the defensive instinct of a cornered animal, he saw only one option. The moment Aron stepped through the hole in the fence, the shooting began.

Suddenly, loud cracks echoed through the quiet woods. The flash of gunfire followed by the deafening barrage that rang out in quick succession was instantaneous. From inside the bank and out on the street everyone heard the sickening pop, pop, pop, pop of the robber's gun. A bullet ricocheted and hit Terry's thick boot grazing his heel and dropping him immediately to the ground. Stunned by the unexpected pain, Terry felt as though someone had hit his foot with a sledge hammer, and he reeled back as bullets splashed into standing puddles and splattered mud wherever they hit. The suspect fired continuously at Terry and Aron as they instinctively ducked for cover. The man refused to be taken.

Not being able to see the suspect ahead, Terry tried to back out of the woods as best he could pulling Aron by the lead back with him through

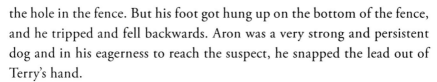

the hole in the fence. But his foot got hung up on the bottom of the fence, and he tripped and fell backwards. Aron was a very strong and persistent dog and in his eagerness to reach the suspect, he snapped the lead out of Terry's hand.

Suddenly, Aron was free.

The dog was enraged. He saw the danger the robber presented and every inch of Aron's body was geared to charge ahead and protect his handler from further assault. The man to whom he was so devoted and to whom he had an unspoken allegiance had been injured before his eyes. With renewed purpose, Aron thrashed through the woods to find the suspect and was soon out of sight. With unbridled fury, he lunged toward the suspect as the branches of springtime growth snapped beneath his weight. And the whole time the suspect never stopped firing.

"Aron did exactly what he was trained to do," Terry remembered, "he ran toward the gunfire to apprehend the suspect."

Like the crisp snap of firecrackers, more shots rang through the trees some ricocheting off of them with a sharp ping and others striking the ground all around Terry. When Terry fell back through the fence, he had fallen flat on his back. He tried to get up, but he kept slipping in a grease pit from a leaky grease dumpster that belonged to the fast food restaurant. Bullets splashed into deep puddles of rainwater that had fallen upon the pools of slippery grease making it impossible to flee. Terry was a sitting duck, and it would only be a matter of time before one of the assailant's bullets hit him.

To increase his chances, Terry began to roll back and forth thinking that if he kept moving, the bullets from the suspect's weapon would not hit a moving target. In a rapid staccato, bullets kept coming and struck everything around him, hitting trees, fence and the dry earth where puffs of parched broken ground flew upward with each strike. Realizing the immediate urgency of the situation, Officer Art Danner crouched low and darted to Terry and helped him back to the only cover there was, two small trees about fifteen yards from the wood line.

Terry thought surely the man would soon run out of ammo, but the barrage was unrelenting. When the officer was finally able to sit up, he fired his weapon back toward the suspect returning fire as best he could.

Officer Moses, just to Terry's right, fired toward the suspect with loud blasts of his shotgun. A full fire fight ensued.

As the shots zinged through the woods, Terry stayed low. Still feeling the sting from the bullet that hit his heel, he knew the man would not hesitate to kill him instantly. Above the steady loud stutter of the fire power there, he heard another sound, Aron crying in the woods. He still could not see the dog at all, and Terry was terrified. Aron's pitiful cries came from right inside the wood line. Ignoring his own injury, Terry tried to go back to the wood line and get him, but the suspect continued to fire keeping everyone pinned down.

Blinded with rage, Terry's only thought was to get his wounded dog back to him. Trying to regain his composure during the continual attack, he knew that recalling Aron was the top priority so he screamed out the German command that Aron knew well.

"Fuss! Fuss!" (Foose) Terry called, over and over, hoping that even in the heat of battle that the dog, wracked with pain, would remember his training and immediately obey the command of heel.

And soon he did.

In the distance, Terry could see the bushes rustle with a sudden slight movement. Terry spotted the brown ears and then the pain-filled face of his dog. He saw his furry, blood-covered friend crawling low to the ground but in a manner he had never seen. Aron was not using his strong front legs at all. Laboriously, the dog pushed against his back legs to move him forward inch-by-painful inch. He was bleeding profusely. As more bullets flew around him, he made the valiant slow effort and cried out as he struggled along propelled only by his back legs. Progress was slow, but he needed to be in Terry's arms.

When Aron got close enough, Terry crawled to him, grabbed him by the tracking harness and pulled him back to cover behind the two trees. Even though he was severely wounded, Aron obeyed Terry's commands with unswerving loyalty. Finally, he was at his officer's side. The dog was saturated with blood, and medical care was urgently needed to save him. But that was not Aron's concern. As best he could, while the two tried to stay hidden on the ground and bullets flew overhead, he pushed his back legs one more time to crawl closer to Terry. Wounded and struggling, he remembered his command and brought himself into perfect position beside Terry on the ground. Then, he laid his head upon Terry's arm to attempt to protect his injured handler with all that he had left. After a small pause, the suspect opened fire on them again. Terry knew he had to get Aron out of there and to a vet, but every time he moved the suspect opened fire again.

Then Terry heard the sound of a car and looked up to see a patrol car racing up behind them. Officer Brian Tomblin, putting himself at great risk, was driving. Crouched low behind the wheel and ducking beneath the windshield, Tomlin took direction from Garret outside the vehicle to direct him to position the car between the shooter and Burnett in order to use the car as their shield.

Stopping near the officer, Tomblin leaned over and spoke with Terry, still on the ground.

"Save the dog," is all Terry said.

With haste but difficulty, Terry and Tomblin lifted Aron into the back of the patrol car, and Terry jumped in beside his dog. He cradled Aron's big head as he held the gravely injured dog in his arms, and he spoke softly in Aron's furry ear.

"Hang on, Aron," he urged softly in the soothing voice so familiar to the dog. "Please, God," he begged, "help us, and let him be o.k."

Blood ran from Aron's mouth, and Terry could feel the blood gushing out from the wound in Aron's chest, and he prayed that they would arrive at the vet's before the dog succumbed to the chest wound. Two bullets had severed Aron's jugular vein. Time was critical.

"He had this look on his face that never in a million years will I ever forget."

Police Dispatch had called the vet's office, half-a-mile away and advised them that a wounded police K-9 was en route. Tomlin turned on all emergency equipment and at top speed, with lights blazing, the patrol car tore through the city racing through intersections trying to save seconds. When it arrived at the vet's, Terry picked Aron up and rushed him inside. The doctors worked quickly trying to stabilize the failing dog, but he had been shot multiple times and was still bleeding profusely. Terry tried to comfort him as he watched them work, but soon he realized that the vet's efforts were futile. The gun shots were too grave and the loss of blood too great. Still cradled in Terry's arms, Aron died on the table.

In shock and profound grief, Terry was escorted from the clinic.

"He died there on that table, and trust me when I say this, a big part of me died there too."

"....a big part of me died there too."
Courtesy of Terry Burnett

There was absolutely no doubt in Terry's mind that if it had not been for Aron engaging the suspect, he and most likely the other officers there would have died. Police reports later confirmed that the suspect had been only five yards away from Terry and Aron when he started shooting. He focused on Aron instead of Terry giving the officer just enough time to move and survive the incident for which he will be forever grateful.

It was all so surreal. Just hours before, they had been sharing sausage cheese biscuits and visiting with Jamie at the start of a leisurely spring day. Most of the morning, Terry had listened to the soft shallow pants of the dog behind him while driving around sipping morning coffee. And he had smiled at his friend who was so full of promise watching him devour every savored crumb of his special breakfast. Now the dog was gone. The back of the car was empty. The tennis ball that Terry constantly carried in the car for reward and training no longer served a purpose. Terry's best friend and his most loyal faithful partner had died doing what he was trained to do. The now-proven police dog never shied from the bullets to perform his job. He would not have thought to do anything else.

Back at the scene, the suspect still refused to give up. More fire power was needed to confront him. The response would escalate to a three-man SWAT team and one K-9 unit. They would go in and get the man out of the woods. A very special K-9 team was chosen, Allen Herald with his dog, Cliff. Allen and Cliff would go in front and approach the hole in the fence to make the suspect move. When and if the suspect moved, Allen was to fall back and let the SWAT team go in to pick off the gunman.

Very quickly, the SWAT team, Allen and K-9 Cliff were all in place. The highway nearby was closed in both directions. Sharpshooters stood atop roofs of the local businesses. The gunfight continued for nearly ninety minutes. With loud bangs, distracting grenades exploded on the ground fired from an overhead helicopter to allow Allen to advance. When negotiators tried to reason with the suspect, he only would let out agonizing moans emitting a loud "Ahhhhhhh" though the woods. With a riveting determination, Allen was adamant that the man would not get away no matter what it took. The shooter was very well concealed and lay in wait hoping an ambush would save him. He felt he could take them all, and if he didn't survive, he would take as many police with him as he could. Volley after volley of rapid fire gunshots bounced off the interstate embankment and between the surrounding businesses.

Allen and Cliff moved with stealth up to the hole in the fence. Allen spotted the suspect through the trees. As Cliff saw him, the man turned and fled from the dog and started shooting again. His ammunition seemed to be endless. K-9 Cliff never got close to the man as Allen pulled him out of the way to let the SWAT team through.

"There he is!" shouted Allen to Sgt. Melvin Brown.

Then everything seemed to happen at once. Allen and Cliff moved further back. The suspect opened fire. Bullets zinged through the trees. Allen felt the sting of one of the robber's bullets grazing under his right arm. And Sgt. Brown, catching a glimpse of the suspect, opened fire. The assailant's return bullet slammed into Brown's bullet-proof vest and then the suspect tried to move out of the line of fire. SWAT officers Jason Bedoe and Mike Garbo who saw the shot hit their colleague rushed forward and jointly opened fire killing the robber instantly. The stand off was over.

For the first time, the woods fell silent. Police crept through the woods, and when they were sure the man was dead, they approached him. The man's guns were finally quiet, lying on the forest floor, but the trees still held the smell of cordite within their twisting branches. The man lay dead with a few thousand dollars oddly fanned out around him in a circle as though it would protect him. Upon the bank robber's tattooed body they found one more thing, a single dog bite.

The community was safe, but at what price? In less than two hours, Terry's whole world was turned upside down. If it had not been for Aron taking the bullets, he would have died right there. It was a hard way to learn that any doubts he ever entertained about the dog's abilities were unnecessary. That one bite proved that the dog knew what to do and did it.

When it was all over, and after seeking medical care for his own wound, Terry sadly returned home to shower off Aron's blood. For three days, he could not remove the odor of blood that clung to him as tenaciously as the memory of his beloved Aron.

"He was my angel," said Terry, "He was the guardian of my life. I can honestly say that in the ten years since the bank robbery, not a day has

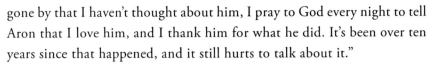

gone by that I haven't thought about him, I pray to God every night to tell Aron that I love him, and I thank him for what he did. It's been over ten years since that happened, and it still hurts to talk about it."

K-9 Aron was due a fallen officer's funeral. His body was taken to the Marshall-Donnelly & Combs Funeral Home, where the owners graciously took care of all arrangements for the fallen dog and on a somber spring day Terry stood at the foot of an ornate casket there to greet mourners. Before they arrived, he placed Aron's tennis ball in the coffin. It had been Aron's favorite reward, but now its presence there seemed like such an inadequate recognition for what the dog had done. But it was part of him and so it was a part of Terry.

"I told my wife that I would not allow him to leave without that tennis ball going with him. He loved that ball so much."

Once fellow officers and the public had paid their respects, the casket was closed and put into a hearse that led a procession through the city of Nashville. Three to four-hundred police units crept along silently with an hypnotic parade of alternating red and blue police lights. Allen Herald with K-9 Cliff drove along in silent reflection.

The sirens that Aron loved that had always signaled an adventure for him were silenced in the cars that followed behind his final ride. Motorists along the way pulled over to let the procession pass, and drivers and passengers in those cars held their hands over their hearts to signal to the police department that they knew and understood the pain of such a loss. As the procession approached the Metro Nashville Criminal Justice Building, the staff and courthouse employees lined the street there, and tear-stained faces watched as Aron passed.

The cars pulled into the parking lot of the K-9 training grounds into Ingo Memorial K-9 Cemetery, where over one hundred dogs were buried. Over six hundred people packed the cemetery and waited there. A little girl holding a bouquet in her tiny hands presented them to Terry saying she had once met his beloved dog. Bright daisies formed into the shape of a bone sat among dozens of sweet-smelling floral arrangements at the waiting grave, all a tribute to the fallen one.

Officers carry K-9 Aron to his grave.

Courtesy of Terry Burnett

Reverend William Dwyer, Police Chaplain, speaks at the gravesite.

Courtesy of Terry Burnett

Metro Police Chief Emmett Turner presents the flag that draped Aron's casket.

Courtesy of Terry Burnett

One hundred K-9 teams circled the burial place as their obedient dogs sat--sometimes barking, sometimes sitting quietly at their sides. Strips of black diagonal tape crossed the police dogs' badges, an outward symbol of camaraderie in the loss. A brief service followed and at the end of it the melodic and poignant strains of Taps floated on the air. The mourners broke ranks and slowly left for the parking lot. A hero buried, they loaded up their own dogs and drove away.

After the crowds went home, the training grounds once more fell silent. There were no longer sobs or soft words of comfort for the family or the bark of so many canines that accompanied their handlers for such a sad occasion yet returned to cars to ride home to finish careers. In that place where Aron had trained, fresh flowers marked the occasion of his passing, and their petals fluttered in the warming breeze of a sun-filled day.

Left behind just beyond a gently-sloping hillside was the peaceful resting place of a brave dog whose career was cut short in the springtime of his life. His journey with his officer had just begun, and they had been destined to travel many miles together. The excitement of the night shift had been just around the corner for him. He was a highly-trained dog, duty-bound to protect the public until one troubled man intervened. In that fateful moment everything changed. There would be no plaques and awards proudly earned over the years, and no array of lawbreakers successfully taken off the community's streets would be credited to the brave dog. There would be no opportunity to fulfill a lifetime of service and retire into the loving home of the man the dog had so honorably served.

The safety of the public and the lives of Nashville's officers had come at a steep price, one that only a dog of such high caliber was willing to pay. It seemed it has always been so in Nashville. Just beyond the brilliant hue of the flowers a few rows back is the grave of another brave dog, K-9 Ingo, former partner of Officer Allen Herald. The dog had been shot and killed by a fleeing bank robber in 1986. Two dogs, eternally young, rest together where they had once frolicked and trained. Theirs was a high calling. Age will not weary them and now in this sacred ground they will never to be forgotten.

There is no amount of Kevlar that can shield the pain of a K-9's loss. For the price of a few thousand dollars scattered on the floor of a thick woods, Aron's life was bought. There is no way to bullet proof emotions to protect from a grief so deep that those outside of K-9 can scarcely understand it. Aron was not "just a dog." He was a pet, a partner, a loyal protector and a friend, all rolled into a creature of great beauty and strength who would sacrifice his very being for the officer who returned his love. A sausage biscuit, a tennis ball and the companionship of Terry was all he required. He was a dog who was proud to wear the badge. Everyone agreed he was, as was proclaimed the day he flew into Nashville, a fine dog.

And now Aron was free.

Aron was given many awards and honors. They include the Distinguished Service Award, Metro Nashville Police Dept., the United States Police Canine Association National Office Monza Award, the 1999 President's Award of Honor-Tennessee Animal Hall of Fame and the USPCA, Region 13, K-9 Max Award, awarded to a dog that saves his handler's life. In addition, the Secret Service presented Aron with an award and a plaque.

Terry and seven officers from the bank robbery incident were nominated by the State of Tennessee for the Top Cop Award, and they all attended the event in Washington D.C.

"As far as I am concerned, that nomination was for Aron. He deserved the award. I was just there to accept it for him."

Terry Burnett accepts the Top Cop of the Year award in Washington, D.C.
Courtesy of Terry Burnett

Each year, the annual "Aron Hero Animal of the Year Award" is presented as a local award in Middle Tennessee and is given to one animal in recognition of a specific heroic action that the animal has performed. The award assures Aron's legacy in the State of Tennessee making him a dog that will never be forgotten.

Other dogs eventually came Terry's way. K-9 Ben came to him three weeks after Aron died at a time when Terry was questioning whether to stay in K-9, and Ben helped make that decision.

"Ben needed me, and I needed Ben."

They worked a full K-9 career together. Ben passed away in 2008 after a long battle with hip problems.

Officer Brian Tomblin, who had driven the car up to rescue Terry and Aron, applied for the K-9 program two years after Aron's death. When he went back into the military full time, he told the training sergeant as he left that he wanted Terry to have his K-9 Lazarus, knowing the dog would be in such good hands.

"We're in our fifth year together," Terry said, "He's been a real pleasure, and I love him to death. He's a good, good dog."

And Officer Terry Burnet would know.

K-9 Saxon

"Welsh Warrior"

The 5th Century Saxon invasion of the British Isles introduced strong warriors that were led by their chosen chiefs. Loyalty to the chief was the greatest virtue. If a chief died in battle, his men would, according to lore, die avenging him, and it was considered dishonorable to leave the battlefield on which one's lord had been slain. Accordingly, the warriors were sacrificed as well, since the chief and warrior were bonded for life and not even death could separate them.

The Gwent Police Department in Cwmbran, Wales, once had such a warrior. K-9 Saxon, so aptly named, demonstrated the brave characteristics of his historical human counterparts—a sense of duty and an unswerving loyalty to his master to which he dedicated his life. Like his ancient predecessors, he showed the same gallant bravery and a determined intent to defend his "chief."

That "chief" was Mike Townley, who acquired Saxon at a time when there was a critical need for dogs in the United Kingdom. In the country of Wales, in particular, there seemed to be complete lack of suitable dogs. Mike's dog, Baz, was rapidly approaching retirement and for two years Mike had been searching the entire nation for a replacement. So great was the need that it was not uncommon for handlers from United Kingdom Dog Sections to pass each other on the motorways as they competed to get to "a dog offer," only to find that the animal had been snapped up by the private sector or deemed wholly unsuitable.

By a stroke of luck, the chief instructor at the South Wales Police Dog section called Mike one day.

"Mike, you just have to see this dog that has been chopped from a course. He is just awesome."

Back on the motorway, Mike drove forty-five miles to meet with the instructor at the South Wales Police Regional Police Dog Training School, who told him that lack of time and money to correct the dog's failings, considered to be nothing serious, were the reasons he was cut from the training program.

Mike approached the vehicle where Saxon was held in a cage. The dog greeted the stranger with a very aggressive and protective growl and continual bark. Having no real home or loving companion, he stood protecting the vehicle, as close to anything he had ever owned.

Protecting his vehicle—as close to anything he had ever owned

Courtesy of Mike Townley

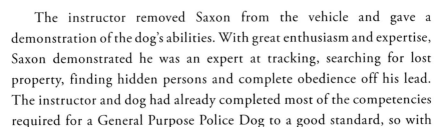

The instructor removed Saxon from the vehicle and gave a demonstration of the dog's abilities. With great enthusiasm and expertise, Saxon demonstrated he was an expert at tracking, searching for lost property, finding hidden persons and complete obedience off his lead. The instructor and dog had already completed most of the competencies required for a General Purpose Police Dog to a good standard, so with Mike watching, Saxon performed with good confidence and with ease.

At the end of the exercise, the instructor gave Mike the lead, and he worked the dog. It was unheard of, having never met the dog, that Mike was able to handle him with such ease. Saxon was driven to work, a natural-born police dog, and he would willingly show anyone who would watch him. Completely impressed, Mike knew he had found his next dog. It took just that one training session to form a life-long inseparable bond.

The instructor had bought Saxon from the South Wales Force, and Mike wrote a large check to the instructor to take possession of his new friend. Using the dog for police work, thus ensuring his own safety, was money well spent. Already affectionately dubbed "Sax," the dog went eagerly to Mike's car. Looking into the eyes of the new dog that was still a bit of a stranger, Mike wondered how many times he would depend on Sax to protect him and what the future would bring. They were just starting down a road together that led to an unknown destination. But from what he could tell, Mike would have a sterling companion for life to travel the road's often perilous twists and turns.

In the heart of coal mining country, Mike's home sat at the top of a mountain overlooking a lush green valley. The white frame residence sat fifteen-hundred feet above sea level and was the highest-dwelling in South Wales. The house that Saxon would call home was a self-sufficient one, using cool spring water and utilizing the power of the sun and wind for power. A herd of goats provided milk and cheese, and the bucolic surroundings were like none that Saxon had ever seen.

The cluster of white buildings on the hillside marks Saxon's ideal home.

Courtesy of Mike Townley

In the remote and scenic panorama, the family grew all their own vegetables and produced organic eggs. From the time that Sax first set paws on the land, he loved the gentle rolling hillsides and the majestic mountains. Miles of open pastures with grazing animals provided the ideal home for a dog that had never known such an ideal location.

At his new loving home, Sax had his own kennel on the hobby farm fully-heated with thick rubber floors and bright lights. But it was not uncommon for him to work his way into Mike and his wife, Caroline's, bedroom or to sleep at the top of the stairs on the landing where he had a good vantage point to protect that bedroom and those of the Townley children.

Saxon learned that when he slept in his kennel and Mike let him out the front doors that it was a work day. On those occasions, he trotted straight to the patrol car and sat down staring at Mike as if to say, "Come on, Dad, let's go."

On a rest day when he was let out of the side door, he wandered peacefully on the grounds to seek a warm spot to sleep in the sun taking not a blind bit of notice of any of chickens, cats, dogs or other wildlife that shared his hill. But when the pups on the farm visited with him, he loved to play with them and ran to investigate any cry he heard if one appeared to be in danger. Above all, Sax held a very strong bond with Mike's 14-year-old daughter, Joy, who like her mother loved the dog dearly. They respected him for what he was and what he did. He was Dad's protector full stop making him an integral part of the family. One of Saxon's greatest joys was to play upon the grassy hill with the Townley children, a pleasure he had not previously known.

Saxon at rest at his new home
Courtesy of Mike Townley

For the first time, Saxon had the freedom to play.
Courtesy of Mike Townley

Just a mile from the local town, the residence was a good distance from the rich industrial and urban areas and was a quiet respite from the bustling cosmopolitan nature of modern Wales. The Gwent valleys, steeped in industrial mining history, were one of the poorest areas in the United Kingdom. What they lost in wealth, they made up for in beauty, and now Sax was a part of it all.

The dog had to cope with every facet of a variety of jurisdictions, from the busy night life in the towns and cities to the sprawling countryside and vast open areas. Gwent was one of the four Police Force areas of South Wales and the smallest. Within its jurisdiction was a very mixed environment, diverse in geographical terms as well as population. If he was to be worthy of the Force, the dog would need to be prepared for all contingencies, and there was no telling what would happen on each night's shift.

Since Saxon had proved to have some failings where he had been trained, Mike immediately began his own concentrated training program to elevate him to a high standard and iron out those failings. Due to the expenses the department had previously expended on donated dogs that had failed to live up to the necessary standards, Mike wanted to know the dog well and wanted to make sure he was well-trained before presenting him to the department for consideration.

As they started training, Mike found Sax to be a serious, hard and courageous animal that needed a firm but fair hand. At home, he was the most affectionate and loving dog that Mike had ever seen. He knew when he was on duty and when he was off, never confusing the two. But Sax could be a stubborn dog. In the past, he had briefly known several "homes" and had been passed from pillar to post with little understanding afforded to him by his previous handlers. Doing much research into the dog's background and previous owners and by tracing the dog's breeding, Mike built a true picture of Saxon's 'being' and psychological make up.

Saxon and Mike take time out to play while preparing for competency testing.
Courtesy of Mike Townley

With patience and understanding, coupled with the correct reward-based training, Saxon responded intelligently and quickly. He developed all necessary skills and soon progressed far beyond the standards required for licensing. After just four weeks, the dog showed all the signs that he was ready to take his competency tests. If he passed, all he needed was to be licensed for his use as an official police dog. So confident was Mike with Saxon's abilities that he planned to breed the dog, hopefully to provide the same high-quality dogs for the Force.

In order to get a fully-independent assessment of the dog, Mike decided to go out of Wales for the test and made arrangements with an English Force to complete the Home Office licensing procedure. On the day of the test, Saxon performed all of the units of assessment to an excellent standard and was on his way to getting his ticket. His last test was the "chase and detain" during which the "bad guy" ran, and the dog was sent to detain him by biting a protective sleeve. By far, it was Saxon's favorite exercise. His speed, power and strength of bite were incomparable.

The "criminal" for the test, a young and very slim officer who was his Force's sprint champion, came confidently out onto the field. Mike had grave concerns for the man. Saxon was so powerful that he was afraid the officer would be knocked over immediately.

"No, it's o.k.," said the officer. "No dog has caught me yet in the distance allowed for the test."

All Mike could do was warn him that Saxon would be that dog and to be prepared for that and the force of Saxon's bite. With Saxon in place, the officer jumped from a tree seventy-five meters away and ran rapidly down the field. Following Mike's obligatory challenge to the man to halt, Saxon was released and thundered down the field to give chase. In a matter of a few seconds he caught the criminal. Not only did he knock him off his feet, but he dragged him back toward Mike like a hunting dog that had retrieved a prize duck.

"Here he is, Dad," he seemed to say proudly spitting the bewildered man out at Mike's feet.

All of the officers watching collapsed with laughter watching the poor sprint champ get up from the ground to dust himself off. They were completely awed by the speed and power of the dog.

"Now that's a police dog!" exclaimed the chief instructor.

Saxon was duly licensed, and he and his proud "Dad" returned home in triumph. Once home, Sax was given a large bone as the family fussed over him and lavished him with praise. As he contently chewed it on the kitchen floor, Mike regaled the family with the events of the day.

Newly-licensed, Saxon and Mike became police partners.

Courtesy of Mike Townley

The peace of the moment was broken when Mike's breathless daughter rushed downstairs and said that a car had just stopped outside the house, and four young men were running from it.

Only half-dressed in his police uniform with no protective equipment or a radio, he called to Saxon. Seemingly ready for action, Sax dutifully spit out his bone and came running. Mike put him on a lead and took him outside to the car. A quick check of it indicated it had been hotwired so likely stolen.

Mike put Saxon into his tracking harness and headed out across the open countryside. As a newly-seasoned and untested police recruit, Saxon began his search. The two tracked the youths across the countryside for about two miles before managing to catch up with them and detain them. They offered no resistance and were promptly arrested for stealing the car.

After arrests were made, Mike and Sax returned to their home where Saxon returned to his flavorful bone, and Mike continued to revel in the fact that he had the best police dog he had ever seen.

When Sax received his long-awaited license, the two were itching to get out on the streets to prove themselves. Once on the street, Sax continued to perform well and nearly every night resulted in a "Saxon arrest." From car thieves to burglars, Sax showed no mercy in tracking down his prey.

Riding around the more heavily-populated town of Newport one night, a call came for aid in the pursuit of a carload of joy riders. For nearly half an hour, the joy riders played high-speed games with a parade of police cars following them. Knowing all the short cuts, dead ends and difficult places where police vehicles could not go, they snaked through the town. The game ended when the joy riders' car ran out of gas.

Doors popped open, and three men jumped and ran. Fleeing from the vehicle, they were chased by two traffic officers. Saxon and Mike followed, coming up behind the officers. Mike could see one of the joy riders just ahead.

"Get out of the way," Mike shouted to the officers as he prepared to release Saxon from his lead to chase and detain at least one of the three youths.

But the officers continued to run on the same path leaving no straight shot for Saxon. The officers fell farther behind the running youth and when Mike saw that they had no chance of catching him, he let Sax go.

Mike's heart pounded fearing for the worst as the dog sped up to the running officers. But unbelievably to Mike and the others in pursuit, Saxon

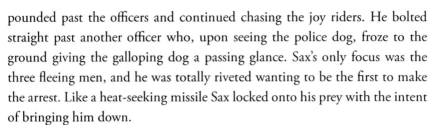

pounded past the officers and continued chasing the joy riders. He bolted straight past another officer who, upon seeing the police dog, froze to the ground giving the galloping dog a passing glance. Sax's only focus was the three fleeing men, and he was totally riveted wanting to be the first to make the arrest. Like a heat-seeking missile Sax locked onto his prey with the intent of bringing him down.

But, the chase terminated at a large fence, which was the perimeter of a scrap yard. Mike watched as the youths vaulted over the tall fence. Saxon jumped up and down impatiently, paced anxiously side-to-side and dug frantically at the base of the fence trying to find a way over. He barked and growled furiously in his frustration to get into the yard. Mike charged up behind the determined dog and put him on a lead. They quickly moved down the fence and found a more suitable place where they both could get over. With great effort, Mike picked up the huge dog and lowered him to the ground inside the scrap yard. The effort had been so great that in doing so, Mike slipped and fell to the ground inside the yard badly damaging his ankle and rendering him unable to move. Mike cursed himself realizing that the other officers in the chase were unaware of his location, and he was trapped inside the fence with the three hostile youths and that caused him great concern.

Sax instinctively understood what had happened and tried to help by licking Mike's face and nudging his legs in order to get him up.

"Good lad--steady now--friendly and nicely now," Mike uttered through his pain as he softly stroked Saxon's back creating some "fuss" to calm him down.

Still unable to move without searing pain, Mike tried to use his radio to call for help, but the battery had fallen off during his fall and was unfortunately out of his reach. Grimacing with pain, he crawled slowly towards the battery. Just as he reached it, he looked up and was alarmed to see the three youths that he had been chasing coming towards him armed with pieces of scrap metal.

As they got closer, Saxon realized the immediate danger and went into a defensive mode in a way Mike had never seen before. His whole demeanor changed from that of a dog that could show his aggression to one that indicated there was no doubt that he would also use it. Fierce and ready, he held the trio at bay.

On an extended lead, the dog circled around Mike barking and growling at the youths who were intent on doing grievous bodily harm to their pursuers. The brazen youths taunted Sax testing to see how far he would go. They threatened to kill both him and his officer.

"Kill the pig and his dog," they encouraged each other.

Saxon would not be pushed.

Deterred by Saxon's protectiveness, the brazen and profane youths resorted to throwing hunks of wood at Mike and Saxon from a safe distance. As the wood sailed towards the downed officer and the dog, Saxon tried to deflect the missiles with his body or catch them in his mouth. But he could not stop all of them, and a few of the hard chunks hit both him and Mike.

It seemed forever to Mike before help arrived, but as long as he had breath in him Saxon would hold the menacing trio off. At last, fifteen officers arrived to come to Mike's aid. Relieved at their arrival, Saxon remained at Mike's side protecting him while the battled ensued. The youths responded to the officers by throwing whatever they could find. Finally, the officers used blasts of CS gas to control the angry youths and to aid in their arrests. Trapped and surrounded, at long last they surrendered.

After the youths were taken away, two officers returned to assist Mike into a waiting ambulance. But Saxon was still feeling extremely protective and highly-charged, and he would not allow anyone near Mike. So with the dog on his lead, Mike crawled sixty yards to the recently-opened entrance to the yard. Officers brought Mike's dog van to the entrance, and Saxon was coaxed into his cage. Only then, could Mike be treated for his ankle injury.

Thinking the injury was not too serious, Mike decided not to go to the hospital but to continue the shift. After an hour of driving, he began to doubt his decision. In considerable pain, he signed off sick and returned home. With Sax safely in his kennel for the night, Mike crawled into the house and went to bed. There in the quiet darkness with only the muted sounds of the gentle night and the lowing of the sleepy farm animals outside his window, he replayed the dangerous event in his mind. He shuddered to think what could have happened to him without Saxon's protection. At the very least, he would have suffered a severe beating, and he dared not think beyond that. Like never before, he was grateful to the brave dog in which he had placed so much trust.

The following day, Mike's wife took him to the hospital where a broken ankle was confirmed. Laid up for six weeks in a cast, both he and Saxon were out of commission. Saxon became quite bored as he sat home with Mike. The family kept him busy as best they could by getting him involved with the chores around the farm, but it did not make up for his avid love of police work. Most nights during that time Sax spent in the house on the sofa next to Mike. Like two old married people, they watched television. Even though he was bored, Saxon knew Mike was unable to work. In his idle moments, Saxon's biggest job was to lick Mike's bare toes and rest his head on the damaged ankle. Mike counted the days until they could return to work.

After Mike's recovery, he got a call that a car had been dumped in a local town, and the men responsible for abandoning it had run off. Glad to be back on the job, Saxon barked loudly into Mike's ear in unison with the car's two alternating two-tone horns providing entertainment on the way to inspect the stolen car. Fitted into his harness in the early morning hours, Saxon worked diligently to find the thieves. The track progressed up the main street of the town, down some alleys, over several fences and through a field of fine Welsh sheep, but then it circled back to the same main street. Obviously lost and unfamiliar with the area, the thieves were not sure where to hide.

Back at the main street, Sax stopped abruptly. He raised his head focusing on the scent on the asphalt, and he started to growl deeply, which he always did when he and Mike were closing in on whomever they were tracking.

Mike scanned the area and saw two men about one-hundred yards in front of him. They stood at the outdoor display area of a used car sales room. Hidden from view, Mike watched them suspecting they planned a break in. With a loud shower of shattering glass, they smashed the window of one of the cars nearest the road, opened the doors and got in.

That was all Mike needed to see. On the lead, Sax raced towards the car as Mike shouted to the thieves.

"Police with a dog, stand still!" he repeated two times, but they did not respond.

Like Mike, Saxon waited to see what the men would do.

"Stand still or I will release the dog!"

At the sound of Mike's voice, the men frantically tried to start the car in a futile attempt to drive away. They hit the single post and wire security fence around the forecourt in the hopes of escaping before Mike and Sax closed in on them, but in haste and confusion the driver entangled the front wheels of the car in the wire preventing the thieves their exit. Gunning the engine, they continued their attempt to break free. Fearing they would break through and get out onto the street to drive erratically in their desperation, thus injuring themselves or others, Mike was all the more determined to stop them.

Another officer arrived on the scene to assist as Mike called to Saxon.

"Down!" Mike ordered, and Saxon lay down near the car.

Cautiously, Mike approached the car and with one swift thrust of his boot, he smashed in the driver's side window. Tinkling glass fell to the ground, and Mike reached in through the remaining sharp shards and unlocked the door. No sooner had he reached in than the driver pushed Mike's head down, slapped him several times and then pushed him back out the window. Trying but failing to maintain his balance, Mike fell to the ground on top of Saxon. No command was needed. Sax leapt to his feet and launched himself through the window clamping down hard on the driver's shoulder. Half in and half out of the car, Sax was not letting the driver get away!

The strength of the dog was tremendous. With a few hard tugs, he completely dragged the screaming man out through the dagger-like broken splinters of glass. Upon exiting the car window, the driver collapsed on the ground. Sax released the bloody man's shoulder but sat next to him staring into his frightened face. With his quarry captured, Sax grumbled a series of low growls to remind him not to move. His tone and expression seemed to say, "Just try it!" Both driver and passenger were arrested, and the driver was taken to the hospital where he was treated for his injuries.

After the incident, all of the officers involved went back to the station for a cup of tea. There was no question that Saxon was the hero of the night, and he enjoyed all the fuss that was made over him by the six officers that he had just met. Once more, Saxon demonstrated his uncanny ability to distinguish the good guy from the bad one and act independently on his handler's behalf. For all the training exercises that emphasized the importance of reading the dog, in Saxon's case it was most often the case that he was reading Mike.

The car thieves were given a small amount of community service as a punishment for their crime, but both were awarded compensation for the stress and injuries they received during their arrest, much to the astonishment of the officers involved in the case.

Many more cases would follow. The night shift always brought excitement, and on a cold winter night, Mike received an urgent plea for help.

"Urgent assistance! Urgent assistance!" came the breathless cry that was repeated from an officer screaming into his radio. Dispatch and other units could not get a word in so urgent was his plea. Mike determined the location of the endangered officer from the channel on his radio related to his location.

Being only a few minutes away from the town and with "blues and twos" blaring, Mike sped to the area. At the location, he beheld a terrifying sight. A mad man with an ax, knife and other weapons had attacked his girlfriend, who then called police, and they too were being attacked by the twenty-two-year-old madman.

Up ahead, Mike could see a male and a female officer who had both been struck on their upper bodies as they battled the man. They were suffering from shock and bruising, but Mike could not determine if their injuries were from the ax.

The madman was so high on drugs that even after they had gassed him and hit him with their batons, he showed no effects of either. Other officers arrived, and Saxon leapt out of the warm car into the bitter night to track the man. Entering into a dark frigid alley lined with stark wooden fencing on both sides, Sax picked up the track fifty-yards down.

Determined to kill his pursuers, the crazed man leapt out from the side of the alley swinging the ax over his head. Saxon started barking sharply as he protectively tried to fend off the man from attacking Mike and the other officers.

"Drop the ax!" the police repeatedly shouted in his direction, but no matter how many times they yelled to him, he refused.

Suddenly, and with great fury, he hurled himself forward to attack Mike. The police moved backward as he approached, and the man went totally berserk. As he swung the ax with all his might dangerously close to Sax, Mike could hear the swish of the sharp blade slice through the air. The next scythe-like swing came too close to Mike, and Sax sensed the immediate danger. With no audible command, Saxon raced forward and bit the man's lower calf. The drugs continued to dull the man's senses, and he did not react at all.

It would be an exercise in futility to use the dog to stop the man, so Mike pulled Saxon off and retreated further back down the alley. Closer to the main road, a group of people gathered to watch the excitement, and their presence energized the man more as he screamed incoherently and threatened to fight them and kill them all. Mike knew that if Sax was to charge again, the man would kill his dog, so he quickly decided that unless it was a matter of life or death, he would not deploy his dog.

The repeating cracks of splintering wood echoed in the alley as the deranged man swung time after time burying the ax head into the wooden fence posts. All Mike could do was hope that the ax would become lodged in the wood rendering the weapon unusable. Then he could safely send in Sax.

But that did not happen. The man made his way to the main road screaming maniacally. So focused was Mike on the man's movements that he tripped and fell to the ground. It was just what the man had waited for. With the strength of many men, the man turned and lunged towards Mike. The deranged man swung the ax rapidly from side to side fully capable of decapitating the officer. The assailant was totally whipped up into an uncontrollable frenzy. From an extended lead, six-feet away from Mike, Sax rushed in to protect his master. With seething fury, the dog attacked grabbing any part of the assailant that he could. He sank his sharp teeth into the man's stomach with vice-like strength, which would normally inflict severe pain. Once again, the man did not react.

Instead, the man shook free and ran into his house and raced upstairs where, unfortunately, he kept a gun. Sharp loud cracks resonated in the alley as uncontrolled bullets ricocheted off anything they hit. From the front bedroom, the man continued to shoot at police and their vehicles with his air rifle. Between moments of silence, which temporarily gave a false sense of security, shots periodically rang out and then once more, screaming at a high pitch, a hail of bullets zinged wildly about the alley.

Eventually, after nine long hours, the man was arrested forcibly and later sectioned under the Mental Health Act. The bravery of the dog could not be overstated that night, and both he and Mike were later commended for their actions awarded with commendation certificates.

Not long afterward, Saxon had the opportunity to show not only his bravery but also an innate compassion. On a crisp fall day, a desperate and suicidal man had left a note stating that he was going to end it all, and his car was found by a hovering police helicopter on a car park off

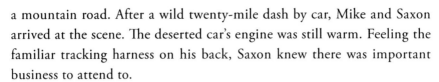

a mountain road. After a wild twenty-mile dash by car, Mike and Saxon arrived at the scene. The deserted car's engine was still warm. Feeling the familiar tracking harness on his back, Saxon knew there was important business to attend to.

For a few miles, the man's path led over the mountain, glorious in its vivid fall hues. Along the mountain path, items of his clothing and personal effects, which he was discarding on his way, were found on the track. It was becoming obviously clear that his intention truly was to kill himself.

Up ahead, there was a steep cliff, and Mike feared the man would throw himself off of it falling eighty feet to his death. The track continued, and a few miles further along Mike found the ominous signs of an empty bottle of gin and a pool of fresh blood. Even farther along, he found a blood-stained kitchen knife and all the man's remaining clothing less his shoes.

As Mike and Sax entered a wood, Mike became concerned. With a huge number of sheep and horses and people who were out for a leisurely walk to enjoy the fall colors, the track was becoming more and more contaminated. Saxon veered off in another direction, and the team found themselves in an area that was off a well-used walk and tourist attraction.

But Sax was totally focused and shortly after entering the wood, he disregarded the numerous distractions, and he soon found the man he sought lying unconscious beneath a tree. Wrists slashed, the dying man sat in a pool of blood.

The animated posture of the hunt subsided, and a more subdued Sax sat quietly next to the despondent man. The dog was a bit suspicious of the man at first and barked at the limp body. But when he instinctively recognized the lack of criminal intent, his compassionate side emerged, and Mike had to restrain him from licking the man's body to give comfort. Mike provided first aid using his shirt as a bandage and then he called for help on his radio. Other officers and an ambulance crew arrived and took the man to the hospital, where he later made a full recovery.

Because of the ability of the dog and the speed with which he performed, there was no question that he had saved the man's life. It was another commendation for highly-skilled Saxon in what had become a very distinguished career.

Formal portrait of K-9 Saxon, a credit to his Welsh heritage

Courtesy of Mr. Karl Pitwon

Mike Townley is a handler that fully understands attachment to a good dog. In the years that K-9 Saxon trod the open pastures atop his peaceful mountain home seeking a warm place to sleep quietly in the sun, Mike had the rare privilege of experiencing the indescribable communion between man and dog to the degree that few outside the K-9 world can truly know. The thought of separating the two would be unthinkable.

Centuries after the Saxon invasion of the British Isles, the Welsh legacy of devotion remains. K-9 Saxon serves as a shining example of how people should treat each other. Unshakeable trust, respect, love and loyalty are lessons a dog teaches well. As in ancient times, the chief and warrior remain bonded for life, and true to the old Saxon tradition whereby loyalty to the chief was the greatest virtue, not even death could ever separate them.

K-9 Rudi

"True Blue Dog of Sherwood Forest"

Nottinghamshire, England, is the home of Sherwood Forest and the legendary Robin Hood. Nestled in the verdant hills of the East Midlands, castles and abbeys dot the land in the scenic heart of what was until the 1980s coal mining country. Each year, when Sherwood Forest holds its famous Robin Hood Festival, jesters, fire-eaters and "rat-catchers" in medieval attire re-create the area's history.

Modern-day Nottinghamshire was not spared its share of rats to catch, but these rats mostly ambulated on two legs instead of four, and they often proved just as hard to catch. Assuming the role of modern-day "rat catcher" was Dave Brown assisted by his ready and able canines.

Dave never had a dog growing up, but he wanted one. His first few pets as he got older turned out to be renegades and vagabonds that no matter how hard he tried to discipline behaved as they wished. This odd assortment of strong-willed canine hobos, previously rejected by society, discouraged him from thinking he could ever possess an obedient dog.

He joined the Nottinghamshire Constabulary as a police cadet when he was seventeen-years-old, and for some time he delivered mail to the police dog compound where he could hear the dogs barking noisily inside. Surely, they were more disciplined than any dogs he had ever owned. He remained intrigued as to just how that feat was accomplished.

Over the years, Dave would find out. On his nineteenth birthday, he joined the regular Police Force and was posted to Warsop on the outskirts of Sherwood Forest three miles from Edwinstowe, the village where Robin Hood allegedly married Maid Marion. Legendary "Major Oak," the now 1000-year-old tree, where Robin Hood and his Merry Men had slept within its trunk, still stood in the town.

It was during that period when Dave was new to police work that he had his first encounter with K-9. At 3 a.m. one moonless Sunday, Dave was walking his beat when a police dog handler sped towards him, and after coming to a quick stop, told him to hop in as the team was off to a burglary in progress. Dave worked with the handler and dog, and in complete awe, he watched an experienced police dog chase and bring down three suspects. He was very impressed with the dog's obedience and skills and afterward seriously entertained the possibility of becoming a handler in the Dog Section.

Taking a German shepherd dog he then bought as a pup to a dog training club, Dave planned to learn the finer points of dog discipline. At the first lesson, Sheba twirled around on the end of her leash like a misguided yo-yo as though possessed by some demonic force. Wild-eyed and protesting vociferously at even the slightest suggestion that she should sit or stay, she snapped and snarled at all the other dogs that were, for the most part, strangely in complete control. Perfectly behaved at home, Sheba's Hound of the Baskervilles-like transformation continued and escalated with each succeeding class, until the dog proved to be a total distraction to other dogs and their owners. Soon, Dave and Sheba found themselves sitting out of most training exercises as social outcasts banned from any meaningful activities. The dog was beyond redemption he was told and soon the two castigated pariahs quietly dropped out of the sessions. Dave took Sheba home where she behaved perfectly once more happy to be home where she had always wanted to be in the first place and leaving him wondering which of them was the true master.

Not long afterward, Dave tried a new tack. He next looked into dog breeding. Naiveté still operating, Dave decided to breed Sheba but found only another training-class dropout for her suitor. Perhaps the new mix of genes, however, would magically create an unusually talented hybrid that would put both parents to shame. Optimistically, Dave put Sheba in a garage with her new friend. He and the other dog's owner peered in the garage window and watched both dogs play. Thinking the dogs were shy with an audience, the gleefully-expectant owners departed to give the dogs privacy. Dave later returned to collect Sheba and took the mother-to-be home.

He waited patiently, but, alas, no pregnancy resulted. Sheba's peer failed again and did not pass on any recessive genes that might have resulted in brilliant offspring. But eventually, Sheba was bred with a paid stud dog and conceived, later giving birth to eleven pups. Dave kept one that proved to be a lay about, completely unsuited for the rigors of police work. If only he could obtain that hard-to-find "good dog." Just as in Robin Hood's time, he found himself surrounded by jesters, but his were of the canine variety.

In desperation, Dave purchased a nine-week-old dog from a reputable breeder and called the dog Rudi. At the kennel, Dave wrapped the little fluff ball in a soft blanket and tucked him in the back seat of the car. Moments later, the young dog crept up to the front seat and climbed on Dave's lap where he promptly threw up his puppy breakfast. Momentarily, Dave wondered if he was not heading down the same road to canine rejection.

But at six-months of age, Rudi was enrolled at several dog training clubs. With an eye on Working Trials, Dave practiced diligently with the dog. At the training clubs, he came into contact with police dog handlers and their dogs, and soon he made an application to join them in the Nottinghamshire Constabulary Police Dog Section after having worked six years with the Traffic Department.

Dave and Rudi developed the most subtle of communication techniques.

"Rudi was an extension of my own senses," Dave said, "Habits, a flick of the finger, a nod of the head, a look, lift of the nose or prick of the ears, were all part of our language. We were a team each complementing the other."

Out on the streets after a thirteen-week training course, Rudi had become the obedient dog that Dave always longed for, and he proved to be excellent in his duties and demeanor. But Rudi had an odd quirk. He just didn't like his police van's blue light.

Dave and Rudi pose beside the police van with its blue light still intact.

Courtesy of Dave Brown

It is hard to say why he objected so strongly to it, but every chance that he got, he demonstrated his aversion to the dastardly fixture. When travelling at a high rate of speed with the typical English blue light flashing atop the van, Rudi felt compelled to work on the light's wiring to the point of disabling the flashing warning light. No amount of camouflage to hide the wiring fooled him. As the European two-tone horns blared loudly on the way to a crime scene, Rudi heard the light's constant whirring noise above his head on the roof of the police van. He then immediately started to work to dismantle the wires. Rudi had learned that with a quick bite through the thick bundle of connecting wires, he could instantly extinguish the light and silence the annoying whirring noise, and he became quite smug after satisfactorily completing his mission.

For that reason, Dave tried to use the light as little as possible. Each time Rudi ripped into the wires, Dave had to file a defect report with the department in order to get the devilish blue light fixed again. But upon occasion, he forgot Rudi's penchant for the wires and switched the light on as he accelerated. That always proved to be a mistake.

An immediate call for a street disturbance came one night when Rudi was at home. Dave hastily returned home to get the dog. After he was momentarily called away on an urgent matter, Dave quickly returned to the task at hand gathering his wits about him to proceed in haste to the call. Speed was essential. Every minute counted if they were to serve their purpose at the crime scene. Dave ran to the waiting van and slid into the front seat as fast as he could. Due to the nature of the call, the blue light was mandatory to clear the traffic en route. He flipped the switch and as the blue light started to whirr and revolve, the two-tone horns blared into the night. Rudi must have sensed the urgency of the moment no doubt picking up on Dave's completely focused manner and official deportment, given that they communicated flawlessly so for once he left the wiring alone.

Dave had driven about a mile and felt so proud that Rudi had finally adjusted to the flashing contraption above his head. All those praises of "good dog!" from training classes and on the job had finally paid off. His mature and respectful police dog had finally learned to leave the wiring alone. It was the pinnacle of obedience success that in the past had always been just out of Dave's reach!

Dave could see the reflections of the brilliant blue illuminate the car's hood and windows, a lovely sight he had not seen for awhile and sorely missed. Trees along the road were a blur as he passed by them at top speed. Rejoicing in the thought that he would not have to file a defect report, he noticed that the interior of the van was unusually quiet. Was Rudi ill? Dave risked a quick look around to the back to check on his exquisitely obedient canine.

There was no dog!

Tires squealing, Dave soon ground to a halt in the crunching gravel, made a quick U-turn and raced back home. What he saw at the gate was a figure standing holding a perplexed police dog on the end of a leash. Rudi pranced about in excitement seeing his uniformed officer return for him.

"Forgot your mate?" said his wife with an exasperated and unforgiving look.

With no apologies to Rudi, he ushered the quizzical dog to the van and stuffed him in. With a gigantic roar and sirens blaring, once more he was off to fight crime. This time, Rudi did not bother the wiring. Maybe the bewildered dog had learned his lesson. Maybe being left behind made him more cautious about ripping apart the lighting wires. This is why the man was the master of the dog. Expert training could eventually fix most errant behavior Dave thought as he drove along smug and self–satisfied that he had been victorious, and there would be no more defect reports to turn in. He could have popped his uniform buttons bursting with pride.

Finally, the van screeched to a stop at the crime scene. Dave tore open his side door and ran to the back to let Rudi out. Dishevelled, Rudi stood wide eyed panting and quite breathless. He appeared relieved that they had reached their destination. Dave saw that not only had he left the van door open to swing to a constantly open position, but the dog's crate door was also left open. As Dave drove at high rates of speed, Rudi had braced himself against the side of the van and dug his toenails into the crate floor holding on for dear life. Wind unexpectedly blew through the van, and it was all Rudi could do to keep himself from being flung out of the open door. Once more, the puzzled eyes searched Dave's face for answers.

It remained to be seen if the two arrived on scene for future calls with the blue light flashing and the four-legged beast in one piece. Short of having Rudi drive, there were nights when Dave thought it was doubtful. But there were enough cases that required Rudi's immediate attention that he braved the light and high speeds to pursue them still confident in Dave's care.

A cool English mist drifted through the air one spring morning teasing out the aroma of rich freshly-dug earth and sweet-smelling grass. Out of the car at 3 a.m., there was not a sound. Dave and Rudi worked stealthily to catch a thief who had been repeatedly breaking into gardeners' sheds to steal tools. The duo arrived at the small rented allotment gardens where local citizens grew vegetables. Over twenty separate plots sat divided by fences and hedgerows. All seemed quiet and undisturbed.

Dave parked the van in a secluded spot so that he and Rudi could creep unnoticed to the gardens. He peered from near a hedgerow, eyes straining against the darkness to see if someone was illegally lurking about, but he saw nothing.

Rudi did. The dog froze in his tracks, and Dave could visualize Rudi's hackles as the bristling coat rose up in anticipation of danger. Rudi lifted his sensitive nose to scent the air. He had detected human scent. His ears stood straight up creating a framework into the darkness like a night scope that Dave could look through. Crouched low, Dave peered through the two pointed ears and down Rudi's long nose to gauge distance and to find what the alert dog had seen move.

Dave never would have seen it on his own as the movement was so slight, but there just three sheds away stood the figure of a man hiding close to one of the garden sheds. The human and canine detectives had been idle for a week, and now their collective adrenalin started to pump getting ready to make an apprehension. From deep in his throat, Rudi emitted a slow menacing growl summoned from the depths of hell that made the hair on Dave's neck stand straight up.

"You there, stop where you are!!" shouted Dave with great authority as he sprang out of his hiding place to make his challenge.

It appeared the man moved again slightly, but it was obvious he had no intention of turning himself in. Panicked at being spotted, he remained weighing his options. Should he stay hidden as best he could or should he run like a rabbit through the gardens to seek refuge somewhere else hoping he could outrun the dog?

Increasingly annoyed at the man's impudence and blatant attempt to ignore his challenge, Dave decided he was not about to let this one get away.

"Police! Stand still or I will send my dog!!" Dave called out with all the bravado he could muster.

Again, receiving no response, he let Rudi go. Rudi relished the command he had waited for and took off in full pursuit. Dave could hear the drumming of the quadruped's quick feet as he ran at top speed through the recently-ploughed earth mimicking a galloping race horse. The moonlight shone just enough to distinguish Rudi's silhouette as he leapt up to take the man down. All four feet off the ground, Rudi sailed through the air like one of Robin Hood's perfectly-directed arrows and landed on the arrogant target. The dog would hang on during the skirmish until Dave could run ahead to release the tenacious hold. Jubilant as he followed behind Rudi, Dave strained to listen. He could hear Rudi's incessant growling as he grappled in the dirt as the non-compliant suspect refused to surrender.

"My God, he's fighting the dog!" thought Dave with alarm. "What kind of balmy thief would brace against the sharp teeth and vice-like jaws of a police K-9 for the sake of a few tools?" he wondered.

Then to his horror Dave heard the ripping of cloth.

At that, Dave leapt like a gazelle over pea patches and potato plants to make his way to the wrestling duo. He could only imagine what he would find when he arrived. The man would be terribly injured and in need of immediate medical care. Perhaps he should summon an ambulance. Dave ran even faster to prevent Rudi from doing too much harm to the stubborn thief.

When he arrived, Dave shined his "torch" on the ground, and the circle of its light traced a path through freshly-planted and very frail seedlings poking out of the rich garden loam. Thrashing around amongst the uprooted plants at Dave's feet, entangled in a fury of wrestling fur and tattered cloth, was Rudi with the poor victim. The man was well-dressed, or had been. He said nothing. There was no blood—only straw. Dave released Rudi from his hold, and the panting dog stood proudly showing off his prey, a disembodied, but not-too-forgiving scarecrow. This would be one for his fellow K-9 officers. The dog had just taken down a scarecrow!

Dave slunk back to the car leading his straw-covered but happy dog, who trotted along merrily at his side. The death of the scarecrow could have easily been the handiwork of one of his former mongrels of unknown origin, but Rudi was his top dog, and Dave shook his head in bemusement at what had just happened. But the human scent had been real emanating from the human clothing the ill-fated scarecrow wore before its demise. In retrospect, the death would not have required a dog at all. A simple match or pitchfork would have done nicely.

The next day, while off duty, Dave, with some remorse, went back to the gardens to do some explaining. In the light of day the whole place looked different and far less intimidating. Before he could say a word, he was intercepted by an irate gardener.

"It's a pity you and your dog weren't around here last night!" the man said with some anger and resentment.

Dave listened with a perfectly straight face.

"I put a lot of time and effort into that," the man said, pointing to the now-scattered bodily remains. "I even used one of my old suits."

He looked ruefully at the twisted and torn figure and spilled remains of straw lying in the dirt wondering what kind of a maniac would perpetrate such a deed against a formally-dressed scarecrow.

"A scarecrow that fine would have fooled the birds and kept them away," he bragged noting once more the quality of his creation.

Dave continued to listen intently and with a genuine air of sympathy.

"Vandals have wrecked it beyond repair," the man ranted, his ire building, "and they must have had a dog with them. Look at the paw prints left in my seed bed!"

The man was inconsolable. The only high point he said was that the vandals had not touched his tool shed or tools. Dave agreed that that was a good thing and as he left, he promised the man that he would do everything in his power to catch the scoundrels who had perpetrated such a dastardly deed against the poor innocent scarecrow.

The straw was no more off of Rudi's sable back when the two were called to search an empty house one dark night. Dave sent Rudi in ahead of him while he waited outside with another officer. Two or three minutes passed, and Dave heard no sound from within. In point of fact, it was eerily silent, and he grew concerned about his dog. As a few more minutes passed, he decided to call Rudi.

"Rudi! Heel!" he called and whistled to attract the dog's attention.

Suddenly, an apparition shrouded in black loomed over both officers. It seemed to be of enormous proportions, and it was not stopping. Like a giant bat, it momentarily hovered above them. Both men screamed and turned to run as the shape hit the ground beside them. There lay Rudi, who had leapt out of a bedroom window two stories up upon hearing his recall. He was not hurt, but the thought that he might be in a future scenario made Dave rethink how and when he would recall his dog.

A time when Rudi did not respond to the recall was when residents of the town's center heard noises coming from the premises of a building where a recent burglary had taken place. When Dave reported with Rudi, he found the building was already surrounded. Numerous challenges had been shouted into the building to entice the burglar to give up and come out and show himself. There had been no reply or surrender, so Dave took a try.

"This is the Police, show yourself or I will send my dog!"

Silence. Dave decided to send Rudi in to take a look around.

"Find him! Where is he?" asked Dave with some excitement to his voice.

Thinking the building was probably empty with the burglar long gone and with no sounds coming from within, either barks, screams or shouts, Dave carefully entered. But he still could not see or hear Rudi.

"Find him!" he continued to call urging on the searching dog wherever he might be.

Now he was getting really worried. As he had learned previously when the dog had launched himself out of a second floor window like a rocket, Rudi was not a dog to ignore his recall command without some form of indication. Dave worked his way through the building finding no trace of Rudi and soon found himself just outside the last room. He hesitated for a moment and prepared himself for what he might find. Slowly, he poked his head into the room. There sat a man well-known to police, and Rudi was watching him closely.

"It's about time you got here," the dismayed man said, "The dog's mugged me for all the sweets in my pocket," he said in exasperation, "and I've only me fags (cigarettes) left!"

It was not the conventional way taught to K-9s to hold a suspect, but it was one that proved beneficial to a dog with a sweet tooth, and it certainly got the job done. Rudi had never even begged for food before, and all the K-9s were trained for "food refusal," so they could not be poisoned, but as Rudi recalled, he had been trained for refusal of meat. He did not recall sweets being on the forbidden list. Evidently, the bribery game he played with the suspect was just ending, and when the sweets ran out, the sweets dispenser would have been bitten.

Fingers of English fog slipped through the night grasping everything in their grip when a call came that numerous cars had been broken into on a car park, and property had been stolen. The thieves had slipped away in the fog. At 4:30 a.m., Dave and Rudi arrived. A quarter mile away, they found an open-top sports car parked and unattended. Dave checked it and allowed Rudi to run free and stretch his legs. Normally, Rudi would not wander more than a few yards away but soon he was missing. Whistles and calling did not bring him back. Then there were muffled barks from near a copse of trees.

Running towards the trees in complete darkness, Dave confronted two motionless figures in dark clothing wearing motor cycle crash helmets. Rudi was circling them ensuring that neither moved. Both men held a half scissor, which they used to break into cars, but had Rudi not been there the sharp implements could have easily been used as weapons to harm Dave. The dog had proved himself to be a loyal protector of Dave on so many occasions during their career together. This was just one of many, and as the years passed, Dave grew immensely proud of his obedient and protective dog.

In the dog's sixth year, Dave went to his kennel to get him ready for a nightshift. There, he found his companion and partner lying dead. Rudi had shown no signs or symptoms of illness, and his death came as a complete shock. A post-mortem report revealed that Rudi had died of Parvo-virus. No vaccine had been developed at that time, and Rudi was one of the first fatal cases in the area. It was a traumatic end to a successful partnership and a tragedy that Dave never got over. There would be no more scarecrows for Rudi to battle and no more blue lights to still. The Nottinghamshire Constabulary grieved for the dog. It had lost one of its most valuable assets.

It was with a heavy heart that Dave, still mourning his loss, trained a stray donated to the department after the dog had been picked up several times. For K-9 Ryan it was his salvation, and he served Dave well for eight years until ill-health ended his service. Once again, Dave needed a new dog. He continued operational patrols with Ryan, who had always been a good tracker but a reluctant biter, while simultaneously seeking a new partner.

K-9 Ryan - Another of Dave's strays that stood proud to serve

Courtesy of Dave Brown

Dave's young son, Shaun, and retired K-9 Ryan

Courtesy Dave Brown

There was an acute shortage of dogs acceptable for training at that time. Any dog offered was brought to the kennels to be assessed. One was a thirteen-month-old German shepherd dog emaciated to the point of looking more like a slender greyhound than the noble shepherd he was. He was a gift dog named Jason from the Gainsborough, Lincolnshire region. Dave peered into the kennel to observe him.

"Who the hell brought this in?" he thought.

The dog had been donated by its owner, a man with a police record who preferred the dog not go to his local police department for fear of it perhaps apprehending him one day. So the pitiful animal was donated to Nottinghamshire. When the police went to pick it up, the dog was tied to a dustbin in the backyard.

Newly released from his prison, the frightened dog cowered and snarled at the back of the kennel. Temperament alone was already working against him, and Dave was not optimistic. With no other dogs to choose from, Dave took a closer look. The rescued animal was a moth-eaten walking skeleton with a tangled coat and dull eyes, and all his ribs were showing. Perhaps, the skeptical officer thought, he could fill him out. Dave tried to visualize what he would look like with more meat and muscle.

With long legs and a long neck he was an unusually tall dog. With a shredded-wheat coat looking as though it had never felt a brush or comb from the day of the dog's birth, all the prospective handlers who saw him had the same negative reaction. The lean dog was nick-named "G. Raffe," and the "kennel maid," employed by the police at Headquarters Kennels to care for the dogs insisted that it be returned to its owners as all it did was try to bite her hand.

Still spitting and snarling through the wire, the stray looked rather startled as Dave opened the gate, but it did not want to come near. After spending days sitting in the kennel winning it over, mostly with food, Dave eventually secured the soulful dog's confidence, and one day the curious creature came to him.

The dog that had been so aggressive trusted no one. But as the reluctant animal softened, Dave named him Laser and took him along with Ryan for a shift in the van. By the end of one shift, he showed Dave he could travel well and could also bark at strangers. But the next day, Dave was told that the dog was to be returned to its previous owner. Dave found himself pleading to keep the furry ragamuffin and explaining why he should be given a chance. The dog had engaged Dave far more than he had realized.

Finally, it was decided that Laser would be kept providing Dave could put weight on him and show the dog was worth the trouble. Laser ate up to six meals a day and slowly gained weight, but Dave dared not let him out in public for fear that as the owner he would be accused of neglecting the dog. Laser had dysentery, but it cleared, and when he was looking a little better, he started to work at night for a week with Dave and Ryan.

Laser was soon introduced to home and family during the daylight hours making it easier for the transition and to prevent sleepless nights for Dave or the neighbors because of a howling dog expressing his emotions in the outside kennel at night. Juggling two working dogs, Ryan was occasionally left at the police kennels, and Laser, affectionately known by all as, "The Hat Rack," was settling down at home. At 4 a.m., in an effort to make it easier to look after two dogs, Dave dropped Laser off at home after a partial shift and secured him in the kennel. Before he could even reach the van, Laser howled out his displeasure, and Dave ran back and took him back out again to finish the shift.

By that time Dave's son, Shaun, became a Special Constable, and the two were the only father and son that "double-crewed" in the Dog Section. Growing up hearing Dave's tales of crime fighting and watching his father's interactions with a whole host of dogs would provide valuable lessons for the novice son.

Dave and the tall, handsome, Laser, testimony to what love and care can do

Courtesy of Dave Brown

Dave, Laser and Dave's son, Shaun, in later years
Courtesy Dave Brown

Laser eventually became more comfortable in his new home. He paid back the generosity extended to him by helping with the laundry. As quickly as Dave's wife hung her wet laundry on the outdoor clothes line, Laser came behind pulling it down, no doubt to see if it was drying properly. He was a fastidious dog not given to attending to nature's calls in his kennel. When nature called, he simply broke out through the wire mesh, and while out and about, he took the opportunity to raid the unattended rubbish bins. After two breakouts and undercover raids in the same week, Dave had to replace the chain link with "weld mesh" to keep Laser in and to end the nightly raids.

Just after midnight one muggy August night, a youth tried to steal a car and was chased and lost from sight. Other police caught glimpses of him but he eluded them again. Dave and Laser searched the area, and forty-five minutes later Laser stopped abruptly and jumped up to sniff the lid of a wheelie dust bin. Was his old affinity for dust bins returning? But this was different. Laser gave a deep growl and as Dave lifted the lid of the container, he saw a well-built seventeen-year-old sitting with his knees under his chin who then popped

out like a jack-in-the-box. All the undercover night-time dustbin research that Laser had conducted in his yard turned out to be well worth the effort.

There was never any predictability determining where lawbreakers would hide. At 3:15 one sunny afternoon, Laser and Dave arrived at an abandoned factory complex. Two men had already been arrested for theft of lead from the roof, and a third man was believed to be hiding in the vicinity. Laser searched the empty building but found nothing.

The roof of the building was dangerous to walk on so Dave summoned the assistance of the Fire Brigade. With a ride in "Simon Snorkel," the hydraulic lift, a full visual search was made on the roof. When the third man was not found there, the brigade left along with all other police officers. But something did not sit right with Dave. His suspicion was that the third man was still there and if necessary, he would wait the man out. So he secreted himself and Laser in a corner of the main factory floor to play a waiting game. With Laser's deadly yet silent reputation, he would not give them away.

After the suspect had not heard a sound for forty minutes, he suddenly appeared at the farthest point away from Dave diagonally across the floor. Both men jumped in surprise at seeing the other. Like an agile spider, the startled man scurried up the wall next to him heading for a hole in the roof. Laser tried to detain him, but the man was too quick and got away through the hole and out onto the fragile asbestos roof.

Dave radioed for the Fire Brigade to return, but by the time they arrived the suspect had once more disappeared into thin air. This time, a big show was made of the entire search party leaving the area, an exercise in one-upmanship to match the suspect's disappearing act. If he could disappear, so could they. A substitute drove Dave's van away adding the element of credibility by sounding the loud two-tone horns for good measure.

Once more, Dave and Laser played the waiting game, this time in another part of the factory just beneath a hole in the roof he calculated would be near where the man had vanished like smoke on a windy day.

Shortly after 5 p.m., Dave heard movement above him. Patience had won the day. Carefully remaining in the shadows where he hid, Dave watched as two feet emerged through the hole. The man continued lowering himself with his face to the wall. Then, the rest of his body slid downward slowly, silently slithering like a snake as he eased through the hole. Just inches away, Laser pricked his ears and gave a fixed stare. Dave took a step forward out of the shadows with Laser on the leash, and as the man touched the floor, Laser touched the man's backside with his cold nose. It was more than a cold nose that made the man freeze.

"Do I need to get him to open his mouth?" Dave asked politely.

Another criminal was off the streets. The dog that had looked so scruffy in the kennel early on continued to perform well. Dave built confidence in dogs and made them proud. Laser was no exception. When the Dog Section needed to publicize their need to recruit new dogs, it was the "Hat Rack," that was chosen to pose for the newspaper advertisement. With Dave's police cap placed jauntily upon the furry head, Laser "smiled" broadly, the image of a content, accomplished and well-adjusted police dog.

"The Hat Rack's" face appeared in newspaper ads
publicizing the need for new recruit dogs.

Courtesy of Dave Brown

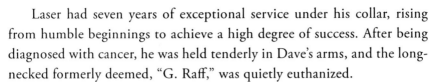

Laser had seven years of exceptional service under his collar, rising from humble beginnings to achieve a high degree of success. After being diagnosed with cancer, he was held tenderly in Dave's arms, and the long-necked formerly deemed, "G. Raff," was quietly euthanized.

Before his retirement, Dave was to work with one more dog. This time, he chose an English springer spaniel named Jerry, who was trained as a bomb detection dog. In 1993, England was still under terrorist threat from the IRA. Due to their bomb detection capabilities, a price was put on the heads of the explosives dogs. Jerry was no exception.

The dog was an agile and dedicated companion that was very good at his job. However, like the other dogs Dave had partnered with, this one occasionally provided Dave with some memorable moments.

The British Royal family had a strong connection with The Dukeries in an area of North Nottinghamshire so the family members visited there often. On the day that Princess Anne was to visit a prestigious and stately church there, Dave and Jerry were called to search the premises before her arrival. Since none of the Royals liked the sight of police dogs preparing the way for them, Dave needed to be thorough, yet quick and unobtrusive.

Just minutes before the arrival of the princess, Jerry's toenails clicked along the old stone floor of the massive church. Off leash, he sniffed in its ancient corners and often in his enthusiasm, he shot out of Dave's line of sight. As Jerry skittered around a corner, Dave promptly called him back. Seconds later, they rounded that same corner together. Like an abstract and prized ceramic sculpture, a malodorous steaming obelisk perfectly displayed and positioned on the cold stone floor confronted Dave. Somewhat sheepish and not nearly as fastidious as Laser had been, Jerry paused to make the same observation. The look on the dog's face mirrored his thoughts.

"Who on earth has done that!" he seemed to say, but the indignant response could not belie just a hint of pride on the dog's part.

At that moment, the old abbey echoed with voices and the footsteps of the royal entourage, which was quickly approaching. Fumbling in his trouser pocket, Dave found a thin plastic glove that he normally used to handle training aids so as not to transfer or cross contaminate with scent. Quickly snapping it on, he crouched down and scooped up Jerry's creation.

Turning the glove inside out, he shoved it back into his pocket just as the echoing of high heels paused in the passageway where he stood. Dave had left the floor spotless, but he could not eliminate the distinctive odor. Quick thinking and with the untimely deposit safely stowed warming his leg, Dave launched into a discussion of the pitiful state of the malodorous floor drains in the old building. Jerry sat angelically below as if confirming every word. Then they made a fast exit.

Dave demonstrates some unconventional training with Jerry in his quest for the elusive, perfectly obedient dog.

Courtesy of Dave Brown

Jerry responds accordingly.

Courtesy of Dave Brown

Three years later, Dave retired, and Jerry lived at home with him as a cherished, but highly-skilled pet. The man, who had so much trouble coaxing obedience from his string of early dogs before joining the Dog Section, later became another of the successful K-9 trainers of the Nottinghamshire Police. He knew dogs well, and he trained them even better. For over his career he had been paired with the best, and despite their differences, the one common thread was their love for him. Humor, love and respect for each other cemented their bond. In Sherwood Forest where Robin Hood took from the wealthy to give to the poor, Dave Brown found the poorest of dogs giving them attention and nurturing their pride. And in the process, he made his formerly poor dogs exceedingly rich.

K-9 Shadow

"The Face of Winter"

He was a one-man dog that did not fit well with his human family, and after only a little over a year, the eighty-pound German shepherd dog that bore the name Shadow would have to find a new home. He was an intelligent dog, headstrong and brash, and his personality did not lend itself well to family living. He continued his life at the home day after day with increasingly poor results. The independent dog was finally donated to the Saint Paul, Minnesota, Canine Unit by his family after he had severely bitten his owner's young granddaughter. The options for Shadow were two-fold the owner had succinctly explained. The dog would be donated in hopes that he could become a police service dog or he would immediately be "put down," as his owner was not willing to risk another serious bite from him on a child or on any other individual.

The Head Trainer for the Canine Unit in 1998, Don Slavik, went to Prior Lake, Minnesota, and screened Shadow at the owner's home on a cold January day. When he stepped out of the warmth of his car, Don saw the dog in question in the yard. With a menacing growl, Shadow instantly charged him. Not deterred, Don tossed a Kong ball about the yard, and he was pleased to see that Shadow showed interest and ran to retrieve it for the moment showing a somewhat playful side. Looking past the dog's initial showy bravado, what Don saw was a strong, confident and tough dog. Those traits were enough to save him and give him a flicker of hope with the Saint Paul Police Canine Unit.

Shadow was about to turn fourteen-months-old as the Canine Unit recruited and selected German shepherd dogs for its spring Basic Canine Handler's School. Mark Ficcadenti, Saint Paul's Assistant Trainer at that time, before becoming Head Trainer the following summer, knew of an officer just entering K-9 school. The student was an outstanding man whom Mark wanted to give the finest dog to train. Mark decided to take a look at the new dog that had been banished from its home so he stopped by the police kennel.

Shadow had been in the police kennel for a week, and ordinarily all the dogs were taken out to play in order to socialize them.

"Not Shadow," said Mark. "No one had the courage to let him out of his kennel for Shadow was just plain mean and nasty. He hated everybody and let them know it in no uncertain terms."

But when Mark by some miracle did get the growly dog out of the kennel, he found that letting Shadow out of the kennel was not the problem. The problem arose when it came time to put him back into the kennel. Plain and simple, Shadow did not want to go back in, and no one was going to make him. Teeth bared, he swaggered about and defied them all.

Mark was a highly-experienced dog trainer, and he found the dog to be a challenge. Mark's calm voice and carefully-measured words had tamed many dogs before Shadow. He understood dog psychology and was no stranger to challenging the aggression he saw in a dog and funneling it into a positive good in the right situation. Mark assessed the situation as he saw it and formulated a training regimen for his new charge. He would need to master the dog and use techniques suited to the unique personality of Shadow. It was time for the trainer to institute some time-honored hot dog persuasion.

The plan got underway. As Shadow strutted with an air of boldness outside his kennel, obstinately refusing to re-enter his cage, Mark tossed hot dogs into the space to bait him back inside. It would be a long process, but Mark was well-armed. The strategy was to first throw the meaty missiles at Shadow's feet since once he was out of the kennel, the brazen dog roamed freely keeping his distance. At first, surprised by the unexpected gifts, he savored all that were thrown his way and then expected more. Mark next

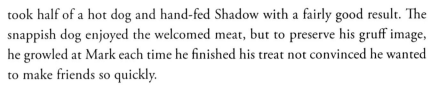

took half of a hot dog and hand-fed Shadow with a fairly good result. The snappish dog enjoyed the welcomed meat, but to preserve his gruff image, he growled at Mark each time he finished his treat not convinced he wanted to make friends so quickly.

"Yes, dogs do bite the hand that feeds them," Mark said, dispelling an old myth, "for it has happened to me before."

Directing the surly dog to his kennel enclosure was the next step. Mark tossed hot dog pieces into the kennel, and Shadow trotted in after them. Then Mark, self-satisfied that he had outsmarted the dog, quickly closed the gate.

But Shadow was soon on to the game. After the first few times that he found himself locked back in the kennel and realized his hot dogs were gone, he changed his own strategy. Afterward, when Mark tossed the pieces of hot dog directly into the kennel, Shadow would only tiptoe part way in, grab the meat and quick as a flash exit before the gate could clang shut. No amount of slight of hand could fool him.

The trainer needed to trump the smart dog in frankfurter finesse or Shadow would maintain the upper hand. But Mark had not fired every shot in his Oscar Meyer arsenal yet. He next led Shadow to the outside kennel, which was much deeper. The trainer would be quicker as the gate keeper as Shadow had a further distance to run back out in the race for freedom. Mark tossed the pieces deep into the kennel run so that Shadow had no choice. If he wanted them, he had to go deep into the kennel to get them. His appetite overcame his recalcitrance, and he willingly ran to the back of the long kennel run to relish what he had come for.

After a week, Shadow was won over by the taste of hot dogs and allowed Mark to gently grab the then more docile dog by his collar and just guide him into the interior kennel. That progressed to feeding Shadow a hot dog as a distracter in order to gently slip a leash on him.

"Once on leash for that first time, it was clear sailing, because he then had some level of trust in me."

When he was less cranky and more manageable, Shadow was allowed to roam free for awhile in the police office to further socialize him, for the next challenge was to muzzle him and bring him into the department's veterinarian for hip x-rays and a general physical before the beginning of spring training.

*Wearing an angry face and a muzzle, Shadow is
readied for his veterinarian's appointment.*

Courtesy of Mark Ficcadenti

It was a gradual process, but soon Mark was able to muzzle the hot dog connoisseur and take him for his check-up and x-rays. Then he waited for the results.

"Shadow is hereby disqualified as a police service dog candidate based on reading of the x-rays," said Doc Wetherhill at the Como Park Animal Hospital in Saint Paul. "He has severe hip dysplasia and will not be able to withstand the rigors of training and do what police dogs need to do."

These were not the words Mark wanted to hear. He had too much emotionally invested in the dog that had recently come his way. He had been so anxious to give the dog to the new K-9 handler to train. And short of that, the general public did not routinely place want ads seeking to find a large surly dog with a propensity to bite. There was really nowhere else for the Shadow to go.

After receiving the bad news, the vet did say that he would send the x-rays off to the radiologist at the University of Minnesota who was considered to be an expert. Unfortunately, the second opinion only confirmed the first, and the expert had annotated, "This dog is unsuitable for police work." The expert said Shadow's hips were so bad that he could not guarantee that the dog would last a day, a week or a month.

With the confirming diagnosis, Mark knew that he could not rightfully assign Shadow to the young officer that waited for him. After some searching, he found another suitable dog and made that assignment. But much debate ensued about what to do with Shadow. Don gave the situation some serious thought and offered his advice.

"If I were you, Mark, I would take that dog. He will be a police dog."

Mark had not seriously considered taking Shadow until Don had suggested it. Just one week previous, myelopothy had taken its toll on K-9 Tyke, Mark's ten-year-old first partner. The old dog had been battling the effects of the degenerative spinal disease since he was four-years-old, and on a recent chilled morning he awoke unable to steady himself on his hindquarters so he was immediately retired. Mark's only option for a replacement for the spring classes was Shadow. He was eager to take on a more serious dog because Tyke had been young and quite a soft dog.

"A harder dog, a dog that seemed like a natural," said Mark, "posed an exciting challenge to me."

The decision was made, and Shadow was now Mark's dog, snaps, snarls, bad hips and all. Mark knew that Shadow had always been and would always be a one-person dog, and Mark's wife, Linda, realized that immediately when the dog was brought home. Shadow had a very hard look to his face that Linda called his "Winter Face," tough and stressed with an expression that kept everyone away. He had used it so often that it became his permanent look, hard and tough all the time. His eyes were yellow, and people believed Shadow to be a wolf mix, but he was simply Shadow, a German shepherd dog that would probably like the fact that the public thought him to be wolf-like. Linda wanted so badly to pet and nuzzle the big dog, but he always kept her at a distance and preferred it that way. When she chanced to come near his backyard kennel, he barked and growled at her reinforcing his message to remove herself from his solitary world.

Solitary, wolf-like Shadow on a cold Minnesota day
Courtesy of Mark Ficcadenti

Still, as often as she dared, Linda went out to the 6x6x12 heavy-gauge wire kennel to present herself as a non-threatening entity. Through the wire, she could see Shadow's insulated dog house just large enough for him to fit in comfortably on the shaved cedar-chip bedding where he curled up on winter days absorbing the warmth of his own body heat. Linda worried about Shadow during the severe cracking summer thunderstorms and during the strong frigid winds of winter, but although he was brought inside when the weather turned extremely severe, Shadow was not bothered by much and showed no distress during inclement weather as he rested in the solitude of his simple dog house.

Linda decided early on that if Shadow was to trust her at all, he would need to figure her out. But it was not an easy task, and time was limited. Most of the time Shadow was with Mark, and when at home, he was in his kennel. Their paths seldom crossed. Shadow was very territorial about his kennel, and he did not want Linda near it. But she had such a small widow of opportunity she had to take advantage of that time he was in the kennel whether he was territorial or not.

Distant and aloof, Shadow stares at Linda from his kennel.
Courtesy of Mark Ficcadenti

Not too closely at first, she sat with her back toward him adjacent to the kennel and began talking, always being careful not to look directly into his golden eyes. By avoiding eye contact with Shadow, he would not feel compelled to snarl, growl or bark to protect his territory. He just sat and watched and listened.

It did not matter what she talked about, she just wanted him to get used to her voice. She talked about the birds and critters in the back yard and about the children and told him how he must protect them. She told him how much respect she had for him, and he seemed to listen intently.

"You have a very special and unusual job, Shadow," Linda told him, "more meaningful than many jobs people have. You are so lucky and privileged to have your job. It's a great life for a dog."

When she ran out of things to say, she would just sit. For six months, Linda held her one-sided conversations with Shadow commenting on everything the dog could see as the seasons slowly changed in his back yard. Eventually, Linda began moving closer—then a little more close— and finally, she started sitting sideways towards him just outside the kennel.

Mowing the lawn brought back the warning snarls and barks, but Linda assured Shadow that he was a good boy with each pass of the mower near his forbidden territory, and after many, many months, he progressed to the point that he no longer growled and barked at her when she cut the grass. Even then, she still did not dare to pet him for the chance of being bitten was too great. So saddened by the dog's lack of any real response to her friendly overtures, she watched from a distance for the most part as Mark alone interacted with the dog, and she remained just barely tolerated.

There was a lot to do to prepare Shadow for a career with the police. Mark knew what the rigorous training would entail. The drive and passion in the dog were there, and he knew Shadow was an extremely tough dog that could work through any difficulty with bad hips. As best he could, Mark would condition the dog and keep him in top physical shape. So when the weather warmed, he took the dog five-days-a-week to Lake Phalen in Saint Paul where Shadow swam daily for nearly forty-five minutes.

Keeping his muscles strong, Shadow swims in Lake Phalen.

Courtesy of Mark Ficcadenti

*The Saint Paul Canine Training Facility named after murdered
K-9 Officer Tim Jones and his partner, K-9 Laser.*

Courtesy of Mark Ficcadenti

*On a sub-zero day, Head Trainer Mark Ficcadenti
addresses a new outdoor training class.*

Courtesy of Mark Ficcadenti

Mark and Assistant Trainer, Jon Sherwood, (foreground) train a new recruit.
Courtesy of Mark Ficcadenti

The exercise was easy on the hips, and since Shadow loved the water, he never gave up due to fatigue. Almost always, Linda accompanied Mark and Shadow to the lake, and protected by Mark's presence, she occasionally fed Shadow treats. He readily took them, but despite her generous offers and attention he always made her aware of the pecking order. Mark was on top, and Shadow was second. Everyone else and everything else rested on the bottom rung of that ladder, and Shadow remained aloof to all except Mark.

Out of the water, Mark never threw the tennis ball or Kong ball knowing that the sudden quick stop when Shadow would pick it up in his mouth would be very hard on the dog's front shoulder joints. Mark continued to modify the exercise program for Shadow, and together they found their own way navigating some unchartered waters to maximize the dog's chances for success.

In training, Shadow never really took a reward, food or otherwise, as many other dogs did. Praise was all he wanted. Shadow required no medication for his hip problem, and anyone watching him work would find no difference in his performance levels. The same was expected of him as the other dogs in class, and he did not disappoint.

"Shadow worked for praise and surprisingly enough he was unstoppable. The reason Shadow was able to perform so well is because he was psychologically and physically tough. Despite the bad hips, his muscle structure was like that of a professional athlete."

Mark had tremendous faith in the dog and soon Shadow became an addition to Saint Paul's Canine Unit. The dog's fearlessness could sometimes cause Mark to watch him in complete wonderment.

Partners ready to patrol Saint Paul
Courtesy of Mark Ficcadenti

Shadow protecting Mark's squad car

Courtesy of Mark Ficcadenti

Sunlight filtered through the cage of the squad car casts a fitting shadow upon the winter face of K-9 Shadow.

All pictures courtesy of Mark Ficcadenti

"No obstacle was ever a hindrance for Shadow to the point I became afraid for his safety. Bounding after criminals without regard for self-preservation caused me, as his handler, great anxiety."

Out on the streets, Mark and his dog faced the same situations other handlers did so often observing the seamy side of life seldom seen by most Saint Paul citizens. On a warm, cloudy June day, Shadow and Mark were called to search in a large house for a man inside who had beaten his girlfriend with a pipe. The suspect, still believed to be armed with the pipe, was hiding inside a large three-story Victorian-style home in a quiet residential neighborhood. After arriving at the house, Mark opened the car door, and Shadow shot out of the car as fast, if not faster, than his contemporaries ever did. Mark knew that once in pursuit, he would run until his objective was achieved. Together, they approached the stately home.

While searching the second story of the house, Shadow turned his amber eyes upward and caught a glimpse of the suspect running down the third floor hallway. Mark saw him very briefly too as the tall skinny man clad in blue jeans and a white t-shirt ran quickly past the threshold. Seeing his prey, Shadow took off after the suspect effortlessly bounding up the long staircase leading to the third floor. The hallway was long and narrow, and as Shadow turned the corner at the top of the steps to pursue the suspect, the man climbed out the hallway window and jumped onto the roof.

By then, the weather had turned, and rain started to fall, soaking the roof and the eaves. Hearing the patter of raindrops hitting the roof, Mark watched through the window as the man moved with some difficulty across the slippery surface. Trying to move quickly, the man narrowly avoided slipping on the slick wet shingles and falling three stories to the ground. With each step, he fought to keep his balance and, after faltering, he soon regained his footing and continued to climb higher up on the roof.

The rain poured down at a steady pace with no signs of stopping. It did not deter Shadow in any way, and without hesitation, he followed after the suspect. Before Mark could stop him, the eager dog jumped out onto the wet roof. Pivoting quickly while teetering on the short roof eave, Shadow scrambled over the rooftop in pursuit. Mark could not always see where the dog had run in the fast pursuit but periodically caught glimpses of him climbing up across sections of the roof. At the heart-stopping times when Shadow was out of sight, Mark could only wonder where he was or if he had fallen to the ground. What if he tried to apprehend the suspect on the slippery slanted roof top? The handler could not go out onto the roof himself since it was too dangerous, so feeling quite helpless, all Mark could do was yell to the officers standing below advising them to catch the falling dog if necessary, knowing that in reality that was an impossibility.

Following in quick pursuit, Shadow chased the fleeing man to the very top of the roof. From there, the man jumped to a lower roof section where he jumped onto the rooftop of a neighboring house. Mark held his breath hoping Shadow would not make the same leap. He knew how driven the dog could be in his pursuits and could only hope good judgment would prevail. Fortunately, the pursuing K-9 never saw the man jump onto the neighboring roof as Mark had or Mark knew he would have followed, potentially meeting his death. Instead, Shadow ran from roof peak to roof peak in a heightened sense of excitement searching for the suspect. Not finding him, the dog raced across the roof and quickly came back through the window as though nothing about his actions was unusual. Mark had watched him, completely dumbfounded. Shadow shook hard to splatter the rain from his wet back before the driven dog ran off again to search inside the house. Mark was glad to have his friend safely back off the roof, and the show was over for neighbors who had been watching the large rain-soaked dog unexpectedly running there. The fleeing man had escaped but only temporarily. He was picked up a few days later.

Rapidly gaining recognition within the department, Shadow became one of the unit's SWAT (Special Weapons and Tactics) Entry Dogs. He was one of a select group of dogs that assisted the SWAT team in searches for very dangerous criminals. Most of the criminals that SWAT sought had committed serious crimes and typically barricaded themselves inside their homes or other buildings. They either had used or were threatening to use deadly force against individuals or the police. After Shadow's inclusion in that select group of dogs, it did not take long to get a call.

Probation officers had gone to the home of a man who failed to register as a sex offender. The man had been tried and convicted in the commission of sexual offenses with very young girls. It was critical that his location was always known.

As his probation officers spoke with him emphasizing that he must register, the man calmly walked into the bedroom of his lower-level apartment, grabbed a shotgun and racked a round into the chamber. With great haste, the probation officers fled from the apartment and contacted the Saint Paul Police Department.

The first thought was to negotiate with the troubled man. Negotiations with him were done via written notes, and it was becoming a very tedious process. With each new "conversation," one of the SWAT members, bracing behind a ballistic shield to protect himself from gunfire, crept to the door to retrieve the man's latest note only to later slip a notepad under the door for more negotiations. The rest of the team, in full protective gear, stood at the ready.

Negotiators believed that the man was going to shoot the first thing that came through the door and also believed that the man was trying to lure them closer and closer to the threshold of the door to perhaps draw them into a line of fire. Six hours passed without resolution, and the negotiators then declared the situation to be a stalemate. A plan to breech the apartment was next on the drawing board.

The worn apartment was small, and fortunately for the SWAT team, the apartment directly above it was vacant. The team studied the identical floor plan, and a new SWAT plan was devised. After two assaults with chemical agents, diversionary devices (flash bangs) would be deployed, and Shadow would be sent in off-lead to locate the suspect. Once Shadow located him, SWAT would make a dynamic entry into the apartment and take the suspect into custody.

That was the plan. But, after two chemical agent assaults failed to flush out the suspect, Mark, along with the SWAT team, prepared to make entry into the apartment via the front door. Two additional flash bang devices would be employed, the first one thrown through the bathroom window and the second device thrown through the living room window. After the second device was deployed, Mark would send in Shadow to locate the suspect, or if the suspect presented himself, Mark would apprehend him.

The round grenade-like flash bangs landing in the apartment would create a sufficient diversion that would allow the team to act quickly. The device would explode with a large report, and then brilliant light, flash and flame would rock the room. The SWAT members hoped the effect would disorient the uncooperative man. There was always some danger deploying the dog when the device was used as injury could occur due to fragmentation

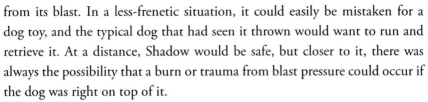

from its blast. In a less-frenetic situation, it could easily be mistaken for a dog toy, and the typical dog that had seen it thrown would want to run and retrieve it. At a distance, Shadow would be safe, but closer to it, there was always the possibility that a burn or trauma from blast pressure could occur if the dog was right on top of it.

Smashing the lower level bathroom window, SWAT deployed the first flash bang device with a deafening explosion. In the dark, Shadow never saw the first flash bang being thrown, but he certainly heard it explode. As focused as he was, he seemed totally oblivious to it. Mark counted to three anticipating the detonation of flash bang number two that was to be thrown through the living room window, but it never came. The team decided to act and not wait for it to be deployed so the door was breached by SWAT, and it was time for Shadow to enter.

"Find him!" Mark yelled to the dog.

With no hesitation, Shadow ran inside, and Mark peeked around the threshold of the open doorway to observe what he could in the thick smoke. Just then, and much to his horror, he saw delayed flash bang number two thrown through the living room window and hit the carpet just in front of Shadow. He knew the explosion would be imminent. Just as Shadow reached the device, the earsplitting magnitude of its blast shook the whole apartment. Expecting the worst, Mark strained to see through the dense smoke to see if Shadow had survived. Up ahead, he saw the fearless dog racing through the smoke without ever having missed a step. Shadow had jumped over the flash bang just as it exploded underneath him and not deterred at all, he headed straight to the back of the apartment. The dog truly was fearless. With his vision limited by the smoke, Mark peered through protective goggles to see Shadow up ahead. In the murky darkness, he spotted his dog at the far end of the hallway standing over the man they sought. Mark watched Shadow, who with enormous strength stood thrashing his head back and forth. Mark knew the dog was making an apprehension. That was the sign Mark had waited for.

"GO!" yelled Mark, and with a thundering crack the SWAT team rammed the door with a battering ram to make entry.

Bulky with bullet-proof vests, goggles and gas masks, they poured in through the entry way to face a sea of smoke. Once inside, they ran down the hall to where Shadow had his man.

The suspect had buried himself under clothing and plastic bags to protect against the chemical agent. After he was placed into handcuffs, they found that within easy reach on the floor next to him he had a .40 caliber handgun. Luck and the element of surprise was on SWAT's side, and thankfully, the man had not used the deadly weapon. Thankfully, as well, Shadow was not injured by the latent flash bang detonation.

Both Shadow and the SWAT team received recognition for their actions on that night that could have proven deadly for all those involved if it had not been for a brave dog that would not let even the explosion of a flash bang directly beneath him divert him from his mission. The SWAT Commander wrote up all the team members and Shadow for a department commendation. That information was forwarded to the United States Police Canine Association's Commendation board, and the incident was voted Patrol Case of the Quarter and was a finalist for Patrol Case of the Year.

Every shift was an adventure, and Mark and Shadow never knew what would come their way. On an eighty-degree July day, the continual shattering of glass caused officers to be called to an apartment building on a report of a naked man smashing out windows. When the first two officers arrived on scene and saw the man, they immediately requested via the radio that an officer armed with a Taser (stun gun) please respond. Having a Taser in his possession, Mark answered their call.

When he arrived, he found a large naked man over six-feet-tall and weighing about 250 pounds standing before officers and clenching his fists. The man was bleeding profusely from multiple areas of his body. He lived in one of the apartments and had for some unknown reason already smashed out many windows with his bare hands and would likely continue smashing more. His body was cut from the shards of broken glass that projected from the painted window frames, and blood dripped from where slivers penetrated his smashing hands. Piles of jagged splintered glass lay beneath the windows on the ground. The raving man was all "hopped up" on narcotics. He was a strong man, and the drugs made him more impervious to pain, enhancing his ability to continue his behavior with great strength despite his injuries. Another officer arrived, and the man was told he was under arrest.

"Get on the ground!" an officer yelled to him.

But the man refused to be taken, and instead, he attempted to walk away from the officers. The response was immediate. ZZZZZT! A blue/white arc of electricity crackled loudly from an officer's Taser to stun the fleeing man. Its two prongs shot out from the device and delivered 50,000 volts of electricity that would have normally caused any man to buckle and fall to the ground from the massive shock. But without losing his stride, the suspect pulled out both prongs that had delivered the shock and had penetrated his chest. Then he continued walking away. His massive girth offered him some insulation from the shock, but immediately, two more Tasers in the hands of two other officers crackled and arced. The double prongs from each hit the target as a third officer let loose a blast from his pepper spray in the hopes of subduing the man. But he remained unfazed. Mark then deployed his Taser again striking both probes into the resistant man's upper and lower chest. The suspect finally buckled at the knees and almost fell to the ground, but astonishingly, once more grabbed both prongs out of his chest and continued on.

Four officers on the scene grew to nine. As they arrived, each saw the man still attempting to flee. A large open gash on the man's foot was quickly creating a pool of blood on the green grass. Soon, he slipped in his own blood and fell down. Then the nine police officers attempted to take advantage of that slip and jumped onto the suspect to try to take him into custody. In the meantime, Mark ran to his car and grabbed Shadow.

"Get down on the ground!" the team repeated over and over as they tried to push the resisting man downward.

Still, the rotund man would not comply, and he threw some of the officers off of him as though tossing rag dolls aside.

As Mark came upon the writhing suspect and pile of grappling officers struggling to subdue him, he saw the suspect, reminiscent of a bucking bronco, go from lying flat on his belly to rise up on his knees despite the full weight of the four officers that remained clinging to him. His ability to resist seemed almost superhuman, and it was futile to pursue that course of action.

"Put your hands behind your back!" Mark yelled as the fray continued.

Again, non-compliance. Mark told the officers to get off the suspect and then sent Shadow in for the apprehension. Shadow, lacking a Taser but armed with a set of sharp teeth and strong jaws, utilized what he was given.

The ferocity of the dog was unrivaled, and he leapt upward with tremendous fury biting the suspect in the stomach. Once again, pain that would have debilitated anyone else did not seem to bother the man at all. Shadow's vice-like jaws were holding the man's stomach tightly, when suddenly the suspect turned and grabbed the powerful dog by the neck trying to twist his head in an attempt to get Shadow to release the bite. Once angry, but now livid, Shadow's grip upon his attacker's mid-section only intensified. Shadow would stay with the fight never surrendering to the pain. His training and instinct would never allow him to do otherwise. As Shadow wrestled with the man, Mark reinforced his actions with encouraging "good boys," and words of lavish praise. The dog was fully committed to see it all through to the end.

When the man would not release Shadow's neck, Mark raced forward with his baton to assist the dog and struck the suspect repeatedly. The angry man lashed out and tried to strike Shadow with his right arm. As the three struggled, Shadow momentarily released the bite and lunged forward again grabbing the suspect's right arm as the enraged and defiant man tried to repeatedly punch the unrelenting dog. But Shadow held the arm tightly. All attempts made by the suspect to disengage himself from the dog were futile. The suspect finally collapsed to the ground with Shadow still on the apprehension and not about to let go.

Eventually, the man began to tire. For officer safety protection, Mark would not release Shadow until the man was handcuffed so the struggle was not quite over. Much of the desire to fight left the man and all he could do was attempt to prevent himself from being handcuffed. With Shadow's assistance, an arrest was made, and the man became dead weight. With some difficulty, he was finally taken from the scene. Five firefighters who had arrived on the scene watched the drama and later said that without "that dog," the cops probably would have had to shoot the man.

After the arrest, Shadow remained frenzied, and he needed some quiet time to return to normal. Mark led him away and back to the car. After all the chaos, the two partners needed a bit of time by themselves.

A search of the man's apartment located a large quantity of methamphetamine. He was charged with felonious criminal damage to property and possession of narcotics. Another danger to society was off the streets.

As a cross-trained dog in explosive detection, over the years Shadow was deployed to "clear" venues for Presidents George H.W. Bush, William J. Clinton and George W. Bush, along with countless numbers of governors,

United States senators, United Nations representatives and visiting kings and queens from a variety of nations. As a "known quantity," Shadow could be depended upon. He cleared and swept the X-cel Energy Center in downtown Saint Paul including the stage and dressing rooms of some of the finest rock bands in the world before they performed their concerts, and he was called upon for venue security for the National Hockey League All Star Game and the Republican National Convention when it was held in Saint Paul in 2008. For five days, Shadow, along with other Saint Paul Police canine teams, responded to calls of "suspicious packages" and unknown devices purposely left by individuals in an effort to create panic and chaos during the event. The dogs' keen noses were the sole indicators of what packages could be deemed suspicious and which others held no danger at all.

Through summer and fall of 2008, Shadow continued to work. As he aged, he was gradually used less and less by the department. But on January 1, 2009, on a brutally cold January night, he was called out. It was well below zero with a cutting below-zero wind-chill. Mark and Shadow rode around the bleak frosted streets during their shift, the dark warm car being their only refuge from the unrelenting cold. Mark had hoped it would be a quiet night, but a 225-pound man in his mid-twenties had chosen the dangerous night to stab his girlfriend and her fifteen-year-old daughter. Then he made his get away.

Dressed all in black to blend in with the night, the suspect lastly pulled a large black hooded-leather jacket on to cover his black t-shirt. Then he disappeared into the shadows. The weather was so dangerous that the police officers on scene were reluctant to initiate a search. Mark was no more enthusiastic than they were, but the man had to be found. So Mark went to the car and pulled out all the cold weather gear that was in his trunk. Before him was an array of attire for all weather conditions. This night he would need the warm parka, stocking cap, heavy boots, gloves and certainly adequate face protection.

Mark knew that the search would be particularly hard on Shadow. As the dog aged, the typical cold of Minnesota's long winters was beginning to affect his work. He was no longer conditioned to work in the cold so he did not hold up well that winter. In the bone-chilling temperatures, he could no longer hold his feet to the ground for very long. The aging dog had always loved the snow and acted like a puppy burying his face in the cold deep drifts.

But in his senior years, it no longer held the joy or attraction for him that it once had. Mark opened the car door, and in the stiff and whistling wind, he let the old dog out of the car to track.

Together, they braced against the cruel and vicious wind heading down the street as snow whirled around them. Braving the cold, Shadow trotted along and seemed to know just where he was going. Putting his own discomfort aside, Shadow followed the suspect's scent for a track that lasted for twenty minutes. The longer it went on, the more excited Shadow became. Mark read Shadow's signals well and knew that the man they sought was not far away. The team stopped at a below-ground-level apartment just two blocks from the scene of the crime. The dog peered into the apartment's dark stairwell and knew that the suspect was hidden there. Suddenly, Shadow became very agitated and began to bark and strain hard against his leash. Just above the stairwell, clouds of condensation from the dog's rapid pants hovered in the frigid air as Mark reached for his flashlight with heavily-gloved hands. He shined his light into the stairwell, and when its bright beam illuminated one corner, it fell upon the man in black who was standing motionless.

"Come out with your hands up!" yelled Mark, and the man, having no avenue of escape, surrendered himself without saying a word.

One cover officer with Mark held the suspect until other back-up officers arrived to help handcuff and secure him in a police car. After the man was taken into custody, the two cold and weary K-9 partners walked through the dark and bitterly cold streets to gratefully return to their car.

Mark returned Shadow to the backseat compartment. They were both glad to escape the paralyzing cold, and Mark was glad the knife-wielding assailant was off the streets. The partners would finally get to go home.

For the successful action that night, Shadow was awarded a citation by Region 18 of the United States Police Canine Association. Four days later, he retired at the age of twelve years and two months and would spend his remaining years at home with Mark and Linda.

Shadow was an exceptionally accomplished police K-9, albeit always a bit rough around the edges, but had had always been an excellent worker and companion. It was in his eighth year that he finally started to mellow, and by almost twelve-and-a-half, he had noticeably slowed down. He had been at the job for a long time. Equally as long was Linda Ficcadenti's attempt to "court" him. After the dog retired, she would finally get her chance.

Shadow had a stellar career as a police service dog serving the City of Saint Paul, and the dog that was never supposed to serve one day had served ten-and-a-half years. During those years, he had always lived outside in the kennel at Mark's home growing the thick fur coat that Minnesota winters demanded, but in the fall of 2008, as his retirement neared, Mark had brought him inside the house to live.

At the age of twelve-and-a-half, snow began to chill the old dog's bones.

.....but sometimes he could still be persuaded by Mark to play in it.

After a long career, the elder statesman of K-9s enjoys his retirement.

All pictures courtesy of Mark Ficcadenti

Before Shadow was fully-retired, he had one more assignment to fulfill. Granada Films, working with television's Animal Planet Channel, visited with the Saint Paul K-9 Unit proposing a series of shows featuring the dogs. At first, they proposed a reality show that would involve Mark's K-9 training class, but after getting to know all the likeable officers and dogs of Saint Paul, they decided to film a series that featured the entire unit.

In order to film the show, a modified K-9 car was created. A dash camera was installed in front of the driver, and a cameraman sat in the passenger seat. When it was Shadow's time to shine, he found his compartment size was reduced by one third to accommodate a sound technician sitting on an installed jump seat there. Shadow was not used to sharing his compartment in the car with anyone, and suddenly he was tucked in closely far more intimately than he would have preferred. He was not gracious to his ride-along guest and glared angrily at the intruder. Sound and camera people knew to expect his grumpy growls as he tried to protect his compartment, car and handler.

Despite Shadow's protests, the English crew assured him they would give him some star power, but the aged dog, all brushed and groomed, rode through the streets of Saint Paul irritated with the whole thing as cameras rolled, and he constantly wore his unfriendly winter face. Each time the filmmakers glanced his way, it produced an aggressive statement on his part which warned them not to glance his way again. They minimized their glances, and Shadow grumbled when he felt it was needed, and together the unlikely group rolled for hours on end through Saint Paul until Shadow's segment was complete at which time he could return to his own patrol car with no further intrusions.

Shadow was a curmudgeon who had become very comfortable living inside with Mark and Linda. But after so many years in the outside kennel, he was having some difficulty transitioning from a streetwise cop to a gracious houseguest. He had never had to orient himself to furniture, lamps, hallways and a whole host of rooms to explore. He was a big dog running and crashing into everything in the house. Shadow was not the easiest lodger to contend with.

Where no K-9 paws had tread before, Shadow wandered through his house. After his retirement, he could be found lying at Mark's feet and moving along with him step-by-step. Once moved inside the house, Shadow's need to protect Mark did not diminish. For awhile, Mark had to put him in a crate at night to prevent him from denying entrance to Mark's twenty-two-year-old son when he returned home late at night. Mark knew his son was home when Shadow growled and chased the young man out the garage door, or when Shadow stood atop the landing near the kitchen growling menacingly, once again, denying entry.

While Mark worked, Shadow spent more time alone with Linda. She began to feed him and shower him with treats, and after awhile, he followed her wherever she went. For the first time, Shadow became more comfortable with people coming through the Ficcadenti's door providing he was properly introduced, and the social, gentle and loving side of the formerly cantankerous dog was finally set free.

After so many years, he finally let his guard down and tentatively at first he rubbed up against Linda's leg or pushed his furry head under her hand to let her know he wanted to be petted. Ear rubs and gentle touches were at long last welcomed and enjoyed. When Mark was not home, Shadow followed Linda everywhere, so closely that she often tripped over him. For every foot she moved, Shadow matched it. He had literally become her ever-present shadow. Three months into retirement, he was transformed. He had not transferred his affection to Linda, but he began to at least share it with her when Mark was not home.

After more than a decade, even though he craved attention and touch from Linda, he reserved the right to growl at her if she "nagged" him. She did not dare push him out of the garbage or away from the dishwasher or anywhere else where he wanted to poke his furry nose. These were all new pleasures for the outside dog, and he let her know he planned to enjoy them. If she spoke harsh words to him to reprimand him in any way, he could still quickly "talk back," expressing his displeasure with a low deep growl. In some respects, he was just too old to change his former ways.

Even after he softened some, Shadow was still capable of becoming all business again any time he got into the car, but at long last, Linda could nuzzle Shadow. She understood his nature and dismissed the territorial aggression that he still liked to display at times, uttering his guttural snarl after receiving a treat from her. The grumpy old man finally accepted her hugs, and for the most part, the dog was content to finally let himself be loved by her.

Finally accepting Linda's love, the Face of Winter begins to melt.
Courtesy of Mark Ficcadenti

In his rebellious years, Shadow had learned to tiptoe into his kennel to retrieve bits of hot dog and now he tiptoed into the Ficcadenti's bedroom to sleep on the floor next to their bed. Having new-found freedom in the house, he sometimes tried to jump up on a bed or a couch, but his aging hips with so many miles on them from chasing Saint Paul's bad guys prevented him from doing so. Sometimes at night as Mark lay in the quiet darkness, he listened to Shadow on the floor softly whimpering, the sounds of an old dog finally expressing whatever he had held within for so many years.

The police dog adjusted to sharing his living space with a four-year-old cat, Georgianne. Up to that point, he had never had any interest in animals whatsoever, but once confronted with one on a daily basis, he gathered enough energy to take a run at the cat, only to learn that she would at first retreat from him only to quickly turn to pummel him unrelentingly with her fast right paw making known her resentment of his intrusion on her Queen Cat lifestyle.

Even with bad hips, Shadow truly had been a "natural" as far as police service dogs went. His "scent" work (building search, tracking and open area search) came unbelievably easy to him, and with regard to aggression, Shadow had been absolutely fearless. Whether growling at Mark after putting his food down and chasing him out of the backyard kennel or confronting armed suspects during high-risk SWAT operations, Shadow's courage never faltered. Because of his bad hips, he was never taught agility, yet over the years he jumped more fences and brick walls while in pursuit of bad guys than most dogs trained extensively in agility.

K-9 Shadow completed a long career against all odds. The veteran police dog defied those who said he could never work as a police canine, and far beyond that, he proved he could perform his duties exceedingly well. Pain never stopped him. He was proof of what could be accomplished when determination and drive overshadowed pain and disability. He was not a dog who mingled easily with the public as most dogs did. In fact, Mark had to exercise extreme care and diligence when other people were around his dog. Other dogs in the unit fulfilled the social public relations roles. Shadow lived to do his job as only he knew how to the very best of his ability.

Mark had more years to work before he could retire with Shadow. After twenty active years in K-9 and twenty-five as a police officer, he continues to acquire dogs for the department and other agencies and to teach the twelve-week Basic Canine Handler's School. Besides training and re-training Saint Paul's twenty-one police service dogs and their handlers, he remains a top consultant in the world of K-9 and was instrumental in the creation and implementation of the *K-9 Cops* television program for Animal Planet. Many more dogs would pass through his kennel, but few more memorable than his unique partner, Shadow.

The Saint Paul Canine Unit was richer for having had such a brave dog for so long. When the night shift was no longer a reality for him, and when the adrenalin rush, fast cars and bright lights no longer colored his world, Shadow was still content in Mark's company. In the dark of night when the criminal element emerged to perpetrate any number of horrendous crimes in Saint Paul, it would be up to the younger dogs to catch them, and on Arctic Minnesota nights, as strong blasts of winter blew down out of Canada, the old dog curled up in the warmth of Mark Ficcadenti's home.

Shadow had earned his place by the blazing fire to warm old bones and lighten his grumpy spirit. The warmth of love in the home began to thaw his cold, stern, winter face, and Linda Ficcadenti finally enjoyed the chance to give the dog all the attention and affection that for so long he richly deserved. And like his beloved handler, Mark, Linda was glad to finally welcome one of Saint Paul's finest home.

"The Peacemakers"

Courtesy of Tony Forliti

Intelligence, strength and beauty—today's police K-9

Courtesy of Russ Hess

1970-2008 USPCA History

About the Author

Marilyn Jeffers Walton is a graduate of The Ohio State University. She has written six books for children, including the successful Celebration Series for Raintree-Steck-Vaughn. Her book, *Chameleons' Rainbow*, won a Children's Choice award in 1986. She is the author *of Rhapsody in Junk—A Daughter's Return to Germany to Finish Her Father's Story*, a non-fiction World War II memoir. More recently, she completed *Badge on My Collar—A Chronicle of Courageous Canines* before writing this sequel. She and her husband, a retired Miami University professor, raised three sons in Oxford, Ohio. She is a member of the 8th Air Force Historical Society and conducts research in the United States and Europe, particularly focusing on WWII prisoner of war issues.

LaVergne, TN USA
20 June 2010
186809LV00002B/49/P